:le,

ıl

How to Be a Successful Housewife/Writer

How to Be a Successful Housewife/ Writer

Bylines and Babies Do Mix

by Elaine Fantle Shimberg

Writer's Digest Books
Cincinnati, Ohio

Library of Congress Cataloging in Publication Data
Shimberg, Elaine Fantle, 1937-
  How to be a successful housewife/writer.
  1. Housewives as authors. I. Title.
PN171.H67S5   808'.025   79-17669
ISBN 0-911654-72-0

Book design by Barron Krody

To my husband, Hinks, for loving, caring and believing.
To Karen, Scott, Betsy, Andy, and Michael, for the loving
cooperation that enabled a housewife-mother to be a writer too.

Acknowledgments

My thanks and gratitude to JoAnne Poston for typing revisions over and over and over, and for serving as research assistant, correspondent, confidant, cat sitter, and pep squad compressed into one slight frame; and to the many housewife-writers who took time off from their writing to share their thoughts with a sister-writer they never met; and to my editor Carol Cartaino and her assistant, Howard Wells, for their patience in teaching me to stretch and reach higher than I ever thought I could.

Contents

Anymore" . . . Coping With Friends . . . When Friendships Fade . . . How to Maintain Friendships With a Minimum of Free Time . . . Program Your Exercise . . . How to Entertain Company So You All Enjoy It . . . How to Answer When Someone Says, "Are You Still Writing?" . . . How to Be Selective About Organizations . . . When You Want to Carry the Club . . . How to Gain the Most from Meetings . . . How to Keep from Writing Too Much for Free . . . Remember That Mother Said You Should Learn to Say "No"

Keep Your Notes . . . How to Handle Your Money

Introduction

Don't risk wrinkle lines wondering where you've seen my byline. Chances are you haven't. It's hardly a household word. (Even around *my* house I'm known as "Mom," "Little One," and "Hey, Where's My . . . ?")

My work's been published in national magazines and magazines you've probably never heard of.

Although my tax return lists my occupation as "Writer," I'm also a housewife, wife, mother, and mistress to a menagerie of pets.

I'm just like you, trying to handle a household with one hand, a house with another, and a writing career with yet another. The key, of course, is remaining in control.

Some women writers object to being called a "housewife-writer." A syndicated columnist I queried ignored my questions on how she had "done it all" (and her obvious qualifications as a writer and mother) and scrawled across my letter in bold words, "I am not a housewife."

Yet many nationally known writers like Marjorie Holmes, Bette Green, Shirley Radl, Erma Bombeck, Judy Blume, and so many others don't mind being covered with the same umbrella.

Even if you have a staff of eight to carry out your every bidding, someone has to give them their instructions and that usually falls to the lady of the house, known in America as The Housewife.

Check magazines on the newsstand and books on the best-seller list and you'll find a great many names of housewives-turned-author.

Next to newspaper people, the occupation of "housewife" probably furnishes the greatest number of writers—although the category of "former politician" rapidly is becoming a close third.

Certainly, it isn't because we housewives have such a great amount of free time on our hands. Nor, I fear, is it because we are so greatly encouraged by those around us. Often we find ourselves defending our "right to write" against those we love most.

Perhaps we write because there's so much to write about, or because we want to touch other people's lives. Or, we write to fill some unspoken emotional need, to express ourselves in order to keep our sanity. Maybe we write because we hate to put "just a housewife" on the blank next to "occupation."

Some women write for money. Some write for fame, to be known for themselves rather than as extensions of others or through others' successes. Some women write to prove to their mothers, their husbands, or themselves that they really *can* do something well.

I write because—it's what I do, because I have the desire. It's not that being a wife and mother isn't fulfilling. I need to be a writer too. I always have. I write because I find humor in the absurdities of daily life. Sometimes I feel sadness too, and I find I can write my tears away. I write when I'm angry and feel I must right a wrong. I write when I'm touched and want others to see beauty and gentleness. I write, as so many other women do, because I must.

But *why* we write really isn't as important as *how*. We housewife-writers snatch at patches of free moments like our grandmothers did bits of fabric to make a quilt. Our time is largely unstructured, and laughingly referred to by others as "our own." It's ours, all right: for carpooling, cooking, cleaning, and kids. And yet, somewhere within our week, we find and make our "writing time."

Writing really blends perfectly with being a housewife and mother. We can blend it in with our job of homemaker, working out of our homes as we oversee small children, feed our families, and remain available when needed. We can write when we travel or when we wait for children, doctors, or repairmen.

Unfortunately, these same advantages can be disadvantages as well. We're too available to people who want to borrow our precious time. Our feelings of guilt for wanting "something more" rise up and envelop us like fog on a Scottish moor. Home is where the heart is—and it's packed with emotion.

Male authors I've talked with find no difficulty writing out of their homes.

"My wife answers the phone, calls me when lunch or tea is ready, and keeps the kids away," a British playwright confided.

He seemed baffled that I find "making time for writing" such a constant struggle.

A male novelist told me, "It's all a matter of self-discipline. You make up your mind that you're going to write and you do it."

"What about the children? Groceries? Cleaning? Repairmen?" I asked.

He dismissed it with a wave of his hand. "My wife takes care of all that. My job is to write. Her's is to keep the home running smoothly."

Letitia Baldrige, former social secretary to Jacquelyn Kennedy and author of *Juggling: The Art of Balancing Marriage, Motherhood and Career*, attributes her success with all three to "a sense of humor, organization and an Irish nanny to help with the children."

Obviously, what we all need is either a wife or an Irish nanny, but since most of us are unlikely to have either, we'd better concentrate on the other two: a sense of humor and organization. It is to this end that I have written this book.

There are many outstanding books on the market today that will help teach you the techniques of writing for publication. Although this one touches on that, its central focus is suggesting ways for you to get your life more organized, manage your home more simply, cope with distractors and distractions, and set up a home office, all with the sole purpose of gaining the greatest amount of writing time and getting the most out of that time.

You'll learn to see and develop the ideas that are around you, how to find facts effectively, and make the most of your merged role: housewife-writer.

This book is meant for mothers with infants, toddlers, and teenagers; for wives and widows, for housewives and "housewriters" of all ages who feel they must write and are willing to seek out new ways to achieve their goal, without endangering their family's well-being.

I have five children (ages seven to sixteen), four outside cats, one inside cat, and two dogs. I have an active husband who keeps me breathless (with love as well as trying to keep up with him) and enough relatives within a ten-mile radius to make the Kennedy Clan feel like a nuclear family.

Yet, by using the ideas and techniques suggested in this book, I've managed to write and sell hundreds of articles, stories, and greeting-card verses in the past seventeen years.

Is it worth it, all the juggling, struggling, coping, and hoping? You bet it is!

Babies, bedmaking, and bylines *do* mix—but you have to keep stirring.

Are You Sure (You Want to Be a Writer)?

1.

"It!"—that elusive something so many of us long for, like the girlish figure of our teens or a self-cleaning kitchen.

"I want to be a writer." We sing it silently to ourselves in the shower. It becomes our mantra as we toss a load of "whites" into the washing machine. It remains a secret between our hearts and our minds. Saying it aloud might be unlucky, like telling your wish as you blow out the candles on your birthday cake. "When I grow up, I'm going to be a nurse."

Nursing, of course, would have been an acceptable career. "Normal" people become nurses, teachers, secretaries, or hundreds of other callings. But writing? That's for drunks and intellectuals! Besides, you're married (or have been), and probably you have a family. You're grown up and a woman now. Aren't you satisfied?

But you're not. You read magazine articles under the dryer, novels under the covers, and newspaper columns as you wait for the water to boil for a fancy gelatin dessert.

"I could do better than this," you think.

You sweep off the front porch again. The leaves are falling.

Tomorrow you'll have to sweep them off again. The kids shout. You're out of milk. You just bought some yesterday. In the distance you hear the steady clacking of your neighbor's typewriter.

Perhaps it is a yearning for something that lasts, something tangible in exchange for our labors, that sets so many housewife-writers in motion. Manuscripts can't be eaten up as soon as they're finished, and they don't lose their buttons. They're considerably more permanent than housework, which is only noticed when it *isn't* done.

But how to begin? Do you just start anywhere, like a traveler dropped down out of the sky into the middle of a bustling city? Or do you preplan for the long voyage ahead? Like any trip worth taking, you'll probably have a greater chance for happiness and success if you take some time to consider where you're going and what you want to do there, so you'll know what to "pack."

What Are Your Motivations?

It's important to know *why* you want to write. You need to identify and examine your reasons if you're to be successful in the role of housewife-writer.

Your motivation probably is different from your neighbor's, and it may not be the same today as it will be five years from now.

Whatever your goals, be certain they're realistic and be sure that your reasons for wanting to add one more role to your already busy life are strong enough to carry you through your apprenticeship and to recharge you if (and when) your work's rejected.

Think about why you want to be a writer *this very moment*. Is it to:

1. make extra money?
2. make a "name" for yourself?
3. fulfill a childhood fantasy?
4. compete with a sibling?
5. "prove something" to a parent?
6. express yourself?
7. have "something" to do with your free time?
8. see if you can do it?
9. bolster your self-esteem?
10. achieve immortality?

There are no "right or wrong" answers. Just be honest with yourself. Be realistic, too. Professional writing is hard work. It's fun—but it takes determination, self-discipline, and patience. Many writers work for years without making a sale. Some, although published, make very little money.

It's doubtful that you'll be offered a $100,000 advance for your proposed (and yet unwritten) novel. Your first book won't get picked by the Book-of-the-Month. There are exceptions, of course. But that's what they are, exceptions. You hear about them because they're so unusual.

But almost anyone with a basic aptitude or talent, market awareness, and persistence, can become a published writer.

Are You Willing to Spend the Time?

How much time? There's no formula. It depends greatly on the type of writing you want to do. Obviously, novels take longer to write than five hundred-word articles.

But it's more than just the writing. There are hours of research, rewriting, editing, and more rewriting. Do you have the staying power? Will you spend the time? Where will you get it?

You don't need to *have* time. You need to *make* it. All successful housewife-writers become craftsmen in the fine art of making time out of air. We're a lot like the left-handed population of the world, accommodating the majority, trying to fit in without looking too odd, but convinced of and accepting the fact that we're a little different. We've learned how to be flexible and adaptable, to get by without bumping too many elbows along the way.

"Women's work is. . . ." Hundreds of authors are busily filling bookshelves with their versions of that complex answer. Women's work always has been extremely varied and usually multi-directional. Our grandmothers were able to sew, put up preserves, and watch the children or help Papa at the corner store. We're experienced in dealing with interruptions, making snap decisions, and running our small business, known as "home."

My English friend, Lisel Gale, says we have "grasshopper minds" that enable us to flit from one subject to another without losing our train of thought. And while I think long stretches of uninterrupted quiet are most conducive for writing, I'll accept as truth that the majority of us learn to work with far less than the ultimate conditions.

Be realistic about what you hope to achieve at your present stage in life. If you have three babies in diapers, no help, and a sick uncle living with you, it probably will be harder finding free time than for a woman whose children are in school most of the day. That doesn't mean you can't make time to write—just that you'll probably have to take "smaller bites."

Along with being realistic about your goals and your time,

recognize that writing is work. It may not seem like it. After all, everyone can write. You just sit down at a typewriter, stick a piece of paper in, and begin to peck at the keys. Like childrearing, everyone considers herself to be a natural in the art of writing.

Many beginners dash off a short story, mail it to *Redbook* or *Good Housekeeping*, and are amazed when their work is rejected. They never would have considered trying to paint professionally or play the violin without some type of proper training.

Writing's no different. It too is a craft. You need to learn its basics and the technical aspects of your particular type of writing: playwriting, fiction, nonfiction, etc. There's a lot of reworking involved; going back to the outline, rethinking what it was you were trying to say. It takes skill and practice, like any other art.

Are You Willing to Take Risks?

I'm not talking about learning to skydive so you can write about it, but the day-to-day risks involved when you set yourself up as different (which you become when you make time in your life for writing). They include being teased and/or ridiculed by those who are resentful and jealous; losing friends who want you to "play" when you must work; rejection from editors who turn down your work when you feel it's the best you've ever done; and having a book on the same subject as yours come out the day you mail your manuscript to that publisher.

"Tell them it's not easy being a housewife-writer," said a number of authors I talked with when writing this book. They weren't being discouraging, just realistic. They know it hurts to have your work rejected. It's a part of you, and regardless how impersonal you try to keep it, it still smarts. Will you cry and quit, or sniffle and continue?

There are risks involved when your writing is published too. Friends may think it's lousy and feel duty-bound to tell you. Your relatives may feel you've written about them and get their feelings hurt.

Criticism hurts even the pros. One author, who received wide acclaim for her latest book, told me she was upset by her single bad review.

"I know it's the only bad one out of many good ones," she said. "But I keep thinking about it and it hurts. I wonder why he didn't like it."

You've got to be thick-skinned to be a writer, and most of us aren't. We're sensitive, emotional, very human beings who love to be loved; and are hurt, shocked, and surprised when we're not.

Are You Willing to Make Some Sacrifices?

Not human ones, although many of us know editors we'd consider handing over. . . . Are you willing to give up something you now have for your writing? It's a trade-off, and each person must determine whether or not what she loses is worth what she is gaining.

It means giving up some of your free time, your personal time, or giving up an extra hour of sleep so you can write. It means telling your daughter that you won't be her Girl Scout leader although you would be willing to help with the creative writing badge. It means making choices of what's important to you, setting priorities, and facing those who think you've made the wrong choice.

Sacrificing means sitting inside, working, while everyone else is playing at the beach. It means missing your favorite television show because you've got a deadline to meet. It means being determined, dedicated, and devoted to your goal. Are you?

How Is Your Energy Level?

It takes strength and stamina to write. I have staggered out of my study after ten intensive hours of writing feeling emotionally drained and physically exhausted. Physical well-being is vital to a writer. That's why it's important to get some daily exercise: isometrics while you're on the phone, running in place every hour or so, parking the car as far away from the store as possible when you shop, or going bike riding. One writer I know rides a stationery bike while she listens to the noon news. I try to jump rope or ride my in-house bike. Other writers swear by swimming, yoga, TM, jogging, brisk walks, and endorsing checks from publishers. The mind and body are closely intertwined. Don't think for a moment you can ignore your health without your writing being affected too.

What are your limitations? It's only being realistic and honest to face any limitations in your life. These need not be thought of as barriers to a writing career, but rather as stepping stones that must be crossed in order to reach your goal.

Have you any physical handicaps, such as deafness, arthritis, visual problems, etc.? Many writers have suffered from these and other afflictions and overcome them. You've seen pictures of armless artists who painstakingly paint with a brush held in their mouth or between their toes. If they can overcome their handicap, certainly you can yours. You might need others to handle interviews for you, or use questionnaires rather than face-to-face interviews. If your hands get stiff from typing, you may have to stretch out your writing hours or use a tape recorder and have someone else do the actual typing. If your motivation is high enough, you'll find a way.

What if you're limited in time? What if you have a chronically ill child, an elderly relative living with you, or you hold down an additional outside job? You still can make time for your writing. It may take you longer, may slow you down a little. But remember the childhood tale of the rabbit and the tortoise. The turtle took his time, but he made it. You can too.

Your limitation is money? You can't afford to squeeze postage and supplies out of your already-stretched budget? Look again. Are there any extras you could cut back on, like cigarettes or desserts? Study your market guides carefully. Don't waste postage on markets that aren't "just right" for your work. Figure your minimum postage costs and see if you can trade your writing skills for postage money with a merchant who may need promotional material, radio copy, or letters to his customers. Other chapters will give more details on ways to get cheap (or free) paper for writing your rough drafts. If you want to write badly enough you'll figure a way to finance it. Everybody needs something written. You just have to find who and what he wants.

What Will You Get In Return
Will it be worth investing all this effort, self-discipline, and countless hours? What are the rewards? The list would run for miles because they differ for each of us. But, universally, writing gives us individuality and freedom. By achieving some level of success as a writer, you no longer take your sense of accomplishment from those won by your children and husband. You become your own person. It makes you more interesting to your family, to others, and to yourself. Your efforts will be recognized and repaid in many ways. You'll begin to see your face, not in the reflection of your shining dishes, but on the jacket of your latest book or in the author's section of a magazine.

Women can invest their lives solely in their families, and many do. But children can turn out badly; husbands leave. When you take the responsibility for your own life (and, along with it, the risks and the chances for success), you'll find you become more confident, more self-reliant, and able to add to your family's emotional well-being as well as their financial security.

Wanting "it"—the writer's mantle—is the beginning. But mere wanting isn't enough. If it were, the world would be overrun with writers. You need to get yourself and your family mentally prepared for your transformation into the dual (or triple) role of housewife-writer (and mother), then put yourself in motion.

Think you're ready for the plunge? Come on in. The water's fine!

How to Organize Your Life (Amidst Chaos)

2.

If you've reached this point, you've probably made up your mind that "today is the first day of your professional writing life." You're anxious to dash off to the typewriter and begin work on your three-part epic novel, *War and Pizza*.

But control that urge, at least until you've got the rest of your life in some semblance of order. Otherwise, it's like trying to serve spaghetti with a spatula. You may have a few pieces in place, but the rest will keep dangling out—and it's these odds and ends that trip you up, making you run back to the kitchen screaming, "It can't be done!"

It *can* be done. It just takes a little organization and preplanning. (Actually, it takes a *lot* of organization and preplanning!) It also takes determination and desire.

Professional housewife-writers have always been a little self-conscious about admitting out loud that we're organized. We have a fear of sounding "holier than thou," or of eroding the myth that you're only creative if you're in a total muddle. We compensate by demeaning our efficiency, waving to the stacks of papers lying about and sighing, "Oh, I'm so disorganized!"

The truth is, we're fibbing. Almost all the housewife-writers I know are extremely well organized. We have to be to get any writing done. It's something to be proud of, a goal to work toward.

Fear not if you sit surrounded by egg-encrusted dishes, piles of dirty towels, and streaked windows. You *can* learn to be organized, to put your house in order both literally and figuratively. It may not take you as long as it did many of us to become professional in your work habits.

You don't have to do it all alone. The first thing every ship captain learns is that there are many hands on board. That's important for a housewife-writer to learn so she doesn't jump ship.

Clue the Family In

Too many of us keep the family in the dark and wonder why we never see the light. It's strange that we're often afraid to tell those closest to us how important our writing really is to our happiness and how sincere we are about it. Perhaps we're frightened of failure—or of being laughed at by those we love.

Yet, our chances for success in the writing field increase greatly when we confide in our families and actively seek their help. It's much more difficult, and often impossible, without it.

Some things may have to be changed around the old homestead, and by confiding in your family, you won't make them resentful because you've changed, or worried that they've "done something wrong" to make you go inside your head so often or refuse to do things you've always done.

You need cooperation from your husband and children. If you explain *what* you are trying to accomplish and why, you'll be more likely to get that vital cooperation and support.

Analyze Your Lifestyle

Think about the way you live, about your lifestyle and that of the entire family. You don't live in a vacuum, you know (though you may feel as though you live *behind* one). Changes in your life are going to affect your family too. Some aspects of your lifestyle may have to be altered a little; others may have to be drastically changed if you are to achieve your goal as a professional writer.

If you've always been a full-time volunteer, softball coach, PTA chairman, and homeroom mother, for example, how do you plan to salvage some time for your writing? Are you willing to drop some of your volunteer activities? If so, which ones? How will you decide between your daughter's Brownie troop and your son's soccer team? What about the amateur dramatics you've always enjoyed? Are you willing to tell your husband you want to drop out of the couples' bowling team?

What about all the time spent together with friends and relatives, shopping, playing cards, or tennis? What will you do? Cut down? Cut out? How will you handle hurt feelings of those who think you're ignoring them?

What if you have a house full of babies and toddlers? Or you're a Windex wizard who likes to see her reflection in everything and enjoys the scent of pine and lemon wafting through the house? What if your husband likes his undershorts ironed? Or he insists on large home-cooked dinner parties on the weekend?

Are you willing to give up some part of your life for your writing? How will you decide what part?

These are all questions we housewife-writers have to face and answer if we're going to become successful writers.

Before you get overwhelmed, follow the example of your toddler and take one step at a time.

First, find out what you actually *are* doing with your life. Try keeping a diary of your activities for one week. Write down what you actually do each half hour. By recording and not just thinking about it, you'll have a clearer picture of how your week is spent.

You may be surprised to discover that you spent two hours arranging the towels and sheets in the linen closet so they all faced the same way (like in *House Beautiful*). You may have devoted an entire rainy afternoon to lining up all the spices in your kitchen according to their country of origin.

Parkinson's Law states, "Work expands to fill the time available for its completion." The best way to cut down on housework is to cut down the time that you allow for its completion. That's an active decision on your part, a decision you must be willing to make if you're going to have time for your writing.

Perhaps you can consolidate some of your housekeeping chores along the lines suggested in Chapter 5 and "find" yourself some extra hours that really were there all the time, just waiting to be discovered.

While you're analyzing your time expenditures, you also must consider your attitudes and values, as well as those of your family.

If homemade bread and ironed underwear are important to your family's sense of well-being, you can't just toss them out overnight, not unless you want a revolt on your hands.

Take time to communicate with your family—especially with your husband. Discuss what really is important, and try to work out solutions together. Joint resolutions usually work better because everyone feels he/she had a voice in them.

What would be the alternatives to the homemade bread and the underwear? You could teach your kids (sons as well as daughters) to make the bread and to iron. They should learn those skills anyway. If the children are too young, perhaps your husband would enjoy making bread with them as a family-fun project while you are writing. If everyone feels it's vital to their happiness that *you* do the bread and ironing, discuss what trade-off you think is fair, what task you're now doing that isn't as important to them.

Also try to discuss openly the changes in routine, style of living and attitudes you can foresee as you take the time you're entitled to, to perfect your craft. Some things must change, something must give. You really can't continue to be all things to all people and still make time to be a writer too.

If you don't tidy up your life before you begin to take on yet one more job, you'll be like the singlehanded taffy-puller. Before long you'll have a real mess on your hands.

Determine Your Priorities

No easy task. First of all, priorities keep changing throughout life. Secondly, *your* priorities might not be the same as your family's.

If you decide that you must have a minimum of three hours daily writing time in order to achieve success, you're going to have to eke them out from your daily twenty-four. Obviously, something else must give way. It's deciding *what* that's the hard part.

Take a look at the list of daily activities you made for one week's time. Go down the list, and number them from one to ten with number one being the most important task for the week. (I seldom get to my number nine and ten! Usually it never really matters.)

What are your top priorities? My number one right now (remember, priorities constantly change) is finishing this book on time. Much further down the list are having lunch with friends, going to a three-hour meeting of a committee I'm on, shopping for some new clothes, and going to Weight Watchers.

I've decided, in order to complete this chapter according to my *self-imposed deadline*, to cancel the shopping, meeting, lunch, and Weight Watchers, all of which sometimes have higher priorities to me than they do this week.

My number-two priority, however, is getting four of my kids ready for camp. Obviously, at some point I will have to make this my first priority. What I've done toward it, however, is to turn much of the responsibility over to the kids. They are to get out the clothes they want to take (following the guidelines on the camp checklist), make a separate list of the items they still need (we never have fourteen pairs of matching socks for anyone, let alone fourteen for each child. Besides, I know only five pairs will ever get worn!) and begin to mark the clothes. I've given each of them a laundry-marking pen to make it easier. I expected to sew the name tags in for the younger two, but to my delight and surprise, they're doing it and think it's fun!

Helping your children become responsible people in their own right is one of the benefits of learning to take control of your own life. Discussing your priorities with your family may help you think them out more clearly. And sometimes you'll find that your family will pitch in and take some of your priorities off your hands completely.

Sometimes it's very difficult to rank your priorities. Sometimes a number six becomes a number three, or a number two drops down to number eight. Nothing is ever black or white. You want to complete the draft of an article, but your husband wants you to go to the movie with him; or your mother's best friend wants you to join them for lunch, but you've got a chapter due. You're bound to disappoint someone—it's them or you. What do you do? You're torn! Decisions mean conflict, and we all like to avoid conflict.

Once you've ranked your priorities, make your decisions accordingly. Sometimes you'll upset others. Sometimes you'll frustrate yourself. Sometimes you have to be flexible and reorder your priorities for a particular occasion. But the important thing to remember is that you have them, and to make each decision separately. Don't get caught in the trap that "since I've goofed up the weekend so far, there's no use trying to write anymore." Or, that because you do accept a luncheon date this week, you have to say "yes" next week. The choice is yours, and it's a new choice each time.

Once you begin to use the priority system in your life, you'll "find" that extra time for writing. It's like fitting an extra bowl into the refrigerator. Sometimes you can just move things around a little, but often you have to throw something out!

Your "found" time may be as easy to discover as writing during the baby's naptime and folding laundry when she's up; or it may be as complex as greatly simplifying your meal-planning, altering your social life, or changing your hobby. One writer switched from playing golf to racquetball simply because "golf didn't give me enough time for my writing."

You'll learn to compromise too. If your husband travels and wants you along but you have a deadline, write your stories in longhand or invest in a lightweight portable typewriter. If you enjoy having loads of company on the weekend, devise ways to simplify your entertaining (and write these methods up for a magazine article).

Eliminate the Unnecessary

Sometimes rearranging the old ways just isn't enough. You still feel frantic and frustrated, without enough time for your writing. It's time to go back to your list of things that erode your hours.

Check Chapter 5 for ways to cut down (and out) housework; Chapter 6 for working with and around your family; and Chapter 7 for ways to deal with organizations, friends, and foes. Look for new ways to handle old problems and things you can eliminate.

Shopping is one tremendous time waster, when you figure your travel time, time used in making the decisions, and then time spent waiting for someone to write up the sale. That's why many housewife-writers order as much as they can from catalogues: from children's clothes and detergent to Christmas gifts and lawn furniture. Most major stores from Neiman Marcus, Marshall Fields, Saks, Bloomingdale's, Lord & Taylor, to Sears, Penney's, Spiegel, and Montgomery Ward publish seasonal catalogues to help you shop at home.

If you must go out, consolidate your trips. Plan "area trips" so you do all your errands in one area at a time. It saves backtracking, which means saving time and fuel.

Nobody's perfect, but many of us try to be. We do all kinds of unnecessary tasks over and over again, trying to convince ourselves that we're really (1) all right; (2) good wives and mothers; (3) capable; and (4) all of the above. Yet, we all can save energy and hours by eliminating these unnecessary "perfection" tasks, such as:

1. recopying the grocery list so "everything's in order" and/or "it's easier to read"
2. rewriting a school permission note to make it "sound better"
3. ironing permanent-press so it "looks better" when it's really wrinkle-free
4. pouring spices into different containers so all the bottles and tins match

5. changing your outfit more than twice before going out
6. ripping out a hem because it's "a little off"
7. making an elaborate dessert because you feel guilty for writing all day and making such a blah dinner
8. polishing the coffeepot to get rid of all those fingerprints
9. remaking the children's beds because "they were lumpy"

If you do any of these tasks or ones like them, you're wasting time. Your family doesn't need fancy desserts, your children's sense of responsibility is far more important than the ability to bounce a quarter on their beds, and of course the coffeepot has fingerprints on it. *People* use it, don't they?

Use this thought as your guideline: If no one really notices what you're doing, stop doing it! That time can be put to far better use if you're going to be a professional writer.

You're not trying to win the Sloppy Housewife of the Year Award. (I'm a shoo-in for that one, anyway!) You're trying to eliminate the negative and unimportant in your life so you can do what's positive and important—your writing.

We all fall into doing a great deal of trivia each day without even thinking about it. You can sponge baby off if there's no time for a full bath. Babies' white high-top shoes don't need to be polished every night. Your canned goods don't have to be alphabetized, and you don't have to scrub the kitchen floor every week. Sounds revolutionary? Revolting? Perhaps, but it's these unnecessary chores that nobody even notices when we *do* do them that eat away at a housewife-writer's day.

Learn to Be Assertive

One of the best expenditures I've made in the last few years to further my career was an assertiveness training course at our local university. Many colleges, hospitals, clubs, and Ys offer similar courses.

Basically, assertiveness training teaches you how to stand up for yourself and encourages you to say "no" when you want to. Sounds easy enough, but for some of us, no is one of the most difficult words in the English language. But that little word can be an enormous timesaver.

For years I had been put on publicity committees of clubs. I didn't want to do it, hated that kind of writing, and found it difficult to be freelancing one moment and offering free material to the same market the next. It got so the local newspapers didn't know when to pay me or for what.

Because I lacked assertiveness, I went to luncheons I didn't want to go to, got on boards of organizations I wasn't terribly interested in, and in general got shoved around because I wouldn't (or couldn't) say "no."

When I did muster enough courage to say "no," I found myself listing so many reasons that I ended up feeling terribly guilty, or was talked into doing the task anyway because "You know what they always say, 'give a job to a busy woman.' " I even took less money than I expected for articles at times because I couldn't bring myself to speak up to the editor.

Being assertive is *not* being aggressive. It's telling people that you can't pour coffee (because you have a deadline), telling your kids they can't have a party on Saturday (when you're proofing your final draft) but that Sunday would be fine, and that you'd be delighted to have Thanksgiving dinner for the entire extended family, but this year you'd like everyone to bring something.

Being assertive is saying that you're important too, and standing up for your rights. It's knowing that you don't have to apologize because you aren't doing what others expect you to do. You'd better learn how to be assertive now if you don't already know. The demands of a housewife's time are impossible otherwise.

"She who doesn't stand up for herself will fall down as a writer." Confucius didn't say that; his wife did—and you know why you never read anything *she* wrote, don't you?"

Know How Your Inner Clock Works

All of us have inner clocks that function uniquely. Some women wake up an hour or two before the family and get a great deal of writing done by the time the house starts stirring. Others stay up long after everyone else has gone to bed.

It's important for you to discover your time of "maximum functioning" and to make best use of it. This time may change as you grow older and your family responsibilities shift.

When I was in my twenties and worked as a copywriter at a radio station, everyone knew it was useless to ask me to write anything before 10 a.m. My mind was fuzzy and the words resisted all efforts to put them into any semblance of order. I put the carbon paper in backwards. I learned to do my "mindless" tasks in the early morning.

Later, when I had babies, the late morning and early afternoons worked best for my creative times. It coincided (which came first?) with the children's naptime and playtime. I was too busy feeding and changing babies in the early morning and too tired in the late afternoon or evening to even think, let alone write, a creative thought.

Now I find that the early morning, as soon as the children have left for school, is my optimum time for writing. I'm more creative, have a high energy level, and the house is quiet. Perhaps in the years to come my creative hours will change again. It's important to be aware of when you function best, to be alert for changes so you can take advantage of them, and schedule your most productive work for when you're most creative.

At this point in my life, my business day is from 8:30 a.m. to 3 p.m. I have a part-time secretary who comes in half-days three times a week to handle correspondence and typing for me. For months she arrived promptly at 8:30 a.m. and worked until 1 p.m. Then she'd leave and I'd write frantically, trying to get some writing done with one eye on the clock for a 3 o'clock carpool, knowing I'd have to dash to the grocery and take one of the kids to:

1. Marcel, the Hair-Stylist (In my day called a barber)
2. The Shoe-In (expensive sneaker shop)
3. zither practice
4. soccer practice
5. soccer drills
6. soccer game
7. pom-pon practice
8. the orthodontist who's had three round-the-world cruises at my expense
9. the stationery store for a folder desperately needed for tomorrow
10. a friend who lives on the other side of town (whose mother doesn't drive)

(Pick all of the above or some of the above. It never is none of the above!)

Suddenly, it dawned on me that I was wasting my most creative hours, that time when I really felt like writing and had the time and the energy to write. Instead, I was dictating letters, filing, and doing busywork. I asked my secretary if she could come in the afternoon instead.

Now I work from 8:30 to noon, writing first or second drafts. She comes in after lunch to clean-type what I've written. Then I dictate letters, etc., and have time to run my errands before getting the children. I know I have to write in the morning. Otherwise, she has nothing to type up and we sit smiling at one another as the meter ticks. That knowledge, plus the fact that my energy level is highest in the morning, has almost doubled my productivity.

If you don't have a secretary or typist, the principle remains the same. Do the creative aspects of your writing when you have the highest energy level and the largest patches of time. Filing, typing, and other busywork tasks can be done when the kids are home, at night, or when you're feeling "written out."

What if you haven't the foggiest idea when your "prime time" is? How do you determine it? Well, it isn't likely to light up in red, white, and blue and play "Here I Am." It's probably the same time of day that you feel like cleaning closets, moving furniture, or trying out a new recipe. That's when "all systems are go" and you should isolate yourself for work. Schedule your writing time during that period for a few weeks. The closets might not get cleaned, the furniture won't get rearranged (which your husband won't mind), and your family will miss the delights of chocolate-marshmallow fluff mousse, but you just may get that article written!

If you don't think you ever feel a spurt of energy, try working during different parts of the day. Give it about a week for each time segment. Record how you felt when you began working, how long you were able to concentrate, and what work you accomplished. Look over your time sheet. Are there any periods where your productivity seemed higher than others? Did the work seem to come easier during these periods? What time of the day held the fewest distractions for you? Rank these different parts of the day from one to ten, with "ten" being the peak of production for you and "one" being when you really are dragging. You should see one section of the day with higher numbers than the others. This is your best time for writing, and you should make every effort to schedule other activities for the remainder of the day. If the entire day is about a "four" for you, perhaps you should see a doctor. You may have a case of the blahs!

If you have no clear prime time, pick the period that's freest from interruptions and make it your prime time.

What if you discover that your prime time is when the baby is fussiest, when the kids are home, or around the dinner hour?

Don't despair. Hire a sitter for an hour or two, trade with a friend, or bribe a relative. Change the dinner hour if you must. The kids can eat carrots and apples to stave off hunger pangs and do their homework while you write. You can work out something for almost any type of situation, if you want to badly enough.

Schedule your writing so you have the most efficient use of the time you have. I usually have many projects going at one time. That way I never get bored. If I bog down on one manuscript or if some mateial I need hasn't come in yet, I can turn to something else. My mind seems to work best this way. But, when I work on any one of the projects, I block out everything else for the time being. Everyone is different. You'll have to discover through trial and error what works best for you.

How to Save Personal Time for Yourself

This is the hardest aspect of trying to combine a career, marriage, and motherhood, at least for me. I have learned to discipline myself to make time for work; be available when needed, to my children; and I enjoy being a loving and supportive wife. But I tend to rationalize that "my writing is all the personal time I need" and wonder why I tend to collapse into bed by 10:30 p.m.

Everyone needs personal time to relax, daydream, thumb through a magazine (for fun, not for article ideas, although it's sometimes hard to separate the two), or just to "waste," do nothing but unwind and recharge the mind.

One way I've tried to create more personal time for me is by making better use of my "dummy time," repetitious work that requires little thought on my part and can be combined with another task such as:

1. folding laundry while watching the news on television
2. waiting for kids to get into the car after school and making lists, sewing buttons on shirts, filing nails, writing letters, etc.
3. thinking of titles or lead paragraphs while doing dishes or running the vacuum
4. wiping off counters or dressers in the radius of the phone cord while talking on the phone

This is a useful form of mind wandering as long as you don't do it when it might endanger you or your family.

One day, my daughter and I were in the car. She was chattering away and I inadvertently began thinking about the unfinished articles sitting on my desk. I mentally was lining them up in order of importance so I'd know which one to work on first when we got home.

My daughter looked over at me.

"You're really not listening, are you?"

I felt heartsick. Instead of sharing this precious time alone with just the two of us (an unusual occurrence in a family with five children), I had "gone inside my head" and left her alone. I apologized, and the errands, which were boring but necessary, became a special time for the two of us to enjoy.

Try to be through with your writing to greet the children when they get home from school. Have an "o.j." break and listen to the news of their day. Then, if there are no errands to run, go to your room to read or soak in a hot tub for thirty minutes. You need this time to unwind. (Make dinner an hour later, if necessary.)

Look in the mirror. It may be the first time all day. Wash your face, splash on some cologne if you use it, and change your blouse. You'll feel like a new person—or at least a more refreshed old one.

After dinner, try to relax. I used to check homework after the dishes were done, then try to write some more. I found that the writing I did then was, for the most part, dull and tired; a reflection of the way I felt.

Now I try to read a few chapters in a best seller, do some editing or needlepoint, or watch a little television if anything decent happens to be on. Sometimes my husband and I, both movie fanatics, will go out to a movie. We also enjoy grocery shopping together. It gives us a chance to relax, be together, talk over our day and share in each other's business successes and failures. His emotional support is very important to me, and we work to cultivate this closeness.

Is there life after 5 p.m.? There is, if you make time for it.

Lists: How to Make Them and Use Them

Mothers don't know everything; it only seems that way because they make lists, and in my casual survey of housewife-writers, I've discovered all are ardent list-makers.

Everyone expects the housewife-writer-mother to store more data than a computer does in its memory banks and to have that information at her dainty fingertips.

"What size shirt does Bobby wear?"

"When is Aunt Minnie's birthday?"

"Did you remember to pick up my shoes?"

"When is my appointment at the dermatologist?"

The list is unending. The only way to remember it all is not to. Put it all out of your mind and make lists. Then, all you have to remember is to look at the list and your calendar. (More about calendars to come.)

Details on the all-important grocery lists, repair lists, and job lists are found in Chapter 5.

Mom's List

This is the list I carry with me on my purse date book. It lists everything I have to do. I carry these lists over from day to day until I finally cross them off. Right now my list reads:

1. appointment with periodontist (carried over six months now)

2. gift for Michelle
3. call or follow-up letter on unacknowledged manuscript
4. neuter cat
5. check on racquetball class
6. recipe from Barb

As you can see, it's a diverse list and contains *all* my activities, not just my writing ones. But I check it each morning and do the most important ones first. The cat and my teeth obviously should be top priority, but neither of us seems to be in much of a hurry to make the appointment. There is a sense of satisfaction when you cross something off, and with written lists you don't have to clutter up your brain with mental lists of things to do.

Permanent List

In the back of my purse date book, I list all the people I give Christmas presents to and what I gave them last year. Then I can buy things when I'm inspired and can check to make certain it isn't the same inspiration I had last year. (I need to also list *where* I put them, as I keep misplacing the gifts and can't find them 'til after Christmas!) I also keep a list of names and phone numbers, in case I want to sent a gift or letter or am out of town and want to call someone. I list my children's most recent sizes, my husband's shirt and waist size, birthdates (and year) of close friends and family so I can remember special birthdays. This purse date book, along with The Book at home, are vital to my well-being and that of my family. If my purse were snatched I'd run after the thief. He could keep everything but my date book.

Remember these important facts about lists:

1. Don't spend time making lists of your lists.
2. Look at them. They're useless if you don't.
3. If you've got a day for errands, put your list on a clipboard beside you in the car and consolidate your travels. Follow an efficient order so there's no backtracking.
4. Carry addresses and phone numbers with you. They can't help if they're on the bedside table.
5. Be consistent *where* you keep the lists for the family. If they can't find the grocery list, they'll never write items down on it.
6. Use lists as memory joggers, and stop trying to remember anything more than you have to.

Make a Date With Your Date Book

I consider the half-day I spent in the stationery store looking at calendars and date books a half-day well spent. I have two calendars.

One is The Book by the telephone that shows two days at a time. Previously I used a full month calendar, but the lack of white space overwhelmed me.

Everyone writes everything down in The Book. It's all there: dates of my husband's business trips, my deadlines, the children's lessons, appointments, carpool schedule, peoples' birthdates (and year), etc. If it isn't in The Book, it won't happen! Don't just write "doctor's appointment." Put a name or initial by it. I once took the wrong child for a checkup!

I transfer this information each morning into my purse date book so I remember not to schedule an interview the day my daughter has an appointment or there's a school track meet. My carpooling schedule and everything else that pertains to me in any way goes into my purse date book.

The purse date book I use is called "The Day-Timer" and has a monthly calendar that slips into a wallet-case. The address file in the back is separate. There are many varieties of date books; some people prefer the flat calendars that hold one year at a time, others the little black book with a page for each day. The best way to pick your calendar is to spend time at a well-stocked stationers and look through them. You must remember to transfer dates from your purse calendar to The Book and vice versa, but once you get used to it, you'll never give it up.

There is one other important advantage of using a pocket date book. Few people carry them so when you pull out yours for a consultation, you have a psychological edge. When a group sets a date, everyone gives in to the person with a calendar. It adds a feeling of mystique! It's also an easy way to say, "Gee, I'm sorry. I have a previous commitment," and hope that your nose doesn't begin to grow.

Make the Most of Your 168 Hours Each Week

What are your goals, your priorities? How will you achieve them? Thinking about them won't work. You must write them down—not to become a slave to time, but to master it. Then review these goals often. Are you headed in the right direction, or have you been sidetracked? What can you omit?

Time is yours to control. The women you most admire, the women who accomplish the greatest number of things have the same amount of time as you—just 168 hours a week. Time is like a blank sheet of paper. It starts out the same for everybody. What you do with it makes the difference!

How to Run Away from Home (When It's Your Office Too)

3.

Last night I went into my study to work. As always, it was spotless. Morrocco leather-bound reference books filled floor-to-ceiling bookcases. Pristine pale yellow wallpaper descended to immaculate off-white wall-to-wall carpeting.

Soothing symphonies filtered in through the well-modulated music system. Ignoring my well-stocked refrigerator, I turned to my secretary, Robert Redford's twin brother, and smiled. He nodded, then lifted the telephone receiver.

"No calls, please. Ms. Shimberg is about to create."

I sighed. Something was tugging at my arm. I opened my eyes.

"Mommy," said a small figure, digging jelly-covered fingers into my stomach. "The dogs messed in the kitchen again."

Welcome to Reality!

Few of us, alas, have my fantasy study. Most housewife-writers I know get by with far less for their "in-house" business ambience. As far back as 1929, Virginia Woolf knew about a housewife-writer's needs when she wrote, "A woman must have money and a room of her own if she is to write fiction." (Needless to say, a woman writing nonfiction in her home is in the same circumstance.)

The fact is, you have to have somewhere to write. Most writing instructors (male) will tell you that one of the joys of being a writer is that you can write anywhere. They extol the virtues of writing as you sit in your vineyard or at your castle by the sea, a simple clipboard on your lap. They neglect to mention you'll spend most of your time runnng after blowing notes and pages and finding that the fresh sea air has taken the glue off your stamps and envelopes. (They also neglect to tell you that it's hard to concentrate when your "vineyard" is filled with kids screaming over whose turn it is to ride the Big Wheel, or when your castle moat is leaking and you can't get the plumber.)

Offices (or any workspace, which we will dignify from here on with the designation *office*) have some features in common. Regardless of where it is located, a proper office should include:

1. an atmosphere conducive to concentration
2. a comfortable place to work
3. storage space for the tools of your trade
4. accessibility
5. availability

The location for your office may vary, depending on the ages of your children, the type of house or apartment you live in, the stage of life you're now in, your personality, etc.

When the children are little, you may want to be close by yourself (in lieu of day-care centers or Grandma), so you can keep an eye on them or at least be in earshot. When they're older, you may want to be as far away as possible. If you're gregarious, you may prefer being in the middle of things, with the chaos around you actually helping you to write. Or, you may be where I am today, at a point where I love to sit in solitude, hearing nothing but the thoughts in my head and the typewriter.

In Chapter 6 and elsewhere in this book, I'll talk more about adapting your writing to the ages of your children. But whatever age they are, it's important to know and understand yourself. If you can't write with distractions, there's no use setting up an office in the kitchen with the toddlers underfoot. Know thyself.

What *you* call a comfortable place to work may be totally different from what *I* think of as comfortable. Some writers prefer to work standing up, writing on top of a dresser or counter top. Others curl up in an easy chair and talk into a tape recorder. Some women take to their beds and write on a lap table. Still others swear by a hard chair that makes them more anxious to "write and get it over with."

I opt for a comfortable chair that keeps my mind on writing, not on my posterior. I like a low desk or table for my typewriter so I don't have to reach up to the keyboard. I usually sit on the floor to proof my writing—and work barefoot!

There are many advantages in working at home. They include:

1. You don't have to "dress up" to go to work.
2. You have no carfare or other transportation costs.
3. You easily can work at night or on weekends.
4. You don't have to take time off if a child is sick.
5. All your reference material and files are always at hand.
6. The telephone is already there.
7. You can check on dinner, kids, or throw a load of clothes into the washer during a break.
8. You can move, if you have to, and take your office with you.

It's the disadvantages of working at home you'll have to face and overcome if you're to succeed as writer-in-residence:

1. People don't really believe you're "working" because you're home. They don't take you or your work seriously, and therefore do not respect your time.
2. You're too easily available to service people, telephone solicitors, children, friends, relatives, etc.
3. You may be too easily distracted by "home chores."
4. It can be lonely.

Can you really make it work so it's possible to enjoy all the advantages? You can! But it takes discipline (ugh! that word again), and it takes determination.

Where to Put Your Office

Ideally, it's nice to have that "room of your own." You can close the door and settle down for business, your business of writing. Your supplies are there. The typewriter (or pad, if you write in longhand) is there too. Your reference books are easily within reach. Your room serves no other function but a place for you to write. That's the ideal. If the ideal is not possible, you have to discover what is possible and make that the ideal for you.

Be creative in your search. One writer I know made herself an actual "closet case." She found a long, narrow closet on the second floor of her home that was used to store Christmas tree ornaments, suitcases, leftover wallpaper rolls, and outgrown clothes waiting to be grown into by another child. She removed the lower shelves, piled everything into the back of the closet, and hung a beaded curtain to divide the storage area from her "office." Then she moved in her typing stand, file cabinet, books, and a $19.95 electric fan, and began writing.

Her kids tell callers, "Mom can't talk now. She's in the closet." My friend doesn't care. She's writing and being published.

I've heard of another housewife-writer who turned a guest bathroom into her "office." She sits on a foam cushion on the closed toilet seat and types on a rolling cart. A piece of plywood fits over the bathtub and is covered with reference books, boxes of paper, and envelopes. A calendar with deadlines in red and important memos are taped to the tile wall. When company comes, she pulls the shower curtain, moves the typing stand out, and hangs up fresh towels!

If you can't find an entire room, settle for part of one. Walk around your house or apartment to determine what space you can commandeer. If you have a husband and/or older children, it's smart to talk it over with them first. You'll get more cooperation, something you need very much, if you haven't taken over the telephone corner where they usually hide to talk in private or the spot where Monopoly always is played.

Don't forget to check out "forgotten" areas of your house either; e.g., the attic, basement, or garage. Some older houses have ample landings on the second floor or separate outbuildings. What about the laundry room or a walk-in closet?

If you decide to claim part of a room that serves another purpose, consider a screen around your area; or hang a curtain on hooks (like the privacy curtains in a hospital ward) or a folding door; or build a divider to partition off your space (your husband can lend support and encouragement to your career by helping out). You need this, partly for privacy and partly to protect your piles of papers from prying eyes and poking fingers. I once worked at a desk where the main telephone sat, and found my freshly typed manuscript covered with doodling when I returned to proof it.

Even a toddler can be taught (with patience, repetition, and a loud voice) to stay out of Mama's office, even if it's only a space behind a curtain or an area marked off by a piece of adhesive tape on the floor.

Some women write on the dining room or kitchen table and say it's perfect. . . until the family wants to eat (which, in my house, is all the time). Still, if that's the only available space, snatch it up before someone else does. Then make it convenient for you and your work. Put a dresser, file, or even a cardboard box nearby so when dinner's ready you can put all your work in one place. Otherwise, you may have to dig through the garbage to find the page stuck to the chicken neck.

Other housewife-writers rave about the virtues of writing on the ironing board. (If, like me, you're a member of the Seven-day Non-ironists, you might as well use the ironing board for something.) It *is* mobile, although a little wobbly.

If your bedroom will hold a typing stand or card table, turn a corner into your office. You can always store all of your supplies under the bed.

Wherever you put your office, remember that it should be yours alone as much as possible, ready and available to you at a moment's notice. If you have to "set up shop" each day before getting down to work, or go down into the basement to get the ladder and carry it up to the second floor where you then climb up to your attic office, you'll probably put the whole thing off. Make it easy for yourself. Writing's hard enough without going out of your way to make it more difficult.

How to Give Your Office an Aura of Dignity and Professionalism

First of all, you must make your "office" look like what it is—a place of business where you do your work. No matter how large or small it is, keep in mind its function: a place for you to write. Keep it and its supplies separate from where you make out grocery lists and menus, where the kids do homework, and where you pay your bills or write personal letters.

I used to have one "catch-all" desk in the bedroom where I wrote, paid bills, typed personal letters, scribbled excuses for teachers, cut out coupons for groceries, etc. After one horrible month, when I misfiled some overdue bills with brochures on Belgium, I decided it was time to become a housewife divided. I put all the bills in a shoe box as they arrived and left them on the desk. I moved my typewriter and everything else concerned with my writing to a corner of the family room. It forced me to go into the "office" to write my personal letters on the typewriter, but my professional equipment was separated from personal and household things.

Having a separate space for you as a writer makes you feel like one. Certainly, having the most elaborate office in the world will not make you a writer. But businesslike habits tend to make you feel more businesslike, and chances are you'll write more easily and more often when you get to the one spot set up for that specific purpose.

What You Need in Your Office and How to Keep It There

It's a lot easier to write about what you need in your office than to explain how to keep it there. I haven't really figured that part of it out yet. But I'll share with you some of the plans that have failed less than the others.

Even the most basic office area needs a place for you to write and to keep supplies. If you have a desk or table, it should be a comfortable height. Typing height usually is lower than regular desk level, so if you're buying something new, sit at it with a pretend (or portable) typewriter to see how it "feels."

A neurologist (whose parents were both writers) gave me a tip that I'll pass along to you. If your neck hurts when you're typing, chances are your typing desk is too high. That means your arms have to reach up, placing an added strain on the neck muscles. I lowered my desk (a Formica slab laid across two drawer chests) just one and a half inches and now have very little neck pain, even when I've been typing all day.

Your typing chair also is important. Both feet should rest comfortably on the floor, and your back should be supported. If you're buying a new chair, try it out for awhile to make sure it "fits." If you're borrowing one from another part of the house, do the same. You'll be spending many hours sitting there, and if your chair is too big or too small you won't feel your best and probably won't do your best either. Take a tip from Goldilocks, and find the chair that's "just right."

I once heard of a writer with an office in his garage who had a desklike platform built along the sides of the garage with four typewriters set up in intervals along the platform. He works on a different project at each of his typewriter stations and keeps all the files, notes, and memos right there beside each typewriter. It sounded hilarious. I almost could visualize a man running from typewriter to typewriter like something out of an old Marx Brothers movie.

Then I stopped laughing and gave it a try. It worked. I now write long-term projects at one typewriter and short articles at the other. There's something refreshing about leaving one keyboard, having a stretch, and returning to the other.

Your office lighting should be strong enough to see by without causing any glare. If you have fluorescents that flicker, check the starter, be sure that tube's resting in its holder properly or, if all else fails, buy a new tube. They're expensive, but they do last a long time.

Natural lighting, especially if it's coming in over your back, is relaxing to work by. Don't face the sunlight directly, as it can cause glare and give you a headache.

My office used to have shutters on the windows, which had to be kept closed because the typewriter sat on the table in front of the windows, blocking them. The room was dark and depressing, and I had to have a lamp turned on even at midday. We took off the shutters (now they're cluttering up the attic because I couldn't bear to throw them away) and replaced them with simple shades. With all the natural light streaming in, I no longer feel as if I'm working in a cave.

Desk lamps, if they're not too high, give good lighting, especially at night. If you're buying a new lamp, ask if you can try it out for a few days. Most reputable lighting companies want you to be satisfied and will let you buy a lamp on approval. If you find a store that won't, look around for another shop. You only have one set of eyes, and if they're tired and strained, writing will be more of a strain than it should be.

Some people like the gooseneck lamp or drafting table lamp you can twist around to shine directly on your work. I always have found them to give off too much glare, even with a low-wattage bulb. If you have one, try it out before buying something new. But never use a lamp simply because "it's there."

It's nice to have an authentic filing cabinet, but it's not a "must." You can buy inexpensive cardboard filing boxes at your stationery store or at a large drugstore. Some women use blanket storage boxes to hold their folders and store them flat under their beds.

You can keep anything in a file cabinet, but the only things you really need to file are your carbon copies of manuscripts. And they *could* be stored in a closet, in the pantry, or on a shelf in the bookcase. Wherever you put your office, try to keep the supplies as close to it as possible.

Typing paper, carbons, and draft paper can be stored in the boxes they come in or in plastic or metal baskets available at a stationery shop, discount store, or office supply shop. There are many second-hand office supply stores that buy furniture and fixtures from businesses that have gone broke. Let someone else's misfortune be your good luck and buy the equipment you need at greatly reduced prices.

Mugs or dividers for silverware keep your pencils and pens united and close at hand. If you still have babies, save empty baby-food jars and fill them with paper clips, rubber bands, thumb tacks, etc. If yours is a "traveling" office, put all these little (but necessary) things in a cupcake tin. Then, when you're through writing, you can put all your papers in a box, lay the cupcake tin in on top, hide the typewriter, and no one will know your secret!

If work space is limited, keep other supplies such as scissors, stapler, letter opener, rubber cement, and correction fluid stored in a shoe box near the typewriter. Hide your postage stamps in a spot known only to you—or there won't be a stamp in the house when it's time to mail out the Great American Novel. Stamps have a way of disappearing like pieces of fudge, until there are none left.

If you have space, a bulletin board is indispensable, if only to remove some of the clutter that gathers on your desk. I post:

1. a calendar (which hangs by the phone) with pins representing deadlines stuck in dates so I don't promise two editors articles on the same day
2. article ideas
3. phrases and sentences "too great to forget"
4. a list of publishers and what they're holding so if an editor calls to talk about my article, I can remember what I sent her
5. a list of most-often-called phone numbers, including editors of newspaper sections, magazine editors, local librarians, resource people, and other writers with whom I commiserate when I'm blue, confused, depressed, or convinced I should have become a real-estate salesman like all my friends
6. housewife-writer cartoons that make me smile, like one that shows a mother at the typewriter with kids hanging onto every limb. The caption reads, "So much for the trilogy. Here comes another 'short short.' " It's so yellowed I no longer can read the name of (or give credit to) the cartoonist.

If you don't have space for a bulletin board (or you're sharing space in a room not conducive to one) pin important information on your curtains (use sharp, thin pins so you don't damage the material) or tape it to the lamp, typewriter, or to a clipboard that hangs on or near your desk. Time spent looking for a phone number or market possibility is time wasted, and a writer sells time.

One woman whose "office" is the kitchen table uses the inside of the cupboard by the telephone as her bulletin board. When she's working, she flips open the cupboard door and checks her schedule, list of articles making the rounds, etc. When her working day is over, she shuts the cupboard, puts everything back into her giant roasting pan, slides it back on its shelf under the sink, and fixes dinner.

"I only use the roasting pan on Thanksgiving," she explained. "It seemed like such a waste sitting there the rest of the year, so I put it to work."

You also can tape memos, deadlines, and article ideas on

windowpanes, on mirrors, and like the woman with the bathroom office, on walls. Be flexible and imaginative. Make your office, wherever it is, as complete as you can.

Be sure to include a wastebasket in your office too. The bigger it is, the more likely you are to throw things away.

Finances will play a large part in how extensive a reference library you'll have. It also varies greatly depending on the amount of space you have available for books, the type of writing you want to do (fiction, nonfiction, etc.), and your interests.

I think every writer needs a good dictionary (hardback, not a paperback); a thesaurus or book of synonyms; and *20,000 Words*, a little book that lists the spelling and division of twenty thousand of the most commonly questioned words. I'm a poor speller and check every word I'm the least bit unsure of. About 90 percent of the time, the word I need is in that book. The meanings, however, aren't listed, so to make certain the word I'm using means just what I want it to, I'll often check the dictionary as well. (If my usage is the third choice, I'll select another word.)

I also have the *World Book Encyclopedia* (used as much by the children as by me); Theodore Bernstein's *Reverse Dictionary* (for when you know what you want to say, but forgot the exact word); a rhyming dictionary; Strunk and White's *The Elements of Style*; various almanacs; *Bartlett's Familiar Quotations*; Bergen Evans's *Dictionary of Quotations*; *Writer's Market*; *Famous First Facts*; and many others.

I do a great deal of writing on women's interests, travel, and medicine, and my library reflects that. When I wrote greeting cards, I collected books on one-liners, humor, and jokes to give me ideas. I haunt the mark-down table and second-hand book stores and often get ten dollar (and up) books marked down to ninety-nine cents or a quarter. If you get *one* salable idea from a book, it's paid for itself.

Other choices of reference books vary greatly. I really can't say what *you* should have, other than if you find yourself checking the same book out of the library all the time (or have to run down to use it there once a month or more), you probably should buy it. It *is* a business expense, you know.

Whether or not to include music in your office is a personal choice. I know women who can write in the middle of a Cub Scout meeting, yet who find even subtle background music a terrible distraction. Others, who hear every click of the clock, are most creative while listening to a rock station. Some find quiet background music helps to filter out household noises like the washing machine, dishwasher, and kids fighting.

If you think you'd like to try to work with music, use the radio or tapes. Records that require constant changing may keep you busier playing disc jockey than writer.

You do need to keep records, though; not the stereophonic kind, but business records. I have a ledger to keep track of all my expenses as related to my writing and the checks as they come in. I also use a file box to record the name and destination of all articles and stories before they are mailed out. (More about these and other types of record-keeping in Chapter 12.)

If you have a movable office (where you have to keep picking up your work and putting it out of the way for another function), try to keep these record books in a drawer nearby or in a box under the bed. They need to have a permanent location so you can find them rapidly.

The subject of keeping your supplies safe from your children and husband would make a book in itself and, to my knowledge, it's a book that has yet to be written.

I have tried reason: "These are Mommy's business things. You can't touch them because I need them for my work."

I have tried threats: "I'll murder anyone who touches my scissors again. Now, I'm going to close my eyes and when I open them, I want to see the scissors on my desk." (When I opened my eyes the stapler was missing too!)

Pencils are especially difficult to hang onto. You can chain them to your desk, have your name embossed on them in gold, or keep them clutched between your teeth. They'll still disappear. I've given up the battle and just keep buying them, knowing full well that a small forest has been felled to help me ply my trade.

Typing paper seems easier to control. I keep it in its original box. I think everyone is intimidated by the official-looking container. My draft paper comes from a variety of sources. Some comes from one of the quick-print shops. The manager gives me paper he's mis-cut or made errors on, and I use the backs. I also have alerted friends of mine who are in business that if they print up new letterhead for themselves, I'd be delighted with their old. Businesses frequently change phone numbers, company names, and/or addresses and don't know what to do with the stacks of stationery on hand. The backs of such sheets are perfect for your rough drafts.

Many newspapers sell newsprint, cut and neatly packaged. One of the papers in my area sells five hundred sheets of 8½ x 11 for under two dollars. Its cash and carry, but well worth it.

You also can use this type of paper for second sheets (carbons) of your work, although I tend to use colored paper for that. I also use colored mimeograph paper for next-to-final drafts so I can tell at a glance which version is which.

While my kids are welcome to help themselves to scratch paper, I'm pretty particular about my typewriter. If they use it, I insist on their returning the margins to the setting I had them on. Nothing is more frustrating than going back to typing your final draft and discovering in the middle of a page that someone has changed your setting. (It's bad enough when I realize I've stuck the carbon in backwards again.)

When the children were younger, they wanted to "play" on Mom's machine. After buying two toy plastic ones that didn't hold up or type, I finally wised up and bought them a used fifteen-dollar typewriter . . . which is still working beautifully for the fifth (and last) child.

The older children now use my portable typewriter. (They prefer my electric but usually I'm using it when they need to type a report). I encourage them all to type their school work. I think it gives them an advantage, especially those with poor handwriting. They like typing, probably because the sound of the typewriter lulled them to sleep when they were little.

Younger children can look upon your work and your office (and supplies) as a competitor—it takes Mommy away from them. Since they couldn't lick it, I let them join me. When they were younger, I gave them a cigar box filled with their own office supplies—crayons, scissors, paste, paper—so that they could "write" when I was working.

I also tried to proof my work when they were doing their homework or watching television. I was "with them," yet working, and that seemed to satisfy everybody.

Now that they're older, I try to keep them out of my supplies, but often find term-paper remains scattered about my study and the caps off of now-dried-up felt-tip pens. As long as they've left enough carbon paper for me to work on the next day, and returned my rubber cement to approximately the same spot they found it, I've given up trying to have "mine" and "yours." Besides, there are more of them than there is of me!

How to Split Your Personality

Don't skip this section. It's vital if you're to succeed as a housewife-writer, especially working at home. Once you have determined your business hours, you *must* do the Superman bit—step into your office and change from mild-mannered mommy into writer It doesn't matter if your office is just the kitchen table. Once you have cleared off breakfast (putting the dishes into the dishwasher or dumping them into the sink to soak), YOU ARE WORKING. Don't hop up to defrost the refrigerator or call your mother. You are "in the office," and you must settle down to your business for whatever time you have allotted as your working day. That's why it helps to have a schedule. You'll settle in faster and find less to distract you. That's also why it's best to have a spot where you can leave everything out, if at all possible. It takes time to get your box of supplies, lift out the pen mug, find your notes and your manuscript. But if yours *is* a traveling office, fight the urge to "organize the box" or cover it with contact paper. Get your work out and start writing.

My husband helps me organize my day. I'm not sure it is a conscious thing with him, and I've never asked. In the morning, just before he leaves, he'll say, "What do you have on tap today?"

I'll answer, "Finish Chapter 4, write two queries on article ideas, and check through those questionnaire responses."

I don't think he even listens to me! But it really doesn't matter. What's important is that I've got my work mapped out so that as soon as he leaves, I throw the dishes into the dishwasher and take something out to thaw for dinner. Then I get to work. By 8:30 a.m., I'm not only *in* my office, I'm writing.

It's unlikely that your husband would break up *his* working day by fixing the plumbing in the men's room at the office or by rearranging the furniture. Don't you do it either when you're working. A housewife-writer has many distractors, and the house is one of them. It's okay to throw a load of laundry into the washing machine, but if you also put it into the dryer, you'll be half-listening for the bell to ring so the permanent press won't wrinkle. You're supposed to be writing. The time to be listening for dryer bells is when you're fixing dinner or making the beds. When you're working, the only bells you're supposed to be hearing are those of inspiration.

How to Convince Service People You Mean Business

When a housewife calls a serviceman for repairs on anything in the home, the usual assumption is that she has nothing to do but to sit around waiting for him to arrive. A woman who works outside her home, on the other hand, often gets these people to come when it is convenient for her (or her husband) to be home, not "whenever." The best way to get this treatment for yourself as well is to tell the receptionist that you work but will take your lunch hour earlier or later, depending on when the repairman can come. If the receptionist is a working woman too, she'll respect your problem.

Before I learned this trick, I was left to the mercy of service people. When they arrived I stood around, waiting to show them how the motor shrieked when it started, or how the agitate cycle wasn't agitating. This usually took an hour or so right out of the middle of my workday and, "since my schedule was ruined anyway," I puttered around the remainder of the day. Now I ask repairmen to come when it's convenient for me, during my lunch break or late in the afteroon when the kids are home and I'm not writing. If you have a great many things that need fixing, perhaps you could schedule them all to be fixed the same day.

Don't let your neighbors make you the "area drop" for deliveries. Sometimes, because they know you're always home, they'll tell store clerks that they'll be out playing bridge, so "drop it at my neighbor's. She's always there." If you don't say no from the beginning, you'll spend your day hopping up and down, signing for your neighbor's package, and then later having to remember to take it over to him or her. (If this advice comes too late, forget to deliver it—and your neighbor will look for someone who's "more dependable.")

Follow Business Hours

All work and no play not only makes you dull, it eventually makes you less effective. Emulate away-from-home office workers, and take time out for lunch.

I used to be very smug about the fact that when I was writing I worked right through lunch. "Didn't even think about food," I bragged. Then I realized that when I did think about it I inhaled the entire contents of the cookie jar!

Now I take a lunch break. Not only am I fifteen pounds lighter, I also enjoy the break in my routine. I feel better in the afternoon and find that I don't have an afternoon slump when I forget my zip code or type two pages before noticing the ribbon's on "stencil."

Remember these rules about lunch:

1. Eat a light lunch so you won't feel stuffed and sluggish all afternoon.
2. No alcohol. It's difficult to be creative when your mind is dulled (or your gregariousness is unleashed) from even one drink. (Besides, alcohol is fattening.)

3. Stick to one-hour lunches. Tell your friends that you have an appointment. You do, you know; with your typewriter.
4. If you eat at home, sit down and enjoy it. Read your mail or watch your favorite soap opera (but make certain you turn off the TV right afterwards).
5. Make the beds or water the plants on your lunch hour if you feel you must, but otherwise just relax.

To Hell With Alexander Graham Bell

The telephone can be both a godsend and a curse for a writer. You need it for telephone interviews, checking to see if a book is in the library or if your pictures are ready, and whether or not an editor is interested in your idea. But if you don't control the phone, it can keep your writing on hold.

Discourage friends and relatives from calling you during your business hours. This is another bit of marvelous advice that I find easier to pass along than enforce. Everyone knows I'm in my office from 8:30 to 2:30. They can "get me" there.

"I know you're busy, but I just want to ask you something," is the way these interruptions usually present themselves. Nine times out of ten, the burning question is, "Will you bake cookies for the sixth grade?" (Answer: No, I don't bake. I buy if absolutely pressed to furnish cookies.) Or, "How was the movie you saw last weekend?" (Answer: I don't remember. I'm working now.)

But the fact is, once the phone rings, my concentration is broken and it takes a while to get back to where I was. Sometimes I've completely lost the phrase or thought I was about to write down. Perhaps you are one of those rare individuals who work best with a dozen preschoolers running around your chair and the telephone ringing itself silly. If so, skip over this section. For the rest of us mere mortals, here are some concrete suggestions that work some of the time:

1. Plead with friends and relatives to call at noon when you break for lunch. Many of them will be busy then and will forget that they had something "too good to keep."
2. Firmly tell those who do call that you're working now, that you'll call back when you break for lunch. This should impress all but the very dullest that you indeed are working, even though you are at home.
3. Buy an answering machine and let your callers communicate with a tape recording. (Most of them will hang up without leaving a message, I'm told.)

4. As soon as you can afford it, put in another phone line. This is your business number, to be given out only to editors, agents, your husband, and to your children who are instructed to use it only in an emergency. Do *not* give this number out to friends and/or relatives. Then don't answer your house phone. Unplug it if you can or learn to ignore it during your office hours.

You may have wondered why I didn't put "Don't answer your phone" at the top of the list. It's because I can't *not* answer it. If it rings, I am sure that either one of the children is hurt or my editor is calling to insist that I take a larger advance! But by having a business number, you transfer those few important calls to one number and let the cemetery lot salesman ring away unanswered.

I did, however, make one concession that it's only fair to admit. To rationalize the extra expense of the business phone, we also made it the children's phone *after* 3:30, when they're home. For this reason, I tell all people I do business with that "I'm out of the office after 3:30." I am. The kids are tying up that phone at this point.

How to Fight the Lonelies

To me, the most difficult part of having a home office is having to maintain self-discipline and fight loneliness. Unless you're actually interviewing someone, you really are very much alone, especially if you have no children or they're in school or grown. That's one reason why it's so tempting to let the gal next door come in for coffee and conversation—and why we sometimes do chat on the phone when we know we shouldn't. People working in an office have coworkers to talk to, or at least are aware that there are other "live bodies" around. Even if you have a solo office, you're bound to see people in the elevator, in the office next to yours, etc.

Some women say that they really aren't lonely, that they enjoy the peace and quiet when everyone else is at work, and the kids, at last, all are in school. Now they can get on with uninterrupted writing. But for others, it can be a real problem, one that can interfere with writing it you allow it to. Here are a few ways to combat the lonelies:

1. If you have small children at home but yearn for the sound of an adult voice, take them to a park or playground for a few hours. You can store up images, smells, and sounds to use in your writing; meet other people; and enjoy watching your children at play. You also *could* use that time to proof a next-to-final draft.

2. Plan to go to lunch with a friend once a week, but set yourself a definite time to get back to work. Make certain your lunch is with someone whose company you enjoy; someone who is enthusiastic

about what he/she does and is interested in hearing about your work too. If you go out with someone who is depressed or bored with life, you'll drag back to the office and not feel much like working.

3. Try to relax and just play on the weekend (or one or two days during the week). Many of us use our time off for grocery shopping, errands, and housework and wonder why we feel tired all the time. Give yourself a chance to unwind and refill the creative reservoirs. Sometimes I've come back on Monday to a page or two that really gave me fits on Friday and found that it almost wrote itself. I've never tried to question why that is, other than having a strong belief in giving your subconscious a chance to work. Save some time during your "days off" for you and your husband to be alone together too. During your work week, you may be preoccupied without meaning to be. He may feel left out—and begin to resent your writing.

4. Accept speaking dates as long as they don't begin to interfere with your writing. You don't want to find yourself talking about writing and never doing any, but by speaking about your work to others, you'll have a chance to be with people, recharge your enthusiasm by talking about something you really enjoy doing, and be more likely to remember to practice what you preach.

5. Join a *professional* organization in your community. Most cities and towns have some profesional groups appropriate for a woman writer. There may be a chapter of a national organization, such as Women In Communications, Inc., or the National Federation of Business and Professional Women's Clubs. There may also be a locally organized author's or writer's club. You don't want to join a club merely to chat about your writing. But these groups can be supportive and informative. Women In Communications is composed of women in broadcasting, newspaper, advertising, and other areas of the communication field. It gives you a broad base to draw upon when you need information and/or interviews, and it will introduce you to women with some of the same interests and problems you have. As long as these groups don't take up an inordinate amount of time, they serve their purpose. If you find, however, that you are constantly running to meetings, talking on the phone, and not writing, then think through your priorities again. (See Chapter 7 for more on this subject.)

6. Each day try to get some exercise. It doesn't matter if you jog, jump rope, or do jumping jacks with the handsome man on television, you'll keep your spirits up if you exercise. While sitting at your typewriter, try touching your head to first one shoulder and then the other. Tense your shoulders and then relax them. Do sit-ups from time to time. You can climb stairs, ride your bike to the grocery, or play volleyball with your kids. As mentioned in Chapter 1, exercise

is important to maintain your energy (and creative) level.

7. *Occasionally* go shopping and just "goof off." I try to do this after I've made a sale, as a reward. As long as you don't get behind in your work, running away from home (and office) won't hurt. LIke going off your diet, you'll enjoy feeling free—and then be more determined to get back to work the next day.

But, for some women, home and office just don't mix. "I keep seeing housework I should be doing," complains one. "I feel guilty when I'm at the typewriter—and guilty when I'm cleaning windows during what's supposed to be my writing time."

"The kids drive me crazy," says another. "I shut the bedroom door and try to shut out their noise as well. But I can't concentrate."

"There's really no place to work," says a third. "I've scoured the house from top to bottom." She hesitates and adds, "Besides, it bothers my husband to see my papers and things lying around. If he can't see them, he doesn't mind."

Where do they run? Some go to their mothers' houses to write, or to the home or apartment of a working friend. I've heard of two housewife-writers who trade houses for their working hours and find that each can ignore the other's phone or doorbell (and housework). Many rent small offices.

A few years ago, I tried an office away from home. I thought it would keep me from getting sidetracked with housework, prevent interruptions, and make me feel "more professional." Briefcase in hand, I left the house promptly at 8:30 a.m. and returned around 2:30 p.m., shortly before the children came home from school. My office was small; I don't think I could have laid down in it, although I never tried. It held a desk, chair, typing stand, and a dusty fake Schefflera. It certainly made others take me more seriously.

One day at lunch I was introduced to a man who nodded pleasantly, as men who meet other men's wives do. He didn't give me a second thought until he mentioned that he had an office in the "B___" building.

"Oh, I do too," I said.

He looked at me in surprise. "Really? What do you do?"

Obviously, the fact that I had a "real" office made me someone worthwhile, someone who "really worked." I didn't imagine the change in him. It was real.

You might think that having the office made my writing better, but it didn't. Despite the fact that I felt more professional, more committed to my writing, there were many disadvantages:

1. It took twenty minutes to get from my home to the office.
2. I had to pay for parking.
3. I needed to "dress" to go downtown.
4. I had to pay rent each month, regardless of whether I had sold anything. The rent had seemed minimal at first. But I was beginning to write longer, more detailed articles. They paid well when they finally sold, but it took longer to write them, which meant more time in between checks.
5. The walls were thin. I could overhear the insurance salesman next door to my office talking to his clients on the phone. I also could hear him lighting his cigarette, or so it seemed.
6. The supplies I needed always seemed to be at home. Although I had a typewriter, dictionary, pens, and paper in both the office and my home, I never had the file or reference book I wanted with me. The library was just across the street, but it took time to get there to find the book I needed.
7. To keep costs down and prevent unwanted interruptions, I had no telephone in the office. It also meant, however, that I couldn't call out from my office and couldn't be reached if the kids got sick at school (they did) or the Newbery Award Committee wanted to reach me (they didn't).
8. Working nights was difficult because I had to get a sitter so that I could go downtown to the office.
9. If the kids were sick, I couldn't go to work at all.

Finally, in frustration, I gave up my office and came home, determined to make a go of it with an "in-house" office. Other housewives, however, rave about the success of their "away" office. In many ways it's harder than working at home—but in many ways, it's easier. Even so, I'd suggest you try the home office first.

Don't be impatient if, at first, you find it's hard to concentrate at home. There's a lot of emotion packed into those many square feet, and you're trying to block it all out and focus in on a little 8½ x 11 inch sheet of blank paper.

Make your office area as conducive to concentration as possible. If you're writing in the laundry room, throw the dirty clothes into the washer (don't turn it on yet) so you won't have to stare at them and start feeling guilty. If you write at the kitchen table, clear it of dishes. And if you have a "room of your own," don't think how dirty the windows are, or wonder if you should wash the dog before you start writing.

Even with an office, you need to have some work that can travel with you; e.g., a filler to write, an outline for a chapter, or a query for an article. These all are perfect "travel companions" as you wait for carpools, doctors, etc. They also write who only sit and wait, someone almost said.

It takes tremendous will power and determination to be a housewife-writer. But you already know that! Don't become discouraged by your failures or frustrated by the constant interruptions. Famous women writers have had them too.

In *Memoir of Jane Austen*, her nephew, James Edward Austen, wrote, "She had no separate study to repair to, and most of the work must have been done in the general sitting-room, subject to all kinds of casual interruptions."

See what good company you're in?

Although I prefer to work in silence and total isolation, I have learned to turn inwards, concentrating on what I am writing, and I succeed to the point that it drives my family wild. They'll be talking to me and I don't hear them. But I also don't hear the TV blaring, dogs barking, or kids fighting, either. And, although I never believed it at the time, toddlers do grow up into reasonably independent youngsters who don't need to be watched every minute of their waking day.

So if you feel you can't write at home, try it anyway. The kids will grow older, not younger, and by the time they're off to school, leaving you with big blocks of writing hours, you'll have developed the discipline and confidence to make the most of them.

Believe In Yourself (and Make It Happen)

4.

"Modesty is a virtue!"

This ancient bromide guided (detoured, actually) my life for many years. It made me ill-equipped to handle compliments from well-meaning friends, hesitant to volunteer for jobs or parts in plays that I really wanted to tackle, and even lost me victories in school elections because I wouldn't vote for myself, even in the face of secret ballots.

Today, through wisdom one seems only to gain through life experience, I realize that if you don't rally 'round your own flag, no one else will either.

We all know women who downgrade themselves at every opportunity.

"What a pretty dress."

"This old thing? I've had it for years."

Or . . . "I love your hair."

"It's a mess. Can't do a thing with it."

What happens? We start taking a second look through *her* jaundiced eye and think, "You know, she's right. She really *does* look a little seedy!"

This chapter deals with the all-important matter of feeling good about yourself, believing in your writing, and keeping at it until you succeed. I am firmly convinced that the main difference between a published writer and a nonpublished one is that the published writer didn't give up. Call it persistence, stubbornness, or self-discipline, as long as you continue to write, to perfect this business of writing, you will succeed. Unlike the guy in the Broadway show, you can't succeed in *this* business without really trying.

It's vital to have confidence in yourself if you want to succeed as a professional writer. Writing, like most art, is subjective. There's almost no way to judge it, other than through an individual's personal taste. If many people like your work, you're a "good writer."

That's quite different from being an electrician. You're successful in this occupation if you can (1) make electrical things work and (2) do it without electrocuting yourself. There's nothing subjective about that! A pro tennis player is successful if she wins more games than she loses.

But what makes you a "good writer" is dependent on many factors. You may have submitted your manuscript to the wrong market or it may have been slanted wrong for that market. Your style of writing may be "out of vogue" just now. (There are "fads" in writing too, you know.) An editor may reject your work because his ulcer is acting up, or his teenager ran away, and he's angry and upset. Or he may have just bought an article on the same subject. Or his wife (whose first name is the same as yours) left him. . . . You have to be diligent and keep writing until you get by this first judge of your work. It's difficult and sometimes it's discouraging, but if you don't keep trying you'll never know if the public thinks you're a "good writer" too.

How to Handle Rejections

With difficulty! It's never easy being rejected in life, and it's no better in the writing business. It hurts! It's knowing that someone else is being judgmental about something that's yours, and there's nothing you can do about it. Most of us are hurt when someone criticizes our children. It carries through with our brainchildren too.

Pouting and crying never have changed a rejection slip into an acceptance. (If I thought it would, I'd be the first to try it.) It also does no good to throw your work away, stuff it in a drawer, write a hate letter to the editor, or sprinkle the manuscript with "Whisper Yes" cologne and send it back.

What *does* help is to figure that even the best editors make mistakes sometimes. *Jonathan Livingston Seagull* was rejected by many publishing houses before it went on to become a best-seller, as was Jacqueline Susann's *Valley of the Dolls*. Taylor Caldwell spent eighteen years trying to get her first novel published. *The Doctor's Quick Weight Loss Diet*, by Samm Sinclair Baker and Dr. Irwin M. Stillman, was rejected sixteen times before it finally was published and became a best-seller. See what good company you're in?

An agent I know has sold many books for her authors the *twentieth* time around, and I have sold many articles on their *tenth* trip out. Sometimes they have to be reworked slightly—or retyped if the editor spilled coffee on a few pages. Believe in your work. Check manuscripts over for any possible changes when they come back and send them out to another market. In fact, I usually jot down a second possible market before mailing a manuscript out to the first one. Perhaps that marks me as a pessimist, but I often feel dejected when rejected, and it's easier to consider where to send your "child" next before it's back staring you in the face.

The important thing to remember is that a manuscript won't sell at all if it's sitting on your desk or in a drawer. In order to be considered, you have to play by the rules, and that includes sending your manuscript out again to another market where still another faceless editor will pass judgment on it.

Possibly there are some writers who are so tough and so experienced that rejections don't bother them. I don't know any like that and personally have not reached that stage.

I take rejections to heart. When an editor writes, "Nicely done. Wish we could use it," I feel like writing back, "So do I. Why don't you, so we'd both feel better?"—but I don't.

I also get upset when I get a form rejection slip. "Couldn't they at least have written something personal?" I moan. The cat just stares at me, contemplating his future with a mistress who talks to herself.

If they write, "We just bought something like this," I kick myself for taking so long on the article, and vow to mail the next query out *before* the article's written.

I'm never satisfied with rejections, and most of my writer friends suffer from this same paranoia. "Did they mean they loved it when they said they liked it or did they mean they only liked it?" We go round and round, contemplating the meaning of life; some unknown "they" two thousand miles away can make or break our morning.

You have to be able to be objective about your writing so you can cut, revise, or totally rewrite in order to improve it. But, on the other hand, you also must believe in it. It may not be as good as it will be a year from now, when you have more experience, but it's as good as it can be now. And you must write, because no one can read your work (or judge it) until it's written.

There must be a slight masochistic tendency in people who want to be writers. We place our ego in the hands of others while we sit home and wait. And yet, when our work's rejected (it's our work that's being rejected, not us), we don't curse the gods or a distant editor but bounce back up again like those plastic dolls with weighted bottoms that kids use as a punching bag. We do because—that's what writers do.

Believing Can Make It Happen

Years ago, when I applied for my first job as a radio copywriter, a station manager asked me, "Are you any good?"

I looked at him in alarm. No one had ever asked me that before. "There are my writing samples," I stammered, pointing to the folder of radio commercials on his desk.

"I'll read them later," he said. "Are you a good writer?"

I agonized for seconds. Would it seem like bragging if I said "yes"? Would he hire me if I said "no"? I took a deep breath. "Yes, I think I am."

"Good," he said, turning to look at my samples. "I'd never hire anyone who didn't think she was good. If you don't, why should I?"

I learned a valuable lesson—that you can't sell yourself to others if you aren't buying you yourself. I must have appeared more confident to the next manager because he hired me right away.

But it's hard to convince yourself that you're a writer when no one is buying your work. Your husband may like it. Your mother may think you're on your way to a Pulitzer Prize. Your best friend thinks you're Beaumont Heights' answer to Erma Bombeck. But you're still not selling your work and you wonder, "Am I good enough?"

Many of us who are being published still wonder. One writer friend said, "Every time I get a check in the mail I cash it quickly, just in case they made a mistake. I still feel that any day now I'll be 'found out.' "

A housewife-writer who has published numerous books for young adults told me, "Every time I get an assignment—not something on speculation, but a firm commitment—I'm sure I'll never be able to live up to the image the publisher has of me, that this book won't be as good as the others, and that they'll find out I've been 'faking it' all this time. My voice shakes, my stomach hurts, my mouth gets dry, and I know I'll never be able to write another word."

I was fascinated. "Then what happens?" I asked.

She looked at me blankly. "What happens? Why, then I sit down and start writing."

The advice comes from so many diverse sources, it must be true. If you're going to be a writer, you must write.

But it's also true that you must have confidence in yourself. If you don't, it will be impossible to develop and practice the self-discipline necessary to get the writing done. It's a little like whistling in the dark. Tell yourself that you believe and start acting as though you do. Concentrate on your goal. Believe in what you're doing, and that belief can carry you.

Sometimes it helps to share your belief with others. Tell friends about your writing. Saying it aloud makes the committment stronger. When someone says, "I hardly ever see you. What have you been doing?" don't stare at the floor and mumble, "I've been working." Look them right in the eye and talk about the article you're writing about abused children or alcoholic housewives for a national magazine.

Chances are about a third of these people will smile, laugh, and change the subject. They think you're joking—but they're not really sure. And they don't want to embarrass themselves by asking.

Another third will say, "Really?" Then they'll stare, and because they're self-conscious and don't know what to say (yes, they might be a little in awe of someone like you), they'll turn and walk away. That, in turn, makes you feel a little self-conscious and wonder if you should have tried that new mouthwash sample after all.

But the other third is a delight. They'll ask what facts you've learned, how you discovered them, etc. You'll get to talk to your heart's delight about something that's near and dear to you. Then—and this is the important part—your listener will say, "Hey, I know someone who had an experience just like that." Then it's your turn to listen, to take mental notes, and add one more bit of research to your work. Your friend feels as though she's contributed something to your article; you've had an interesting exchange of ideas and experiences; and both of you have learned a little of what communication is all about.

For years I felt self-conscious about "being different" and seldom talked about my work. I wasn't exactly a closet writer, but I was close to it. I felt embarrassed about "what I did," like someone who has thousands of pairs of shoes stuffed in the closet but has a compulsion to buy more, or who eats a dozen doughnuts at one sitting. I just didn't like to talk about my writing because I didn't know how my revelation would be received. Like a mother protecting her weakest child, I surrounded my writing with arms of silence.

Be Healthy and Wise

You need to maintain a proper diet in order to keep up your energy level. Never overeat; it just makes you sleepy. But a good breakfast is important. Stay away from fad diets. If you need to watch your weight, make certain you eat balanced meals and fewer calories. Some writers may argue that they function best on coffee for breakfast and a hamburger for lunch. I disagree. You plan balanced meals for your family. Why slight yourself?

In order to accomplish everything she needs to do and a little bit more, many housewife-writers steal from their sleeping hours. They go to bed early, get up at midnight, write for two hours and go back to bed until the kids get up for school. Others stay up until three in the morning and write.

"I can get along fine on four or five hours of sleep," one prolific housewife-writer boasted. Then she wondered why she was so prone to colds and flu which, in the long run, caused her to lessen her writing output. Adequate sleep is important to good health, and a writer who also functions as housewife, mother, lover, cook, etc., needs good health habits as much as anyone doing hard physical labor.

Temper Time Demands With Realism

Be realistic about your time demands. Don't set impossible schedules for yourself. Too many would-be writers get carried away by enthusiasm at first, attempting to spend far more hours at their work than they can afford. Then they become discouraged when they fail to stay on schedule and give up.

It's far better to plan just one hour a day for your writing (and feel as though you've been given a treat when you can stretch it to two) than to consider two hours a "must" and constantly feel frustrated.

For some reason, writers, although enamored by words, seem obsessed with numbers.

Beginning writers, frustrated by their lack of sales, will complain "But I wrote two thousand words a day" . . . "I typed fifteen pages yesterday" . . . "I have six articles in the mail."

The problem with working toward a numerical goal is that you become less concerned with the quality of what you're counting. Be realistic, counting minutes and hours instead, and you'll be able to focus in on the words you're selecting (even if it means using one writing session to complete a single paragraph, as long as it's a paragraph of value).

Concrete goals are important, and perhaps it's easier for some people to calculate the minimum number of pages they'll write per day and rigidly stick to it. I personally feel much less inhibited by working during my "writing period" and concentrating on what I'm trying to say. Sometimes it's only four pages; sometimes, it's twenty. But that's okay for me. Every oven's different and sometimes cakes take longer to bake one day than the next.

While you need to develop self-discipline, in order to stick to your self-imposed writing schedule, you also need to be like an old girdle—flexible, but firm. Life's not predictable. Families have problems, illnesses, and needs that must be attended to NOW. That means you must make allowances, put "tucks" in your scheduling so you can let them out when needed, giving you extra hours to meet deadlines and still cope with the unexpected. A housewife-writer's life is filled with surprises, and if you let them throw you, frustrate you or stop you, you'll never make it to "Go" and collect your two hundred dollars.

Coping With Procrastination

Are you a procrastinator? Welcome to the crowd. Most of us are, and it's something we have to be on constant guard against. Each morning I can think of at least twenty reasons in as many seconds why I "need" to do something other than write.

Luckily, procrastination is not a fatal disease. It can, however, be chronic, and can only be controlled, not cured. The best way to control it is through practicing self-discipline. (Don't make a face. That isn't as hard as it sounds.)

If you procrastinate because you're overwhelmed by the enormity of your task, try subdividing it into smaller sections. Little bits are never quite as threatening.

I had to totally reorganize and rewrite one chapter of this book. I found myself incapable of beginning the job for two full days. I'd go into the study on time, but rather than work on the chapter I'd transfer names and addresses into a new address book, put plant food on my dead cactus, rearrange old copies of *Reader's Digest* into chronological order, and wash out the mugs holding my pencils and pens. I did everything imaginable to keep from facing that chapter.

My deadline was at hand. I knew I had to do something. So I outlined the chapter, writing the main idea of each section on a slip of paper. Then I spread all these scraps on the floor and moved them around until they (at last!) followed in a natural order. (A strong wind would have set me back days!) Then, taking each piece of paper in its turn, I wrote a paragraph or two explaining the idea. Before I knew it, I had outsmarted myself. By making confetti out of my chapter, I had been able to work on it, piece by piece, rather than trying to tackle the whole thing at once. I was able to stop procrastinating because I was only faced with a series of small and nonthreatening writing tasks.

Often we procrastinate because we have so much to do we don't know where to begin—so we don't.

"I've got a column to write, this article to finish, and a chapter due by the end of the week. I'll never get it all finished." (Just typing this makes me feel anxious.)

There's no way anyone can do everything at once. You can't possibly concentrate on that many things at one time. This predicament happens often in the life of a housewife-writer. People think she's preoccupied, but actually, she's trying to figure what to do next as she pins up the hem on her daughter's cheerleading uniform, hears the bill collector coming up the walk because she forgot to mail the checks she so carefully wrote out, and the next voice she hears will be her editor on the phone saying, "Where's the manuscript you promised?"

This is the time to set priorities. Write down all your deadlines (both writing and family) and take most important things first. By zeroing in on one task and giving it your full attention, you can accomplish wonders, and less time is spent worrying about everything and doing nothing.

When you procrastinate, you let things pile up. It means massive disorganization and more stress and frustration in your life (already filled with enough of both). Try a little behavior modification to shake up the inertia. Give yourself a treat when you've accomplished something.

"I'll finish this draft and then fix lunch."

"I'll retype the article and call my girlfriend."

Give yourself deadlines and make deals with yourself—be a tough taskmaster. I talk to myself constantly—"Come on now, finish this up"; or "Get back to work. That's a pretty long coffee break." People may think I'm a little nutty, but they expect it when you're a writer.

Each day write down what you hope to accomplish that day, as well as the major goals you're aiming for. "I want to write a book," is too big a bite for anyone. You have to break it into smaller pieces so you don't choke. But by writing it down as your goal, you'll know it's there, and by also jotting down the daily steps necessary to get there, you'll reach the goal sooner. Books are written by chapters; chapters by pages; pages one by one. It's as simple as that. Post your goals over the typewriter so that whenever your mind wanders, you'll spot your goals and get back on track.

Remember that procrastination only makes your job harder. If you have to tell an editor that you can't handle an assignment, call her first thing in the morning. The longer you wait, the harder it becomes. Rewriting's no fun either. But the longer you put it off, the larger it becomes in your mind. Do it now—and get it done. Procrastinate and you've got the same task staring you in the face tomorrow.

Get Thee to a Typewriter

It always comes back to this, doesn't it? If you want to be a writer, you must write. Erasmus, a Dutch scholar, said in 1508, "The desire to write grows with writing. . . ." Fan that desire with sincere belief in yourself and your ability, not blind faith, but conviction tempered by application of proven writing techniques, steadfastness of purpose, and a willingness to put in the hours necessary for success. You *can* do it, and confidence in that fact will be your guiding force.

When people asked if I were "still writing," I'd nod my head and change the subject. It was so much safer.

Now, because I've been exposed by publication, I have no secret. I'm very visible. So, like the slightly pudgy girl who dives into the water before anyone sees her (so they'll be dazzled by her strong strokes and less put off by her rounded tummy), I speak right up.

If you *don't* believe in yourself, if you won't speak up, if you really think you're battling against impossible odds, you might as well quit now. You'll never succeed as a writer if *you* don't think you can make it.

That doesn't mean that you'll never have doubts. Most of us do at times. There are so many facets involved in writing and selling, so many steps where you can be tripped up, that you'd be crazy *not* to feel a little uncertain. But, like *The Little Engine That Could*, thinking you can, acting as though you can, and taking the appropriate action often can make it so.

Belief in yourself ignites your creative power, driving you ever toward your goal of becoming a professional writer.

"Where do you get your ideas?" (One of the most common questions asked.)

I try not to dwell on where I "get things." As long as the ideas keep coming and the words keep flowing, I'm not about to probe or overanalyze. When you believe in your work, in your overall goal, and in the particular piece you're writing, your subconscious filters through to the surface, filling in the dry spaces, like water rushing down an irrigation ditch.

Believing in yourself, in your ability to succeed as a writer, keeps you plugging away during days when nothing sells. It makes you strive for improvement even when you're selling everything you write. It keeps you working on a definite writing routine, helps you organize your life so you can make time to write, and gives you the energy to write, even when you're exhausted from looking after a home and family.

It enables you to give yourself a good talking-to when you panic, like my friend, when faced with a definite assignment. It means being able to answer, "Are you a good writer?" with a confident, "You bet I am. Maybe not as good as I'll be someday—but I'm good!"

"What if I believe in myself and I still don't sell anything?" a young woman once asked me. She had put a deadline on her talent—"If I don't sell something by . . . ." Who's to say that if she had kept working one month more she might not have sold an article? Perhaps her writing was terrific, but she was submitting to the wrong market. Her biggest mistake was in putting a time limit on her belief in herself.

If you don't believe in yourself, who will?

Writing Breeds Writers

Epictetus, a philosopher of about A.D. 110, said, "If you wish to be a writer, write."

It sounds so simple.

But making yourself sit down and write is probably the hardest part of being a writer. We're afraid to start writing because maybe our finished product won't be any good, or people may laugh, or . . . you fill in the blanks. So we postpone our debut until we "have time to write."

But nobody is looking over your shoulder. No one will know if you're writing but you. No one will know if you only write one page. It's important to begin.

When I was in school, I had a part-time job working in the address-o-graph department. I sat at a giant, dirty, noisy machine that looked like a printing press crossed with a typewriter. I shoved metal plates into a slot and pounded out name and address labels, typed backwards (so when printed they would face frontwards). I was so bad at it that I was embarrassed for anyone to see how many plates I had ruined. I began stuffing them in my purse and lugging them back to the dorm to throw away in secret so no one would know.

But when you're sitting at your typewriter, it's just you. You can throw away stacks of first drafts, and no one will ever find out. If you wait until you can do it perfectly, you'll never begin. There has never been (nor ever will be) a book, play, article, or any other piece of writing so perfect that it couldn't have been made better by some little rewriting here or there. But who needs perfection? Who would really recognize it if we found it? And what would we all do afterwards if we did?

So don't use perfection as a reason not to get started. Do your best, and if it doesn't turn out exactly as you would have wished, do better next time. But at least, you've begun. If you're perfection-prone remember the tale of the cabinet maker who decided that he would build a perfect chest. When it was completed, it was truly magnificent. But he wanted it to be without flaw. He sanded it and sanded it, wanting to make it totally smooth. When he had finished, the chest was sawdust beneath his feet.

But even once you overcome your initial fear and/or awe of beginning, there are a thousand and one other reasons not to get started. I know why "this isn't the best time for me to write" as well as you do. I can out-procrastinate anyone on my block. I have excuses for not writing that I haven't even used yet! But I try not to listen to any of them.

Probably the most insidious form of procrastination comes in the guise of letter writing. (We're sitting at a typewriter and we're writing. What more do you want!) But lengthy, chatty letters to friends and editors, though fun and less stressful to write than manuscripts, won't sell. It's tempting when you're writing to a writer-friend to "tell" the story or article idea you're working on. Often this waters down your enthusiasm when you finally do sit down to "write for real." It's important to keep in touch with friends, especially when they're writers who can comfort and encourage you in your work. Just tackle that type of correspondence *after* working hours. Then you can write about all the sales you're making.

I'm all right if I can get myself to "assume the position" (with me, it's sitting at the typewriter. You may prefer lying on your back on the waterbed, writing on a clipboard with your special astronaut write-upside-down pen). Then habit begins to take over. I almost can feel the change coming over me, like a woman in the TV commercial who finally finds the "right " toilet bowl cleaner.

I stare at the typewriter keys and begin to carry on a two-way discussion with myself, one worthy of any split personality, stating all the reasons why I really can't get any work done today because . . . then I shrug impatiently, tell myself I've heard all those tales before, and begin, slowly, to write.

Inspiration Be Damned: Full Speed Ahead!

Most writers agree that a regular routine, even if it's no more than an hour a day, is better than writing only when the "mood strikes."

Inspiration seldom comes when you wait for it. Like a recalcitrant child, you have to seek it out, cajole, and, finally, get tough. Writing's like getting water from a pump. You need to prime it a bit first before anything starts flowing. But a pump's only as good as the condition of its parts. Any housewife who is trying to include writing in her schedule needs to be aware of its physical demands.

How to Do Housework Faster — (or Not at All)

5.

Nothing can erode your writing hours as much as housework because it's "always there." Regardless how perfectly you do it today, you'll have to do it all over again tomorrow. And, worst of all, it's never totally done. You always can find something else lurking in a dusty corner or damp crevice that needs your attention. Some women spend all day cleaning, scrubbing, washing, and waxing. Yet, chances are their homes don't appear to be any more sparkling than the houses of women who give theirs "a lick and a promise." Whoever said life was fair?

When a writer friend and I surveyed nearly five hundred women (full-time homemakers as well as women employed outside the home) for a book we were writing, we discovered that working women unanimously agreed that their housekeeping standards had changed.

One woman reported, "I no longer feel that my house has to be as immaculate as my mother's was. It only needs to be reasonably clean. That's good enough for me."

Said another, "I do only what has to be done, what

shows. . . . There are closets I haven't straightened in months, and I'm afraid to see what's collected in the attic. On my days off, when it comes to choosing between a full day of spring cleaning or a picnic with the family, I'll pick fun every time. The housework will get done eventually, when it needs to badly enough."

A housewife-writer looked thoughtful as she ran her fingers over a houseplant. "I know I could be doing more housework . . .but there's no end to it. Sometimes I feel a little guilty when people come over and I know there may be cobwebs somewhere. But there might be cobwebs at their house too! Besides, I'm starting to get work published, and my family's content with things as they are. What more could anyone want?"

Think about the standards you impose on *your* housekeeping. Are you aiming for the unattainable goal of perfection? Does a spotless house make you feel like a "good wife and mother"? Are you trying to keep your home the way you *think* you remember your mother did hers? Are you "competing" with a sister, sister-in-law, or cousin who's known far and wide as "The Perfect Homemaker"? Are you married to a man who equates an immaculate house with your love for him? Are you using housework as an excuse to keep you from writing?

Understanding *why* housework's important to you is vital if you're to control it. By removing (or at least being aware of) its emotional aspects, you can deal with it practically, efficiently, and realistically, which must be done if you intend to salvage enough time in your day for writing. It's an "either-or" proposition, because time saved from one can be recycled for the other.

Put Housework In Its Place

By mentally and physically putting housework in its rightful place—a chore to be done, but only when it's convenient for you—you'll find the compulsion to get it done eases. You'll discover, for example, that you can just as easily dust, vacuum, and do laundry when the kids are home from school as in the morning, and that often they'll enjoy pitching in and talking about their day as you both work. They'll have a better sense of what running a household requires if they take an active part in it too.

If you determine that your only uninterrupted time for writing is in the morning, convince yourself that it's "all right" to leave the dishes in the sink and write. The dishes will still be there when you break for lunch. You'll do them faster and with a sense of satisfaction if you've done your writing first. If it makes you feel any better, find someone whose house is messier than yours and think of hers when you start to feel guilty.

Forget about scrubbing your kitchen floor on some self-imposed schedule. In her book *How to Be a Mother and a Person Too*, Shirley L. Radl says, "If my feet stick to the kitchen floor, I mop it."

I have gotten by without mopping for two weeks by washing up the sticky spots. Eventually, of course, you'll scrub it, but only when it's convenient for you or so sticky or dirty that it's easier to mop the whole thing than "touch up." All Grandma's rigid routines of "Monday is wash day, Tuesday is ironing, etc.," were not set up for the housewife-mother who also writes.

Make housework fit into your writing schedule, not the other way around. Do only what needs to be done *as* it needs to be done, then do it as efficiently as you can. I call this "planned procrastination." It means, "There's a method to my madness."

Draw up a list of chores that need to be done. Then see if they fall into any logical order. Some women do the bulk of their grocery shopping on Friday (when the supermarkets are most crowded). Others prefer to do it on an off-day, like Tuesday or in the evenings. I split my bedchanging; Monday we change the beds downstairs, Wednesday upstairs. I most often do laundry on those days so it "makes sense." But the secret of success with "planned procrastination" is in being flexible. Grocery shopping *can* be done a different day, the beds *can* be changed on Tuesday, Thursday, Sunday, or (horror of horrors) not at all that week.

Sometimes I find myself too wrapped up in an article to do grocery shopping. Usually there's something I can find to feed the family, and the shopping can be done another day. Some days I'm too tired from writing to clean the room I planned to tackle that day. There's always tomorrow!

Don't let a rigid schedule of chores organize *you*. You're supposed to organize them! Streamline your housework in order to have time for writing. Most people don't inspect your home with a white glove. If it's neat and you're content, they'll be far more impressed with the smile on your face than the shine on your floor. People aren't supposed to eat off your floor. That's why we have plates. (If the plates are dirty, use paper!)

How to Streamline Your Housework
   1. Eliminate the unnecessary.

2. Simplify what *has* to be done.
3. Do what you *have* to do faster.
4. Let others (family or paid help) do some of it.

What do you *have* to do? Really, very little. About the only household tasks that must be done are having food for your family to eat and clean clothes for them to wear (and you don't necessarily have to be the only one responsible for either). Everything else can be "faked" a little. Does that sound shocking? It shouldn't. Magicians have always known that their tricks really were not magic, but illusion. So, with a little preplanning and sleight-of-hand, you can learn to make many once-necessary chores vanish into thin air.

Don't Clean Your House, Strip It

Begin by taking pictures of every room in the house, and study each photo carefully. Then ask yourself, why is this room "dirty"? Chances are it's not dirt you're looking at, but *clutter*. Most of us become acclimated to the mess around us. The junk piles up bit by bit, like tiny silent snowflakes, until suddenly we realize we're snowbound.

But the camera isn't fooled by "comfortable" clutter. It sees all the photographs, road maps, and magazines on the kitchen counter as well as the sweater, gym bag, and soccer ball on the family-room floor. It uncovers a stack of unanswered mail teetering on top of your dresser, along with the messy array of perfume bottles, nail-polish remover, and tubes of ointment for some long-forgotten itch or pain. Study these photos of each room and write down what needs to be thrown out, hidden, or rearranged.

Begin with one room and work through to every other room in the house. If your children are old enough, let them do their own straightening, but make sure they have adequate storage for their things. This includes baskets, buckets, plastic washtubs for little cars, doll furniture, and blocks; bookcases for books, puzzles, games and records; cigar boxes, metal bandage boxes, or matchboxes for crayons; drawer space or plastic washtubs for T-shirts, underwear, socks, shorts, etc. Don't overorganize. Kids can toss socks into a drawer without too much trouble. It's doubtful they'll get them into a little divider within the drawer. Have closet rods lowered for small children so they can hang up their own clothes, and put hooks everywhere, inside and out of the closet, so they can hang up ties and towels, belts and balls (put the ball in a mesh bag first), jackets and jeans, etc.

Check the photographs to see if you have too many things sitting around gathering dust (proving to anyone who has nothing better to do than checking up on you that you've been too busy to dust) and making the room look neglected. Put some of these things away, along with miniature collections (if you can bear to box them), tiny ashtrays that hold ashes for only one cigarette, all but two of your favorite tabletop pictures, and empty-but-decorative candy dishes and vases. Sometimes this reduces the choice to the Wedgwood vase your great-aunt gave you for a wedding present or the one your nine-year-old made in ceramic class. Let your conscience be your guide.

Look at the counter tops in your kitchen. If they're anything like mine, they're cluttered with cookbooks, old newspapers, a screwdriver, obsolete athletic schedules, dog collars, plant food, failed diets, a new paintbrush, vitamin-pill bottles, and empty canisters. Wouldn't kitchen cleanup be easier without all that to wipe around?

What about the bedroom? Is your dresser covered with the kids' school papers, back issues of *Reader's Digest* you haven't gotten around to reading yet, your son's water pistol, a dried-up box of cough drops, someone's dirty comb, a brown button, and a black sock? If you can't bear to throw these things away cold turkey, put them into a drawer or a "tidy box" (more about this later in the chapter).

By clearing off counter tops, dressers, desk tops, and coffee tables, you'll not only have an easier and faster time dusting when you do dust, but things will look neater even when you don't. Remember, illusion's the name of the game.

If You Have to Dust, Water, Polish, or Feed It, You Don't Need It

Notable exceptions to this rule, of course, are your husband and kids. And to be totally honest, I must admit that at this point, I have approximately two hundred ceramic, wooden, fabric, and metal hippos inhabiting my house, not to mention two dogs, countless tropical fish, four outside cats, and one inside cat. (The latter is what makes our tropical fish "countless.") Perhaps this makes me even *more* expert on saying that if you don't already have animals, don't get them. Cats can keep themselves clean but need *you* to clean their litter boxes—often. Pet chameleons excel at hide-and-go-seek and have the advantage of blending in with their hiding place. Birds delight in tossing the shells from their seeds outside the cage onto the floor and may attack any hand foolish enough to venture into their cage, even under the guise of cleaning it. Gerbils, hamsters, and the like specialize in getting loose and getting pregnant. One friend lost her son's snake in the shag carpet. Another friend had her exercise session disrupted when her sister's Pomeranian got his long furry tail caught in the spokes of her exercycle. In the noisy few hours until the police came and released him, she missed the interview it had taken her five weeks to arrange.

I could go on for pages, but the message is clear. You need *fewer* diversions, not more, if you're going to combine housewifery with writing productivity. If you need something soft and cuddly to hold, buy a teddy bear or pamper your husband. If your kids think *they* can't live without something to pet, moan about the traumas induced by your allergies—and buy your neighbor's kid a kitten for Christmas.

Live plants need watering, fertilizing, misting, and transplanting when they grow too big for their pots (which is about the same rate as my son outgrows his sneakers). They also require, so I'm told, someone to talk to them and are all too likely to shrivel up and turn brown despite your monologues.

Fake plants, on the other hand, just sit there and collect dust. Mine also have the tendency to drop their plastic leaves.

If you feel you must add a touch of nature to your home, have the best of both worlds (natural and "artificial") by using dried ornamental plants and grasses, such as dried leaves, pussy willows, sea oats, pods, feathers, cones, etc. These require no dusting, watering, or rearranging, and thrive on loving neglect. They're a perfect "state flower" for the housewife-writer.

Collectibles, like artificial plants, also have to be dusted—and usually polished as well. Small *objets d'art* on display in your home had better mean a great deal to you. Try to avoid copper, silver, or glass collections as much as possible. If you harbor squirrellike tendencies and *have* to collect things to feel secure, put them under glass so they can be admired. Or, learn to love them, dust and all—unless you do your best creative thinking while you're dusting.

Think of the time needed to care for an object or any home furnishing along with its cost when you're shopping. Window shades and curtains require less upkeep than venetian blinds. It's easier to sweep a floor or vacuum a rug than having to do both in a room with an area rug and some floor exposed. Glass tables are lovely but require more upkeep than wooden ones.

If No One Notices It, Don't Do It

Since writing is a lonely, difficult and, at times, tedious labor, we all tend to procrastinate as long as possible. Rather than procrastinating on our housework, however, to make time for our writing, we do the reverse and find all kinds of ways to get distracted by our house.

"I couldn't get any writing done today. I had to clean the bedroom," one writer-friend told me very seriously.

When I pressed her for details, she confessed that she had put some photographs she found lying on the dresser into a scrapbook, then taken all the books out of the bedroom shelves and rearranged them according to subject. (That probably would have been greatly appreciated if her husband was a Dewey Decimal freak. As it was, he didn't even notice until he looked for a book he was reading and couldn't find it.)

He also didn't notice that she had covered all of her shoe boxes with leftover bedroom wallpaper and rearranged the underwear in her dresser. She noticed, however, that it was time for the kids to get home from school and she hadn't even uncovered the typewriter, much less typed on it.

Sometimes you do need to tackle those tidying-up tasks—but save them for a rainy day when you've just completed an assignment and dropped it into the mail, or for when you're stuck for an idea on how to get your heroine out of the damp dungeon you put her in on page 202.

Murphy's second law says that "Everything takes longer than you think." Don't figure that it will "just take a minute" to straighten the playroom, water the plants or put the winter clothes in the attic. It will take much longer than that and you'll end up wondering what became of the writing time you had promised yourself. Remember your priorities, and do the writing first. For some strange reason I don't understand (but I'm sure has a scientific basis), you'll be able to do those other tasks faster later.

Ask yourself, "*Will anyone notice if I don't do this at all*" Some of the tasks you've tied yourself down with make no impression whatsoever on the rest of your family. So why do them (unless they give you some sensational feeling of satisfaction)? Who knows (or cares) if you rotate your sheets, iron the tea towels, repaper the shelves in the pantry, or polish that ugly tea set you hate and keep on the top shelf just in case Aunt Lilly ever comes to visit?

"*Will anyone notice if I don't do this today?*" If not, postpone it if you need the time for writing.

If you feel you *have* to do something, *is there an easier way to do it*? In many cases, there is. Throughout this chapter I'll refer to many shortcuts I've discovered for myself (and swiped from other housewife-writers).

Can I get someone else to do it for me? The "someone else" need not be paid help, although as soon as you can afford to hire an extra pair of hands (even once a month), you should do so. It could be in the form of a cleaning service, laundry service, lawncare person, etc. Decide what you are most "in need of." What tasks take the greatest amount of your time? What do you hate doing most of all? What distracts you most from your writing? What chore frustrates you the most? If you had a fairy godmother, what would be your wish?

One housewife-writer I know found carpooling to be the greatest distraction in the world. Rather than hiring help for the housework, she paid for a responsible teenager to run errands after school and take her kids to their various lessons, games, and medical appointments.

"I like the way I take care of my house," she said, "but I hate driving."

Another writer found cooking the elaborate meals her family loved took more time than she wanted to spend. She found a full-time homemaker with two small children who was delighted to make some extra money. This woman comes in two mornings a week and prepares gourmet dinners. Think about *your* "needs" and find yourself a helping hand.

How to Use Delivery Services

There aren't many delivery services left in today's world, but make use of what there are. Although you'll pay more, you'll save time—and *that* time, well-spent, will result in bigger sales that will more than pay for your delivery service. I use a laundry that picks up and delivers for my husband's shirts and the sheets. It's expensive, but so is the time it takes to wash and dry sheets from five twin beds and one king-size one. If there were a grocery that delivered, I'd consider using that as well. Don't forget florists, drug stores, department stores, and specialty shops that deliver.

If you have children, you already have homegrown help. Since you offer them room and board (and a whole lot more) why not put them to work? Even toddlers can help by setting tables, putting away laundry, and feeding pets. But you must give them the opportunity and be patient as they learn. It may mean lowering your standards a little and knowing that you could do it faster and better. But stop aiming for perfection and try for happiness. You'll be giving your children a sense of fulfillment. (Of course, sometimes you have to shout a little to get them to realize how lucky they are to be learning responsibility! See "Job Lists" later in this chapter.)

Don't be afraid to ask for help; this really is the crux of the situation. When it comes right down to facts, most of us feel guilty asking for help. "It's *my* job," we think and try to balance everything as we dart in and out from under our mother, wife, housewife, and writer hats, like a hummingbird in a flower garden.

But there's no reason why the other members of the family can't or shouldn't pitch in and learn to use the washing machine, stove, and other household appliances. Other hands can be *your* greatest timesaving source.

Some husbands accept a share of the workload. Others won't. They feel that their job is to earn the money and yours is to run the house. They take it as an insult that you want them to do "women's work." If you have such a husband, hand over the "male" jobs: changing lightbulbs, making repairs, and pulling furniture out so you can occasionally clean behind it. Sometimes they'll fool you. When we lived on the beach, my husband loved cleaning the sliding glass doors. He spent hours wiping off the salt spray and polishing the glass—and woe-be-it to the first person putting fingerprints on "his" doors!

It's harder with the kids. Suggesting that they help usually doesn't work. You've got to demand it—"I said 'NOW,' not after the TV show." Then you've got to follow up to see that it's done—but don't be too critical or you'll get the job back fast.

Be clear in your instructions. Sometimes we just hand over a task, assuming the child knows how to do it properly. It's worth walking them through it the first few times before you let them "solo." Most kids will complain a little ("Mary's mother doesn't make *her* empty the wastebaskets"), but you'll eventually discover that they really are proud of their skills.

This was brought home to me vividly by my thirteen-year-old. She reported quite scornfully that a youngster on her team didn't have a clean uniform.

"Her mother was out of town and she didn't know how to use the washing machine. Can you imagine? And she's *my* age."

There's nothing like this type of aside to lift mountains of guilt just when you're sure you're about to be arrested for violating the child labor laws. The truth is, in "the olden days," kids were expected to help with the chores. They were a vital part of the family work force, and in fact this is a lot of what made a family *feel* like a family. Ask farm children. They'll tell you with pride about the hard work they do alongside Mom and Dad.

In addition to helping with the workload, the family can actually *reduce* the load itself. Anyone who's lived out of a suitcase knows that a shirt can be worn more than once, and slacks until they stand up by themselves. (This does not apply to those children who seem to attract dirt on their way out of the bedroom.) But, for some reason, once we return home to the washer and dryer, we toss things into the hamper even though we've worn them only a few hours.

Ask your family to think about what they throw into the laundry. Could it be worn again? Or is opening the hamper lid easier than hanging it up? (With some youngsters, your problem may be in getting them to let go of a favorite shirt, even though you promise to give it back the instant it comes out of the dryer.)

Get help with the laundry in any case. Otherwise it will ooze over your entire day, like the protoplasmic monster in a horror movie. Have the kids help fold and put their clean things away. Don't be tempted to wash "a little" every day. Establish washday routines and stick to them when you can.

"Tom Sawyer" the other chores. If you have young children who are eager to help, make it seem like a treat. Look at them thoughtfully and say, "Well, maybe you *are* old enough to run the vacuum."

My seven-year-old thinks it's great to be allowed to empty the dishwasher, snap the green beans in two, shuck corn, scrub out the sink, and move the hose around to sprinkle the lawn. The older ones enjoy having a turn to fix dinner, changing their own room around (after cleaning it), and helping decorate for a party.

When they balk, level with them and say you'd appreciate their help and you need it. Give them a choice of chores, and be sure to say, "thank you." If they're old enough to drive, turn the grocery list over to them. It's a good way for them to learn the price of food so they stop complaining "we never have steak anymore" and "why don't we ever have fresh raspberries?" Give your sons as well as daughters the opportunity to plan and cook a meal for the family. There's no reason for any youngster over ten to be ignorant in the kitchen. Many begin much younger with scrambled eggs, french toast, and hamburgers, soon working their way up to full-course dinners.

Most of my children have a culinary specialty. A friend once asked them about it.

"I'm the brownie-maker," said my oldest daughter.

"I'm the omelet-maker," boasted the oldest boy.

"I'm the bread-maker," said the youngest daughter.

"I'm the hot dog-maker," said our little guy.

The middle son was silent. "What about you?" asked my friend. He thought a minute, then smiled. "Me? I'm the trouble-maker!" Don't turn the children into slave labor, but let them join the family team. Sit them down with you and your husband and discuss the need for shared household responsibilities. It's their home too.

Learn to Control Your Space

This is one way to make housework easier. Many of us have our kitchen utensils in the same spot we put them in the day we first moved into our house or apartment. Yet our family size may have changed, our eating habits altered, and our interest in cooking waned.

For years I climbed up on a kitchen stepstool to get the electric frypan down from a high shelf, even though I used it at least once a week. On the other hand, the paella pan (that I couldn't live without, handcarried home on the plane, and have used twice in five years) sat in the easy-to-reach drawer below the stove.

Poor thinking? Bad planning? More likely, just "habit." Not until a friend pointed it out to me did I even realize that it would be far simpler to reverse the location of those two items. Then I looked at my kitchen with a different eye and became more aware that many of the locations and storage areas for my things were wrong, causing me to spend almost twice as long in the kitchen as I needed to.

It's easy to accumulate kitchen gadgets as they come on the market. Most of them claim to be timesavers, and many of them are— providing they're out where you can get to them. But for that you'd need a kitchen counter the size of a football field. In addition, many of the kitchen electrical "toys" serve a highly limited function or duplicate the function of at least one other.

For example, I have a wok and a deep-fat fryer. Yet, when I make Chinese food or fried foods, I usually grab the electric frying pan. For some strange reason, both the wok and the deep-fat fryer sat in front of the slow cooker I used weekly. I was moving the wok and fryer every time I took out the slow cooker.

I also had an electric hot dog cooker, which someone had given to me as a gift. I used it once—then returned to boiling hot dogs in a saucepan. But the hot dog cooker kept its prominent position on the shelf.

When I really started to examine my kitchen tools, I gave many of them the old heave-ho. I threw out the hand grater (which was only used when I grated carrots) because I now have a food processor (bought with the proceeds from two articles on spring cleaning) that grates carrots faster and more efficiently and leaves my fingernails intact so that I can break them on the typewriter instead.

I gave away most of the carving knives, since I keep washing and using my "favorite" one anyway. I gave away a set of chipped breakfast dishes, put the salad bowls near the sink where I fix salad, and put all the lunch box supplies in a drawer next to the refrigerator so the kids had everything in one place to make their lunches. I "wasted" a day rearranging the kitchen—but I figured that I saved more time in the long run by organizing and controlling my space.

What's more important, I did my kitchen reorganization on a day when I had just finished one major writing project and hadn't yet begun on the next. I didn't do it right in the middle of a hectic deadline with massive changes required on a manuscript. Nobody does that? You're wrong. My two older sons decided to rearrange their bedrooms right in the middle of exam week.

Has your family unit changed while your kitchen remained the same? If your children are grown and away from home, do your still have the large saucepans in front of the little ones you use daily? Do you lift out *all* the mixing bowls to get to the one you want? How many wasted motions do *you* make in the kitchen?

My "instant statistics" (the kind you make up because you believe them to be true) tell me that 85 percent of the time a woman wastes, she wastes in the kitchen.

Think about controlling your space in the other parts of your house too. Does it take you an hour to get everything together to pay bills? Why not have a "bill box" where you put all the bills, stamps (so they don't get mixed up with those you use for your writing), pen, envelopes, address labels, calculator, and checkbook?

What about your linens? Is the linen closet far removed from your bedrooms and baths? After running up and down to get sheets out of the upstairs linen closet for the downstairs bedrooms, I paused to catch my breath and collect my wits. I moved the sheets for my husband's and my bed downstairs into a bottom drawer of my dresser and our little guy's sheets to a shelf in his closet. *House Beautiful* may have an artistically stacked linen closet, but we *live* in our house. Convenience is what really makes a house beautiful.

What about the laundry room? Is the mending kit in your bedroom? The marking pen in the study? Rags for wiping up spills under the bathroom sink? The cleaning hints stuck under the phone book on a kitchen shelf? Put all these things in a drawer, pail, or basket beside the washing machine. Have one box, jar, or can for lost buttons. Then, when you find something wanting a button, you'll know where you put the one you found under the couch cushion, and the needle and thread will be right beside it.

This theory also works in your office. Are the things you never use in the top file and those you use every day down below, making you do deep-knee bends to reach them? It's a good way to stay in shape, but every motion wasted is time lost. Is the dictionary in the children's room, the stamps in the bedroom or buried in a junk drawer? Are your reference books nestled on a top shelf you can't reach?

Control your space by:

1. Rearranging according to use and convenience.
2. Throwing (or putting) away what you don't need, use, or have overwhelming emotional attachment for. Ideally, of course, you should throw things away if you aren't going to use them. But most of us, being human, vacillate over certain items for no "good" reason. We think we "might use it," or it stirs up memories, and our arm seems paralyzed every time we try to throw it away. It's no use asking a friend to come help you decide. The friend would say, "Chuck it!" and thus ruin a perfect friendship. That's why I still have an orange-colored chipped pitcher from my childhood vacation cottage, a broken potato whip that belonged to my grandmother, my high school letter sweater, and a shelf of old medical books that belonged to my husband's father. Please don't analyze what all this "means." I use them only to show you that you're not the only one who has difficulty in parting with "things." If you can't discard them outright, at least put them away.
3. Buy duplicates of things you need to put in two (or more) places, rather than chasing all over the house for them. Two-by-two worked for Noah, and it should work for you. Buy two rolls of tape when you need one, two bars of soap, two packages of toilet paper, two ball-point pens, etc. When one is used up (or lost), you still have the second to use until you can buy two more. This backup system works in two ways: you don't find yourself totally out of something when you need it, and it saves steps. I follow the same two-by-two policy in my grocery shopping and always buy two of each "must have" item. Then, when I use the last of the coffee in can number one, I write "coffee" on the list before opening can number two.

It doesn't matter if you put an item in a place that seems crazy to other people. As long as it's where you need it, leave it there. (That's why I have pencils in the bathroom, bubble gum in my study, and a stapler in my kitchen.)

You'll learn to save time by organizing and controlling your space so you control it, not vice versa. There's a reason why the military has a prescribed place for every item in a serviceman's footlocker, and why the scalpels, sutures, and scissors used by a surgeon are laid out in exactly the same way each time. It's so critical time won't be wasted looking for something.

On Your Mark, Get Set, Go If There's No Way to Avoid It

At some point, some things have to be done. You've put them off while you were finishing your article or cleaning up a chapter. But sooner or later, the house is going to need some cleaning up, too. When you do a chore, make certain you organize it efficiently and sensibly so you don't make more work for yourself.

For example, clean the refrigerator out *before* you go shopping. There'll be less to take out, and you may discover five bottles of olives shoved to the back so you don't need to buy a sixth. Clean the refrigerator out *before* you scrub the kitchen floor, just in case you drop an egg or the family-size catsup bottle. Sweep out the fireplace *before* you run the vacuum in that room. Wash out the tub *while* you're letting the water run out. Water your plants *before* you dust the tables they're sitting on. Clean a bedroom *after* you strip the bed and *before* you make it so you can pile all the junk on the mattress without getting the sheets or spread dirty.

If you find yourself retracing steps, or having to repeat a chore in a short span of time, think about whether or not you could put individual tasks in a different, more logical order. Take time to write it down, if necessary. It will save you time in the future.

"Doubling" is another way to save yourself steps. It's doing two things at once, what we housewife-mothers have always done. I know I've seen pictures of colonial mothers standing by an open hearth stirring a pot while they rocked a little one. I've done the same thing in modern times.

You can cook while waiting for the dryer to ring, clank, or moan, whatever it does to tell you it's through.

In the "olden days," before prefolded diapers or disposable ones, I used to fold diapers as I watched TV news. You can do the same now with your laundry.

Let your kids play in the hose on a hot day—and wash the car at the same time.

Not only do I wipe the tiles while I'm in the shower, I also wash out the soap dish, rinse out my pantyhose, and outsing Barbra Streisand.

Make cleaning out the garage a fun time for all. Organize a garage sale with the throwaways and let the kids have the proceeds. (Or, keep the proceeds yourself and buy a new typewriter. On second thought, if you want help, you'd better split fifty-fifty.)

Keep a supply of postcards or notecards in your purse or glove compartment of the car so you can write a note when you have to wait.

I have vivid memories of my childhood when I sat on a little stool and my mother put my hair in pincurls. We had fantastic conversations then. We didn't realize that it was "meaningful communication" or "bridging the generation gap." We thought we were just talking. When I grew older and could do my own hair, we continued our talks as we did the dishes. I still think these moments, when you're doubling your time, can be the most effective talking times. Often a child is less self-conscious when he/she is doing something with his/her hands, and before a bed is made, silver is polished, or soup is made, will find that telling mom wasn't so bad after all. Naturally, sometimes you need to give your undivided attention, but I've had many good talks with my kids when we've been working side by side.

Bed Making

Beds create more problems than any other piece of furniture in the house. And I'm not talking about sexual problems, either. It's the great debate over *making the bed*!

Some women consider bed making a vital daily task. For them the bed *must* be made before the day gets too far along because . . . well, because "mother always did." For them not making the bed symbolizes losing control, not getting started "right," or inability to cope with the new day. One friend, whom I consider to be totally noncompetitive and noncompulsive, says she is driven to making the bed as soon as her teeth are brushed.

For others, there is little or no emotion attached to bed making, and they usually make beds if, and when, they get around to it. Sometimes beds never get made and no thunder rolls; no lightning crashes.

I never make beds on the weekend. (I keep thinking I might get a chance for a quick nap sometime. I never do, but hope springs eternal. . . .) During the week, I either make the bed or pull back the covers and rationalize that "it's airing." (That's a euphemism for "not making the bed.")

My children make their beds occasionally. I figure their rooms are their business (a totally hypocritical theory, as I become very hostile when their rooms get so messy I can't walk in without tripping over Tonka trucks, records, and schoolbooks). I've discovered that kids tend to make their beds if:

1. They're having friends over.
2. They want to avoid starting on their homework.
3. I've asked for volunteers to set the table.

If you feel strongly about bed making, you have three choices:

1. Buy comforters for yourself and your kids so you all only have to toss it over the bed. There's no hassle with top sheets, blankets or spreads. The Europeans have been using these for years.
2. Keep the children's bedroom doors closed so you can't tell if the beds are made or not or if they're made but look as if a body is buried under the covers.
3. Make them all so you can bounce your quarter but do it quickly and get it over with.

How often to change the sheets is another emotional bed topic. At college, they handed out cot-size sheets that were supposed to fit twin-size beds; we were told to put the top sheet on the bottom and put our fresh sheet on the top. I always got confused and never could figure why bother at all. We change sheets (top and bottom) once a week. More often and the kids will think they're in a hotel and want to ring for room service. Less often and the sand starts building up. To resolve this dilemma, ask yourself the question, "How often do I want_ to wash sheets?"

Why all the fuss about making the bed? Just that it takes more time to make it than not make it—and for each extra bed you make, it takes that much longer. Make it if you must. But if you don't make it, don't waste the time saved by feeling guilty.

Sell the Iron (Or, Clothes—Dirty and Clean)

Irons have been known to serve a variety of purposes. They can be used as doorstops, paperweights, bookends, or, used in pairs, as barbells. But the housewife-writer who plugs in an iron is going to find herself pressed for time.

Never buy anything that requires ironing. The cotton industry is working very hard to tell us that cotton is terrific. It is. I prefer cotton to polyester—but I won't iron it. You have to make choices if you're going to make time for writing. This is one of them.

Naturally, if given *their* choice, the members of your family probably would prefer that you ironed everything. Sheets look and feel better when ironed, although you can sleep soundly on them unironed. Pajamas probably feel better ironed and possibly underwear does too. But no one in my family will ever find out, unless they learn to iron themselves (which one of my daughters has). Perhaps that's your clue. Ironing should only be done when the person wanting it can do it him/herself.

If your husband insists on cotton shirts (as mine does), send them to a laundry. It costs more—until you sell the article you'll write instead of doing the ironing.

When you buy new clothing, look for permanent-press labels or buy the dressy T-shirts. T-shirts look great with slacks or skirts and require no ironing.

If your children are little, buy clothes they can dress themselves in; no back zippers, tiny buttons that resist the efforts of little fingers, or snaps. I always loved sailor suits and insisted on dressing my first two boys in them. Then I wondered why they interrupted my writing every time they had to go to the bathroom. They couldn't manage the buttons. They also kept losing the tie, got the white suits filthy, and thoroughly hated them. I'm convinced neither of them will ever join the navy!

I also bought my little ones shorts and shirts in red, white, and blue. Then, no matter what they picked out, they "matched." (As they grew older, they learned that the spectrum included other colors.)

For awhile I "color-keyed" the children, buying red for one boy, blue for another, pink for one girl, and yellow for her sister. When the fifth child came along he got all the hand-me-downs and looked like a rainbow. But until then it certainly made sorting laundry a breeze!

Don't over-buy for your child. The less in the closet or dresser, the less to take care of. If a child won't wear a hand-me-down (and some kids can be very stubborn), give them away. Of course, special outfits, like the sailor suits, you can wrap and "save."

Unless your boys needs sports jackets for school or church/ synagogue, save your money until they're in their teens. A navy sweater over a dress shirt and tie looks quite dressy. Look around for a friend who has a boy slightly bigger than yours and ask if you can have the jacket when it's outgrown. Boys' jackets are extremely expensive, seldom worn out, and almost never out of style.

For girls, make it easy on yourself. Have a dressmaker make a few solid color permanent-press skirts, and buy blouses and T-shirts. This is especially good for preteen girls who have trouble fitting into off-the-rack dresses.

Shopping for children's clothes can be a tremendous time waster, when you figure travel time, time used in making the decisions, and time spent waiting for someone to write up the sale. That's why many housewife-writers order as much as they can from catalogues. You can shop at your leisure and find unusual gift items and most of your children's clothes when you let your fingers do the walking. Sears and Penney's both offer excellent quality, and it's easier on the nerves than dragging small children through a store. Older youngsters may rebel and want to do their own shopping, but younger ones love to open their "presents" from the catalogue service, even if it contains nothing more than p.j.'s and blue jeans.

If you have more than one child, write his or her name and size on each article of clothing. It makes laundry sorting easy; and when it's time to hand an item down to the next offspring, you'll know if it's a regular, slim, or husky.

When your children get to the stage that everyone wears the same size, color, and type of sock, leave them in a pile near the dryer and it's every man (and woman) for himself!

If you find a store you like, tell the saleswomen to call you when what you need is in—or pull some items of your size so that you can come in to try them on.

One last tip, made to order for the housewife-writer but taught to me at a jeans shop in Arizona: If you need to shorten cuffs on slacks but don't have time to hem, use masking tape. They told me it would last for seven washings. (It lasted for twelve!)

"Concorde" Your Cooking

I used to be something of a gourmet cook and spent hours in the kitchen preparing meals that were eaten in fifteen minutes by those who ate it—and complained about for thirty minutes by those who didn't.

"What's this yucky sauce?" I'd hear, and watch my finicky offspring scraping beautiful noncurdled Hollandaise sauce onto the salad plate. No matter how hard I tried not to, I kept taking it very personally.

"I *could* have been writing instead, you ingrate," I'd mumble, pouring an extra serving of Hollandaise on my vegetables just to show how good it really was. A voice whispered back, "Then why weren't you?"

Once I worked almost a full day creating a cake-and-whipped-cream dessert that looked like something out of a magazine. In fact, that's where I had gotten the recipe. Proudly I carried it into the dining room and waited modestly for the applause.

"Mother!" shrieked one daughter. "You *know* I can't eat that. I'm on a diet."

"I think I'll get some ice cream," said a son.

My husband looked at me apologetically. "I'm sorry, honey. I'm really stuffed."

I sat down, determined to eat the whole thing myself. "They don't appreciate me," I mumbled into the mocha frosting.

"Did you make it for them . . . or to keep from writing?" said the voice.

I've always listened to voices (especially since I first became aware that I talk to myself). Now I write approximately thirty hours a week, and I have learned to streamline my cooking. Our meals are well-balanced, we all like what I fix, and I'm not gaining weight. Something *must* be right.

You need to spend some time thinking about your cooking. Does your family really enjoy fancy cooking? Do *you* get creative satisfaction from it? Are you using it as a means to procrastinate? If your family really does enjoy it—and you like fixing it—don't cut it out from your life completely. Declare one night "gourmet" night and spend that day creating something marvelous from one or more of your collection of cookbooks. That way you won't feel guilty when you fix nourishing but fairly plain meals the rest of the time. Pamper your family from time to time. You'll gain more cooperation from them in the long run.

If your children are old enough, you might sneak in another gourmet night by encouraging them to try their hand at a dinner, or let your husband play chef. Communication with your family is vital. Food is an extremely emotional subject, and it's foolish to try to guess what your family feels about their meals.

For some families, getting "carry-out" Chinese food or pizza is a treat. You don't always have to cook to make dinner special. My kids think TV dinners are great (my husband doesn't!), so often if we are going out, I "splurge" and let them have that. It also doesn't hurt to let the kids have something from a fast-food chain occasionally if you're really rushed for time.

The key is in being flexible. When my children were babies my grocery cart was always filled to the brim with jars of strained baby food and junior baby food. But, regardless of the number of little jars I kept in stock, I never had the right one for a specific meal. Rather than make a special trip back, I learned that baby didn't really care if he had oatmeal and applesauce for dinner—and strained meat for breakfast.

(If it didn't bother baby, it shouldn't bother me.)

Try to cut down on preparation of your meals. One way to streamline your cooking is to use some of the timesaving devices available. Crock Pots, slow cookers, microwave ovens, and pressure cookers all can save you hours of kitchen time, time that you can spend far more profitably in your office. Food processors that dice, chop, and mix save mess as well. Naturally, you don't have space or money for all the newest cooking devices. Talk to your friends, especially those who work outside the home, to discover what they use. Mentally list the pros and cons of each.

Remember, to get the most from this equipment you must learn how to use it properly. Many people use their microwave ovens only for grilled-cheese sandwiches and reheating! When all else fails, read the instruction manual that comes with the appliance. After all, some writer spent a lot of time writing it. You'll discover how it can serve you best—and then be better prepared to come up with some ideas on your own.

Don't turn up your nose at convenience foods either. Some of them can save you tremendous amounts of time. Frozen vegetables that you add to soups or stews make a fine busy-day meal. Just add them to the chicken or meat in your slow cooker about an hour before serving. Chopping up all those vegetables would have taken at least an hour. Naturally, you'll add any leftover vegetables you have in the refrigerator, but the frozen ones make sure there's plenty for everyone.

Canned fruit can be turned into a fancy dessert (poured over ice cream) or a salad (served with cottage cheese) or if you're really busy, just serve it as it comes out of the can. Frozen one-serving dinners (TV variety or packages for the microwave) are ideal for youngsters who come home from practice long after the dinner hour is over and everything is cleared away—or when you have someone coming home for lunch and peanut butter and jelly just won't do.

I don't use cake mixes. It's faster to buy a ready-made cake, although we eat very little cake. We always have fresh fruit around, little boxes of raisins, and carrot sticks for nibbles.

I serve a lot of raw vegetables: cauliflower, celery, carrots, squash, and cherry tomatoes. The kids snack on them and I throw them into the salad along with any leftover cooked vegetables. You can add leftover meat, chicken, fish, or ham and have a fantastic lunch or salad course! We steam fresh vegetables too.

Don't use convenience foods if the idea of it bothers you. But you might reexamine your motives. Are you equating "good mothering" with "homemade"? Do you feel you must "doctor up" convenience foods with something you've made from scratch, or combine a number of convenience foods to make it "all right"? Most of us are very emotional about food. That's why it's very easy to get stuck in, and on, the kitchen.

Learn to simplify your recipes. In Alan Lakein's book, *How to Get Control of Your Time and Your Life*, he discusses the "eighty-twenty principle." According to him, "80 percent of the dinners repeat 20 percent of the recipes."

I know it's true. Whenever I have a full day of writing, I fix my regular "deadline" meal. It's roast chicken parts, instant rice, canned asparagus or green beans and fresh fruit. Dinner takes five minutes to prepare and no thought on my part. I always have the "fixings" in my pantry and freezer. The kids see this dinner and say, "How did the article come out, Mom?"

Make a list of ten complete dinners your family likes and that require a minimum of preparation. Use chicken parts rather than a whole chicken (so you don't have to carve it), hamburger mixed with canned Chinese vegetables, a bowl of fresh fruit and cheese for dessert. Make sure these dinners don't use many pots and pans to help you save time on kitchen cleanup. As long as it's good, filling, and there's enough of it, your family really won't know or care that you spent ten minutes on it or ten hours.

Ask your family to help suggest menus for variety. We all tend to get stuck in a rut. Usually, especially in a large family, there are few things *everyone* likes. If you can coordinate some likes into each menu, you'll be able to serve meals with something everyone is bound to like, and you won't end up being a short-order cook.

Make out your list now. Be certain that you always have the ingredients for your deadline meal in the pantry, and then get out of the kitchen and into the study.

Save those complex, many-step recipes for the weekend, or let the kids try them. Better yet, throw them away and pretend you never clipped them out in the first place. No one (but you) will ever know you did.

Don't forget to use the two-by-two system in the kitchen. When you're cooking make twice as much stew, spaghetti sauce, meatloaf, soup, etc., and freeze half of it for another time. Freeze it in the freezer-to-oven-to-table containers, never metal if you have a microwave. Two housewife-writers who live next door cook on alternate days. One day one makes the double batch for her buddy who spends the day writing! The next day they swap jobs. (I've never tried this. *My* writing buddy would go out of town the day she was to cook for me.)

Have a Gift Box

Although gift buying and wrapping isn't part of cooking or cleaning, it *is* a chore that can interrupt a productive writing schedule, especially if you have young children who are invited to a great many birthday parties—and the invitation comes the day before the party.

Rather than running out to get a gift every time your child needs one, buy an assortment the next time you go to a discount store. Keep an eye open for new and clever things at the drugstore, novelty shop, stationery store, etc.

Keep a large box or basket filled with gifts appropriate for the ages of your children's friends: toy cars, coloring books and crayons, bubble bath, games, jewelry, billfolds, etc. This also is a good place to put duplicate gifts *your* child receives.

Also keep cards (commercial or homemade), wrapping paper or the comic section of the newspaper (sports page for older boys), tape and scissors in the box. Then the next time you have an occasion that calls for a gift, your child can rummage through the box and "shop" there while you finish your article or chapter. It may not be as personal as going out to buy something special, but it saves time—and gas too.

Have a Tidy Box

This is probably one of the world's greatest timesaving devices and makes "tidying up" a breeze. Keep a covered box or basket in every "public" room. In the family room it could be a brightly colored footlocker or wicker basket. In the bedroom, use something that slides under the bed or can be used as an end table.

As you walk through a room, put magazines, catalogues, odd sneakers, and keys that you find lying about on the floor or cluttering up the tables into the box. This removes the clutter in minutes and gives you a central "lost and found" depository. It saves you from hundreds of "Hey, Mom! Have you seen my_____?" (Fill in the blank.) They know (or should know) to look in the tidy box.

Of course, you immediately grasp the one weakness of the tidy box. Eventually it overflows and you have to empty it. Usually you dispose of 75 percent and put the rest back in the box.

I don't believe in using a tidy box in kids' rooms. Their room *is* a tidy box, and the less you have to wade through the mess, the better. Some of my kids are extremely neat: hang up their clothes, put dirty things in the wash, vacuum their rugs without being told. I have others who can lose a pair of jeans for months in the midst of the disarray. For the most part, I believe in the ultimate goodness in people and the ultimate realization by youngsters that things are more easily located in a reasonably neat room. I tend to be a little messy myself so am self-conscious about complaining too much about their rooms. But let me find a dirty dish in the family room or sneakers in the kitchen, and I can be the Wicked Witch of the West. I yell, scream, give the "it's everybody's responsibility to help" pitch . . . and often, I pick it up myself. Well, nobody's perfect!

Lists, Lists and More Lists

These three types of lists can greatly ease your household chores.

Grocery List. Hang it on the refrigerator, pantry door, or some conspicuous and specific place. Have every member of the family old enough to write add to it. If there's a drugstore near the supermarket, hang a second list for that too and make both trips at once, saving time and gas.

In the beginning, you may have to remind your family that IF IT ISN'T ON THE LIST, I WON'T BUY IT! If someone says, "You didn't buy shampoo," you can throw back, "You didn't put it on the list." Strict adherence to this rule will make believers out of your family very quickly. It also will save *you* from being the "fall guy" when someone runs out of toothpaste. Most important, you'll be teaching your family responsibility.

(Try to shop at the same grocery. You'll whiz through much faster because you'll be familiar with where they keep things. My record: twenty-eight minutes flat for the main shopping!)

Repair List. This can be a clipboard, card, or chalkboard, as long as it too hangs in plain sight near the back door. Record everything that needs to be repaired on the left side of the sheet and those out being repaired on the right. That way you won't forget to call the TV man again and won't leave your good shoes sitting at the shop for two months while you turn the house upside down looking for them.

Train all the family to pin notes on their clothing requiring dry cleaning. Memos such as, "motor-oil stain on right shoulder" or "please mend tear in left pocket" prevent articles from coming back cleaned but still stained or still torn.

Put the responsibility for these notes on your family and off your shoulders. You've got enough to do.

Job List. We have a children's rotating job list that runs on a weekly basis. The duties include: table clearing (serving dishes only as everyone clears his/her own plate and silverware), scraper, dishwasher, garbage/sweeper, and free.

Once we used a daily rotation, but I discovered I was spending hours writing up the elaborate chart, explaining why we always seemed to go out on Wednesday when someone was free anyway, etc.

Then I had a paper clock, with hands pointing to the various jobs like we used when I was a kid at camp. But my kids are craftier than we were. They moved the hands around to suit themselves and we had terrible rows; and when I used index cards marked with chores and alternated them under the children's names, they shuffled the cards.

My foolproof method now is to use a wall calendar with numbers one through five written in the first of every week. Each number corresponds to the job sequence for that week.

Other families report success with job jars, voluntarism-under-coercion, and the old badger game (where you keep badgering them to get busy). The important thing to remember is that you're trying to organize your child task force, not get an *A* in chart making.

How to Compete With the "Perfect Housekeeper"

"What do I do?" wailed a housewife-writer. "His mother was a perfect housekeeper. She washed his socks before they hit the ground, her cakes were so light they floated off the plate and her . . . ."

I sympathized. It's hard to compete with a mother-in-law who is (or was) perfection personified. Convince yourself that a person's memory of things is not always the way it was. Maybe she had a staff of twenty-eight, maybe she *could* cook but she was a lousy conversationalist or . . . well, be thankful it she didn't write too. If you can't win points against a childhood memory, be a strategist. Figure what's most important to him and go for that.

If clutter annoys him, hide it. Keep the area around "his chair" spotless; use candles at the dinner table (so he doesn't see the laundry's piled up in back of him). Keep a few extra pairs of his socks to throw in as ringers when you get a little behind on the wash.

One woman caught on to the system very quickly. As long as she served her husband's vegetables in a side dish (the way his mother did), he never complained about the rest of the meal.

Governments have been doing this for years. It's time we

housewife-writers caught on. It's called *appeasement*.

When It's Time to Clean . . .

I seem to have left discussion about actual housecleaning to the last in this chapter . . . . Describing how to clean, what to use, etc., would fill a book. In fact, it does; a rather good book by Shirley Conran called *Superwoman*. (Actually, it tells more than I want to know about cleaning my house.)

Below are my "A to Z Mini-cleaning" tips for the housewife-writer. They're all proven methods to get jobs done as quickly and effectively as possible.

A

ashtrays:	Each smoker is responsible for his/her own ashtray. If a guest left it for you, dump the contents into the garbage, drip a drop of liquid dishwashing detergent into the ashtray, and let hot water run over it. It will come clean untouched by human hands.
attics:	Never tackle an attic without a box (for giveaway items) and a giant plastic bag (for throwaways). I've never seen a great deal of sense in cleaning attics. They're fun for kids to rummage through on rainy days. But if the ceiling's creaking, maybe you better take a look at what's up there.

B

baseboards:	Use the proper attachment on your vacuum, if you have one. Otherwise, sweep them with a stiff broom. If you have inside pets, outside dust storms, or shedding carpets, you may need to clean them often.
basements:	Basements seem to get a greater workout than attics. Bikes, sleds, and Christmas tree decorations may be stored there. Often, the laundry is there too. Many husbands set up shop in the basement, a situation that *can* create a substantial mess that you must not assume responsibility for straightening unless there's a fire hazard. Unless your basement's finished (paneled or otherwise made livable) it is probably filled with paint cans, picnic baskets, and other part-time paraphernalia. Keep them off the floor and organized with metal shelving. Sweep the floor and knock the cobwebs down from time to time.
bathtubs:	I see no reason for Mom to be the sole scrubber of the tub. Keep a sponge dangling from a mesh bag on the shower

head and let each bather wash the tub out after use. Little ones love this particular job, and many times I've yelled, "It's fine. It's clean. Now get out of the tub!" The older ones can be reminded that dorm mates find "ring around the tub" far worse than "ring around the collar." They might as well get in practice now (while it's a help to you).

books: If you have a few, take them out from time to time and blow the dust off. If you have a full library, use the vacuum attachment. Try to keep your books free from moisture, and keep them upright so air can get to them.

C
closets: Volumes could be written on closet-cleaning, depending on what type of closet it is. All closets need to be dusted occasionally or wiped out, and that's best done by taking everything out. In a clothes closet, the rod should be wiped off with a dry rag. The floor should be swept or vacuumed and only things used, needed, or too dear to discard should be put back. I find shelf paper to be a double bother. You have to clean it and the shelf as well. If your shelf is really so awful you don't want to put anything on it, paint it with a high-gloss paint so you can just wipe it off.

counter tops: Wipe stains (such as purple price marks from groceries) up before they can set with a mild abrasive, such as Spic and Span. And keep them from getting cluttered!

D
drapes: A drapery expert I shall always cherish said "Never clean draperies. Just take them down once a year, take them outside and shake the dust off." You also can vacuum them if you have the proper attachment. Dust rots draperies eventually. If your "drapes" are really curtains and they're made for the washing machine, go ahead and wash them—but be sure or you'll find yourself with an armful of limp and shrunken curtains.

E
electric toaster: Don't pry stuck English muffins or bagels out of the toaster with a fork. You'll electrocute yourself and break the toaster as well. Unplug your toaster, turn it upside down, and shake lightly. (Note: if you keep your toaster on a little tray, you can carry the whole thing to the sink, open the little tray door on the bottom and shake all the crumbs into the sink.)

F

floors:
My ideal would be carpeting on everything but the kitchen, with plain vinyl there with no crevices that take hours to pry dirt from. No shag carpets in the kids' rooms (they lose pieces of erector sets and contact lenses). Use a dry mop on wood floors; sponge mop on vinyl ones (change the water often); and an upright vacuum, if you have one, on the carpets.

freezer:
Take everything out and put it in a picnic cooler or wrap in newspaper. Turn freezer off. Leave door open. Wipe out with a sponge dipped in water and baking soda. Clean freezer when it's running low of food, if possible, and be sure to empty the drip pan on the bottom.

furniture:
Wipe plastic coverings with damp sponge. Use mild abrasive if necessary. Take cushions off sofas and sweep or use vacuum attachment. Vacuum cushions and plump them up before replacing. Greasy spots on backs of chairs can sometimes be removed by using a diluted shampoo solution and a toothbrush. Try on a hidden part of chair first to see if fabric is colorfast.

G

garages:
Should be cleaned when there's no room for the car, or kids need money and/or something to occupy them. Metal shelving can double storage space. Throw away empty or dried-up paint cans. Return disposable bottles to grocery. (Let offspring doing the returning keep the money.) Take newspapers to recycle area. Put all repair equipment (hammers, bicycle pump, screwdriver, etc.) in one spot so everyone can find them. A pegboard is ideal for this. When everything is out, sweep floor with a pushbroom. Then, if it's really dirty, turn hose on. Consider garage sale if you have a great many disposable items, or take them to a second-hand store if you're rushed for time.

H

hairbrush:
Wash out once a week in shampoo. Use comb to remove hair from the bristles. Dry gently on a towel. Many kids who wash their hair at least once daily never think about washing their hairbrush. If it's really dirty, soak it in vinegar water.

I

icecube tray:
When you notice little fuzzy things floating in your iced drinks, it's past time to wash out the icecube trays. Just empty the ice out and rinse in warm water. Never put in

the dishwasher or use hot water. You'll take off the coating on them.

J

junk: Keep unidentified keys for one year. If you still don't know what they unlock, throw them out. Go through other junk drawers on a monthly basis and try to discard at least half. If you see something that you know belongs in another spot, put it there.

K

kitchens: Because we spend so much time in kitchens, I think they have to be cleaned on an ongoing basis. One cupboard near my phone is always clean and neat because I tend to it when I'm put on "hold." When you reach too high or bend too low, ask yourself, "Is this item in the best spot for me?" (It varies, as people do. Some women keep the drinking glasses by the sink. Others keep theirs by the refrigerator. Who's "right"? They both are.) Keep one area for your entertainment supplies: ice tongs, candles, cocktail napkins, etc. Organize your kitchen as personally as you do your office.

L

lamps: Dust the shades with the vacuum attachment or gently with a clean rag. Be sure to use the proper watt bulb in each lamp. I once burned a shade because I had used a one hundred watt bulb and it only needed a sixty.

laundry room: Keep detergent in a covered plastic container. You can keep it filled from the super economy box, if you want, but you'll use less and spill less by scooping it out of a smaller container. Keep bleach and other poisonous supplies in a high (and preferably locked) cupboard if you have small children (or grandchildren). Be careful when you use bleach. "A little dab will do you." Spray spot removers used before you wash an item will often keep the spot from setting. Cold water removes blood stains. If you *do* use an iron (despite everything I've told you), be careful. Electricity from the iron and water from the machine can be an extremely dangerous combination.

M

magazine racks: Go through them once a month. Clip out any articles you want to keep. Try not to keep magazines less recent than the last two issues. Like most of us, I don't know what to do about *Reader's Digest* or *National Geographic*.

mops: If you use string mops, rinse them out in warm water and white vinegar after use. Otherwise you'll just be moving dirt around from one spot to another.

N

night stands: Go through once a week discarding all strange-looking items without bothering to wonder how they got there. Right now mine has a skate key, black shoestring, two half-read "dirty books" (more badly written than "dirty"), a whistle, and a prescription I never bothered to get filled.

O

oven: Two luxuries I once thought ridiculous and unnecessary are automatic garage-door openers and self-cleaning ovens. In regard to the latter, I take it all back. A housewife-writer I know demonstrated hers. She still doesn't clean the oven very often, but when she does, it's just a matter of pushing a baffling number of buttons. I have a relative who doesn't have a self-cleaning oven, but she doesn't have a problem cleaning her oven. She just doesn't do it. In between are most women. Despite all the television ads of beautifully dressed women cleaning their ovens, it still is a dirty job. Try out the various sprays. Make sure you have *plenty* of ventilation or use your child's scuba equipment. Wear gloves to protect your hands, and never cook anything messy in the oven for at least a week after you've cleaned it. It's too self-defeating.

P

pans: To clean a pan that had food stuck (or burned) in it, sprinkle in some dishwashing detergent and let it sit in the oven overnight. My mother and I used to call this "oven surprise." We forgot abut it and were surprised when we opened the oven door a few days later.

pillows: Every so often (depending on if you have a long-haired cat or your kids eat popcorn on the couch) put the throw pillows in the dryer on low heat. It "fluffs" them up. Some people wash bed pillows and put them in the dryer too.

R

refrigerator: Turn it off and take everything out. Throw away any brown lettuce (it's supposed to be green) and mayonnaise with rust spots on it. Wipe the shelves off with baking soda and water. Throw out any graying leftovers. Put all similar-type food in one spot so you can find it easily and not buy more of the same. Turn the refrigerator back on. Be sure to empty the drip pan and, if you can get to the vent, vacuum any dust or dog hairs from it so the motor won't have to work overtime.

rugs:
Although I like my upright vacuum for heavy cleaning, I adore our little carpet sweeper. The kids do too. It's easier to get them to sweep up in the dining room with that than when we had an electric broom that had to be plugged in and emptied. The carpet sweeper has to be emptied too, but it's quicker. You can buy a child's size or regular size. The smaller one often is handier.

S

shoes:
Everyone can polish his own shoes if you have one spot where all the polish, rags, and buffer are stored. Keep extra shoelaces there too. You can clean white patent-leather shoes with toothpaste if you run out of polish.

staircase:
Although I believe in putting bundles on the side of a staircase, so you (or someone else) can take them up on the next trip, I am careful to keep the steps clear of obstruction. A tiny car or other toy can cause someone to slip and be badly hurt. If your steps are carpeted, make sure it's tacked in firmly. If not, make sure they're NEVER waxed.

spring cleaning:
I don't believe in it.

T

telephone:
Dust the dial as you talk and occasionally, wipe the oil off the receiver and ear piece.

television:
When your reception gets fuzzy, try dusting the screen with a clean, soft cloth.

toy chest:
Occasionally go through (with child) and throw away broken toys, puzzles with less than two-thirds of their pieces, and games with missing parts. Put toys they've tired of in the attic. A month later, they'll seem like new. Watch for toys your child may have outgrown. Pass them down to younger offspring if in good shape or, if you're out of offspring, to friends or thrift sales. Toys can be recycled too.

U

upholstery:
Clean spots off as they occur with a mild detergent solution. Mend tiny tears so they don't grow. In both cases, if it's beyond you, call in an expert. His or her services are bound to be cheaper than recovering!

V

vacuum:
Most experts recommend you vacuum before dusting because you stir up dust. I've always figured you

dropped dust on the floor when you dust so dusting came first. I think it's a toss-up. Do whichever way makes you feel most efficient. Do empty the bag and put a clean one in *before* you vacuum, in case you make as big a mess as I do.

vases:
Rinse out with baking soda between "refills."

W

walls:
If you can possibly afford it, I highly recommend covering kitchen walls with a vinyl-type wallpaper. Grease spots and fingerprints easily can be wiped off with a damp rag as you talk on the phone—unless you have a large kitchen or a short phone cord. Children's rooms should be painted with a semigloss paint. The walls can be wiped off and the kids can cover their walls with posters, pennants, and pictures that kids want on their walls. If they want a change of color, it's easy to get out the paint roller and paint away. People who wash walls say you should wash up from the bottom so dirty water doesn't run down. I just keep washing spots off as I see them and change one hundred watt bulbs to seventy-five so nobody notices. I'd rather paint than wash.

wastebaskets:
I keep plastic and paper liners in my metal wastebaskets so they don't rust if anything wet gets thrown away. Plastic ones can be rinsed out when needed. Most people err by buying wastebaskets that are too small. Buy big—and buy many if you want to encourage your family to pick up as *they* go too.

windows:
Sometime *somebody* has to "do windows" and it probably will be you. Try to enlist your husband or a teenage child to climb up the ladder to do the outsides, but the insides can be done with a vinegar-and-water solution. My kids love to help when I use the spray-type cleaner, but they usually leave the window looking even more streaked. (Sliding-glass doors probably are best left a little streaked so no one walks into them.)

X

xylophone:
Clean this and other hard-to-dust items like sculpture, blinds, and lampshades with a feather duster. I got one as a gift and thought it was funny, an anachronism. But I used it so much that I bought a second one. Grandma knew a good thing when she saw it.

Y

yucky jobs:
"Yucky" things have to be clean too. Sometimes one

woman's "nothing-to-it's" is another woman's "yuks!"
You could spend all your energy finding someone to
trade off jobs with—or do it quickly yourself. Garbage
cans are one of my yuks. I prevent them from getting any
dirtier than necessary by using plastic bags to line them,
and make it easier to wash them out by using plastic
heavy-duty "cans." My second household "yuk" is the
toilet, brought about by years of washing out diapers in
it. It's best solved by keeping brushes in every bathroom
and once a week pouring a little cleaning solution like
Pine Sol in. Let it sit until you think about it, give a good
scrub with the brush and forget about it. (Note: If you
have sons, ask them to remember to be gentlemen and
clean up after themselves!)

Z

zebras: A man came home from work and found his wife busy
scrubbing their zebra. "I've been working all day and it's
still not all white," she sobbed.
He took her in his arms. "Some things don't have to be,"
he said gently.
Leave the "everything-must-be-clean-and-white" to an-
nouncers in television laundry-soap commercials.

If you've been following along, you might wonder what happened
to the "Q" lising in my household tips. That stands for *questions*, and
if you still have some, you'll probably find the answers in Shirley
Conran's book, *Superwoman*, or in one of the Heloise books now
available in paperback.

Don't let the house run you. Granted, chores have to be done—but
they *all* don't have to be done, nor done every day, nor done only by
you.

I have a plaque in my kitchen that reads, "My House Is Clean
Enough to Be Healthy and Dirty Enough to Be Happy." It's dirty
enough for me to get some writing done too, and that makes *me*
sparkle.

Caring for (and Coping With) Family

6.

"You've got a wonderful husband and great kids. Isn't that enough?"

A friend once said this to me. (At least I always thought of her as my friend.) Yet she hit me right in my insecurity blanket of guilt. I don't know about you, but I still find comments like that hard to handle.

I *know* it isn't a matter of right or wrong, what is or isn't "enough." I also know that I don't *have* to feel guilt. But I do.

I rationalize: "I'm happier when I write, and a happy mother is better for her kids." I make justifications: "If I weren't writing, I'd be into volunteer work. At least I'm home this way." I lavish extra attentions on my family to "prove" to them that I really love them very much even though I sometimes get very caught up in my work. The truth is, they already know I love them.

Why then do so many of us worry about "what people think?" We say we really don't care—but we do. Our antennae constantly quiver to catch even the slightest whisper of doubt that we're not doing a proper job as wife and mother.

This phobia isn't reserved for housewife-writers. It afflicts in epidemic proportions most of the married, female working world. But, at least, they travel under a greater aura of respectability. *They* go to an office (i.e., *they* work). We stay at home and still want to claim working women's status. How suspect.

Lois Gould wrote an article, "How Can a Woman Sit at a Typewriter When There's So Much Work to Do?" in the April 14, 1977, *New York Times*. She said, ". . . nobody ever checks on whether I've written five pages today or only three, or none at all. Whereas there are all those booming male voices on TV telling me, 'Eyes are on your floors! Spots are on your stemware!' " She understood the problem. She was writing out of her home.

How can you cut down on guilt? (Every woman knows you're never totally free of it.) It helps if you're realistic. Analyze objectively, think through exactly what you are and aren't depriving your family of because you're writing. Be honest. Obviously, some things are bound to be different. After all, you're taking one, two (or even six) hours out of what used to be an uninterrupted stretch of being "on call" to your family. You're taking some of *your* time back for yourself. There! I've said it. Did that really hurt so much? Aren't you entitled to some of your own time? Of course you are.

There are benefits to reclaiming some of your time for yourself. It will prevent overindulging your children and trying to do everything for them. It will make it easier to "cut the apron strings" and let them test their wings a little. Your life won't be totally tied up in your children's lives and interests. Many psychologists agree that women who have other interests in their lives adjust better to the "empty nest," suffer less difficulties of menopause and have fewer signs of depression. See how healthy writing can be!

But you need to be aware of and even write down the changes you foresee in your family's life. Which ones are most emotionally packed? How can you handle them?

How to Keep Hubby Happy and Helpful

One woman, who finally succeeded in getting her first article published, told me she found it very difficult to make time for her writing.

"My husband likes to dine formally," she said. "He expects a four-course dinner with homemade bread and fresh-baked pies. I spend half my day in the kitchen. I've tried to work out a compromise, but he's immovable. In his mind, my love and his dinner are hopelessly intertwined."

This is a problem, but not one that can't be resolved. If this husband is as rigid as he sounds, perhaps it might be easier to acquiesce on this point, but then find another area of compromise. Maybe they could agree on home-cooked meals four times a week and then eating out the other nights. She could have those days for her writing. Or, she could agree to the home-cooked meals but send him off fishing on the weekend without her so she could write then.

If he's not willing to give an inch, there may be underlying reasons that have nothing to do with her writing. If you have such a mate, don't throw up your hands in despair, or throw him out either. Be honest. Explain how important writing is to you and your well-being. Ask for his help in arranging a schedule that works for you without making him feel threatened in any way. He *should* be cooperative because he loves you; but, if he isn't, don't take his stubborness for lack of love. More than likely, it's lack of understanding. Blame it on his mother, and figure you may have to write when he isn't around and hide all the tools of your trade under the dirty clothes when he's home. (He'll never look for them there.)

Sometimes husbands become jealous of the time their wives are spending at the typewriter, away from them. They feel left out.

"I could understand it if my competition were 'another man,' " said one husband. "But it's a Smith-Corona!"

Some housewife-writers circumvent this problem by asking their husbands to help with their writing: editing, proofreading, or even typing. There are husbands who help as their wives' photographers or illustrators, and there are many cases of husband and wife working side-by-side as coauthors.

Other husbands are baffled by the entire writing mystique and are supportive—but at a distance. One husband, whose wife writes "household humor," admits he never reads her work.

"I don't understand what's funny about it," he said, "but as long as the editor keeps publishing it and her readers like it, I don't *have* to understand."

Some husbands read everything their wives write and mumble, "That's nice, dear." Others make constructive suggestions that can strengthen manuscripts or add to their salability. A few transfer their resentment toward their wives' preoccupation with writing to the manuscript and tear it apart. There is no cut-and-dried "husband reaction" because each marriage is different and so is each husband/housewife-writer relationship.

Many women find new problems when they begin to be successful.

Strangers recognize *her* name, and her husband becomes "Mr. Housewife-Writer." A man secure in his own right can easily cope with situations like this, laughing it off or ignoring it entirely. But other men may feel threatened by their wives' prominence.

A woman can best handle this situation by acknowledging that she did write *Desire Under the Kitchen Sink*, chat briefly about the book, and steer the conversation to a more general subject. Don't mindlessly underplay your success "for your husband's sake," but don't monopolize conversations either. People may be more interested in how Jane Fonda may play the plumber in the movie version of your book than in your husband's sale of five thousand white-buck shoes to a Dartmouth shoe store. But remember you still go home with the "guy that brought you," and he knew you way back when . . . . Besides, you love him. Include him in the conversation just as you would want him to include you at the Saddle Shoe Convention. It's just good manners.

Without a doubt, a supportive husband is one of the greatest assets a working woman can have. Without it, the juggling and scheduling involved in working, running a house, and managing children (if any) become an almost overwhelming task.

This is especially true for the housewife-writer who has, in addition to the usual stresses, rejection slips and deadlines to contend with. There also is the frustration that comes with having to work when there's so much else to do and everyone else is having fun—and the frustration of not working when you know you should be. A supportive husband can be the extra ingredient that makes the difference between the woman who is successful in her writing and one who can't seem to get her career off the ground. If you have such a man, treasure him.

Most men are supportive to a point—but they still want dinner ready when they come home, clean clothes in the dresser, and a wife around when they want to talk—or even when they don't feel like talking but want company. If they'll cook or do the laundry, you're fortunate. Many rebel at this kind of "help."

I try to be available after dinner to join my husband in the living room. He'll read and I'll do some editing or outline in longhand. I prefer working on the typewriter, but I've made this compromise. We enjoy being together, even though we're both doing different activities, and we're available for conversation if either is in the mood. I used to use this time solely for needlepoint, but found that by adding an extra hour or two for editing, I can increase my writing volume substantially without shutting hubby out, and that's in between helping with homework, answering phones, and getting snacks.

We both try to avoid making phone calls at night or getting involved in long discussions when someone else calls us. We also plan very few evening activities that don't include each other or the children. We lead extremely busy lives in the daylight hours and need the evening together to "touch base," unwind, and breathe the same air.

Sometimes even the best of plans doesn't work. When you have a tight schedule—too many revisions in too short a time, or a child gets sick the day before your manuscript is due and you just got the typewriter back from the repair shop—call for help. That's a four-letter word you *should* use around your family.

Ask your husband to bring something in for dinner or take the kids out while you work. If he's supportive and/or understanding, he'll lend a hand. But he has to know. Too many of us attribute "mind reading" to our husband's long list of attributes and then wonder why he didn't volunteer when we needed him so much. Don't play martyr and try to go it alone. Husbands like to feel needed too.

How to Fight for Your Time With a Minimum of Conflict

You can be as disciplined as a West Point cadet about your writing schedule, but when a family crisis or special occasion comes up, you have to be flexible. On those days, even your best planning and scheduling isn't enough. Rather than trying to write and doing it poorly, sometimes you just might be better off delaying it a day or two.

When I spent a few days "on the road" with my family, we checked into a motel with faulty air conditioning and cell-size rooms. We spent as much time away from our rooms as possible. The first night I tried to do some writing in longhand (there wasn't room to set up a typewriter), but the room was stuffy, dark, depressing, and smelled of carpet-cleaning solution. I finally said, "To heck with it," and gave myself a vacation. At first I felt guilty. Then, like a dieter on a binge, I enjoyed my freedom.

But old habits are hard to break. I discovered myself writing leads, ideas for future articles, and even doing some outlining in the little notebook I always carry with me. If I had tried to force myself to work, those ideas never would have found me—or is it the other way around?

"I planned to write today," I think as I fall into bed, exhausted, "but—unexpected guests dropped in; a child fell roller skating so I spent the day at the doctor's office; the kitchen caught on fire." All these were actual events that kept me from completing work that I planned on a particular day. But flexibility is vital to any housewife-writer. You have to roll with the punch (even when it's Hi-C on your white carpeting) and figure that tomorrow *has* to be a better day.

If you have days like mine (and I'm sure you must), try not to let them get you discouraged. It will only make you tense, irritable, frustrated, and old before your time. Tell yourself, "Tomorrow I may write twice as much and it all will be twice as good as it would have been today."

But, and this is important, don't think I'm trying to say that you should give up on a day without a fight. If you think you can salvage even a little time, do it. We all know it's easy to find excuses for not writing. So try—but if you can't, relax and put if off until tomorrow. Then *do* it, when tomorrow's TODAY.

Part of being realistic is not expecting things to be the way you'd like them to be. You must work around things that are.

Be assertive about your working hours. Tell the family that Saturday morning from eight to ten (or whatever works best for you) are your "do not disturb" hours. Plead for isolation unless they have something very important. Of course, your definition and theirs of what is important may be vastly different. Don't ask for permission to work, just for cooperation.

Kids are very intuitive. They'll sense your hesitation if you feel you must apologize when you're working. Be firm in your requests for cooperation. They understand "fair play," and when you explain the rules—that you need their help to get your work done—they should be helpful. Children really do want to please you. Usually when they mess up, make noise, or barge in it's because they forgot; nothing more sinister than that.

Barring the unusual or the bizarre, stay on schedule. Everyone will respect your writing more if *you* do. If the kids see you in the kitchen making a salad when you're supposed to be writing, they won't take your schedule very seriously.

While I was working on this book, the children were on holiday from school. They kept running back and forth through the house, standing outside my door arguing, and playing air force in the hallway by my study (with my door being the supply depot).

I tried to concentrate, but kept being disturbed by bombs bursting outside my door. Finally I called them together.

"This book is very important to me," I said. "I really would appreciate your help in getting this chapter finished."

They took on the challenge and for two days tiptoed whenever they came even close to my closed door. They spoke in whispers. At the end of the second day, one son asked if I had finished the chapter.

I had the decency to blush. "I—ah, I didn't work on the chapter today," I admitted. "I was working on my column."

"Mother!" he exclaimed. "You were supposed to be working on your book!"

I felt properly chastised and went back to work on the book. I could tell that they were disappointed with me. They had taken my work seriously—but I hadn't!

When you're working, don't feel you have to apologize for it. Set the timer for the younger children, being realistic, of course, for how long they can play without checking back with you.

It's important for your family to know that you're available if they need you. That's one of the advantages of working at home. And, although I keep stressing the importance of sticking to a schedule, I don't want to undermine the need for being on hand when you're needed—emotionally as well as physically.

That's one of the reasons I seldom do any typing at night. It seems to make the rest of the family feel isolated. It's not that they really need me for anything, but there's something about a typewriter clacking away in another room that fascinates some and disturbs others. I've noticed it in myself when my son is typing. Just as whispering tends to make your ears perk up, the clacking of keys makes me wonder, "What's he doing?" I know what he's doing. He either is typing a school assignment or one of the stories he likes to write. But it puts my curiosity on a "ready alert."

My family knows if I'm typing at night I mean business, it's an emergency, and I prefer no interruptions. If you find you must work then—because it's the only time you can or you have to meet a deadline—then announce it to one and all, so they'll ignore you for the "time out" you've requested. Otherwise, they'll pop in and out with Latin translations for you to check, excuses for you to sign and, if you're surrounded by toddlers, worn blankets and balding bears for you to pat.

I find I'm much more available for discussions if I'm just sitting with a notepad (or my needlepoint) in the evening. It's more condusive to confidences. The family knows I'm interruptible then, "off-duty," and just Mom. I also try to be available when the kids first come home from school. It's hard for them to respect a closed door when they're dying to tell you they made cheerleader—or need to say that they didn't. You always can go back for another hour of intensive work later in the afternoon, but don't keep them waiting too long or they'll stop telling you their problems and successes.

How to Do Your Share with PTA, Carpools, and School Activities

If you have school-age children, you're probably going to want to do *something* at their school. They want you to and you'll be made to feel guilty if you don't, either by yourself or others. But also realize that many children, especially the younger ones, want you to help at school but really aren't that upset if you don't.

My youngest said that his class was going to a local amusement park. Five mothers were needed to help with the class. "I think I can get you picked if you volunteer now," he confided.

I was torn. I was behind on an assignment and really didn't have a full day to spend at the amusement park. Yet I felt compelled to volunteer. I procrastinated about three days and finally called the teacher, offering my services without much enthusiasm.

"Oh, I'm sorry," she said. "We've already got more than enough mothers. But thanks for offering."

I turned to my son, expecting him to break into tears. Instead he said, "Oh, that's all right, Mom. Too bad you'll miss the fun." And he ran off to play. Moral? Kids don't always desperately want what *you* think they do. Sometimes they just want to see if you'll do it. It really doesn't matter what "it" is. They just want the reassurance that you'd be willing to do it. I try to get the kids to level with me. "Is it important to you that I do it?" If they say it is, then I try. Many times they'll say it really isn't. (Then you've got to figure out if they really mean it!)

Because we feel guilty for being different, housewife-writers often jump to conclusions and read meanings into our kids' requests that aren't there. A simple, "Will you be home when I get home from school?" leads us to explaining that we were only gone once this week because an interview ran over when a "yes" would suffice.

We worry what others may think about us too if we don't come, do, drive, or whatever everyone else is doing. I voiced my feeling to one son after I had declined to drive across town to see his soccer game.

"Gee, Mom," he said. "Most of the parents *don't* come to our games. I wondered why you wanted to drive so far." If in doubt, ask.

Naturally, each situation is different, and you have to consider the child, the event, and the time you have available before making any decision. Basically, however, I can offer these rules:

1. In the fall, immediately volunteer for one "spot job," anything that has to be done only once, even if it takes the best part of a day, such as eye exams, a Halloween party, or talking about being a writer to an English class. Then you're through for the year.

2. Refuse to be head of any committee, homeroom mother, or anything else that puts you "in charge." Someone will back out and you'll have to do the job; you'll spend time on the phone finding helpers; it makes you too visible. Be happy to be an Indian—an invisible one, if possible.

3. Always say what you *will* do and play down the "won't." Chairmen usually are delighted to hear that someone is willing to help out. They won't realize the job you agreed to do wasn't what they had hoped you'd accept until they've hung up.

4. Never qualify your answer. "I'm sorry, I can't," will do. If you add that you have a deadline this month, they'll call you again for next month.

What to Do About Birthday Parties

Try to talk your children out of extravaganzas. If you can't, take them to an ice-cream shop that specializes in kids' parties or to a movie so there's little preparation and no cleaning up afterwards. Older children enjoy taking a few special friends to a fancy restaurant or a pizza parlor.

Before I began writing full time, I planned a Scottish birthday for my seven-year-old daughter. We handmade little Scottish paper dolls with the party information written under their kilt (plaid material stapled over the figure).

Each guest was requested to wear a kilt (plaid skirt). I found a baker who agreed to frost a cake in plaid. As the Shimberg clan colors seemed to be unrecorded, we settled for pink, blue, and green, my daughter's favorite colors.

It was a lovely party, but not one of the little girls realized the hours of preparation that went into it. Today I'm wiser. The kids have movie, skating, or pizza parties and we're all more relaxed.

My daughter read this and disagreed.

"I remember that party," she said. "It was fun."

"Was it worth all the time it took?"

She shrugged. "I don't know. But I remember it."

She had me there. If she still remembers that party, it *was* worth all the time and effort. Special memories are what life is all about. Ask any grandparent.

Let me just say, in my defense, that if you have parties for your kids, make them special for the child, and not just bigger and more spectacular than the one your neighbor or sister-in-law had.

Our family birthdays are celebrated in style at breakfast with cake or pie, depending on the birthday person's whim. It gets them started off on their special day feeling very special; and, when they were younger, it gave them new toys to play with all day (so Mommy could do a little writing).

What to Do When the Kids Complain, "You're Always Working!"

1. Don't feel guilty.
2. Put it into perspective. (You must do points "one" and "two" simultaneously for them to be effective.) What the kids usually mean is that you are busy right this minute when they want you to play Candyland or drive them to the drugstore or review geometry theorems.
3. Try to keep the guilt and/or anger out of your voice and calmly tell them you'll be at their disposal in thirty minutes, an hour, etc. For little children, set the timer and tell them to let you know when it rings. (Note: Put the timer up out of their reach. Kids are sneaky and *have* been known to move the timer up!)
4. Consider the charge. Perhaps they mean that you're busy when they first get home from school and need to tell you about what an unfeeling teacher said to them, or how they scored the winning goal in soccer, or that THE BOY smiled at them today. It really helps everyone if you take a breather and are available. After they've "touched base," chances are they'll get a snack and go play, listen to music, or start homework, and you can sneak in another hour of writing.
5. If they're old enough, get them to talk about their feelings. Find out exactly what bothers them about your working. Maybe they feel you don't care about them. Maybe they want your ear. Perhaps they're jealous of your career. Communication is the lifeblood of a writer, and what better place to start than with your family?

Why Kids Bicker When You're Fighting a Deadline

Because they're kids.

Because they like to get your attention.

Because they sense *your* tension.

No, it doesn't only *seem* that they're worse then, they really are. Screaming at them does no good. It only adds to the noise level and makes everyone (especially you) feel lousy.

If your kids are little, put each in a different room and have them draw you a picture. Tell them you'll judge the entries when the timer rings. (Of course, you'll give blue ribbons to all involved unless you want to create another incident.)

If the kids are older, try reason. Remind them that Daddy has his work and you have yours. You're glad you can do yours at home so you can be around if they need you, but they have to help make it work. Compare your deadline to their term paper due date or cheerleading tryout and try to get them to relate to your problem on their level. Appeal to their sense of honor, responsibility, decency, and, as a last resort, guilt. If all those fail, send each on his or her separate way—and if they both want the same way (i.e., the room with the television), send them outside or to their rooms.

I also am not above throwing myself at their mercy ("please help me!") or bribery, in the line of duty.

Once I was working on an article for Essence. I was typing my final draft, and my clean typing is painfully slow. I could hear fighting in the background. Suddenly, the door flew open and one of the "defenders" came in to lodge a complaint.

"Play a quiet game," I said with sudden inspiration. "If I don't hear any noise, I'll treat everyone to ice cream."

There was instant peace. I got the manuscript typed and mailed. We all got ice cream cones and the kids considered that article "theirs." When it sold, they couldn't wait to see "their" article in print.

I have let Monopoly games go on well after bedtime because it kept things quiet and I could work; I have let them make fudge on rainy days although candy, presweetened cereal, and bakery goods (other than oatmeal cookies) are banned from our house. I have also (I blush to confess it) occasionally suggested they call a friend to see if they could spend the night.

While I was completing this book, I found myself alone for three days with my seven-year-old. The older kids were away, my husband was out of town on a business trip, and school was out. I had a great deal of writing to do and a minimum of time.

"Tell you what," I proposed. "You keep yourself amused during the day and let me work, and we'll go out for junk food at night."

It worked!

Any port in a storm. Accept that they are kids, and most kids bicker. If you weren't under stress, you probably wouldn't even notice.

What to Do When the Kids Get Sick

The Shimberg Law of Probability states that the incidence of children getting sick increases proportionately to the nearness of a deadline.

If your sick child wants you near, move your work into the sickroom. If they're little, let them pick out stories for you to read at the top of the hour. The remainder of the time, they'll probably be content just to have Mommy close, even if she is pounding a typewriter.

Sometimes I'll read my work aloud as I proof it. It helps me feel the pace of my work and amuses the sick child too.

You can let a sick child stamp your return address on envelopes, file negatives, or sharpen pencils. (A box of old jewelry or Christmas cards can provide hours of amusement too.) Naturally, if they're really sick, the way some kids get from chicken pox or strep throat, you'll have to remember your flexibility plan and try to reschedule your work for another time.

How to Hear Your Family Tick

Sometimes your family will say that they're delighted with your work when, in truth, they subconsciously resent it. How can you tell? By listening to what they say and don't say, and what they do and don't do.

For example, if they steal your scissors, carbon paper, and stamps, and write math assignments on your final draft, they may be just plain thoughtless—or they may be trying to tell you something.

Do they continue to pop into your study when you've asked for quiet hours? Do they call from school and ask you to bring forgotten lunches and/or gym suits? If so, tell them to beg some lunch from a friend. Most kids have plenty to share and if not, one day without lunch will remind most youngsters to take their responsibilities more seriously the next time. Does that sound terribly cruel? I don't think so. If you start covering for your children, they'll take advantage of you and, what is worse, never learn to look after themselves.

Perhaps the kids feel angry that you make them take the bus to swim practice, or worse, walk or ride their bikes. Maybe your husband feels neglected because you no longer bake or knit him sweaters. He doesn't say so, of course. In fact, he *says* he's proud of your published work. But then at a party, when someone compliments him on losing weight, he says, "It's not from dieting. My wife's just too busy playing writer to cook for me anymore. I'm just wasting away." That's the voice of resentment talking.

Other women writers tell of put-downs from so-called supportive mates, men who *really* think they are supportive of their wives. Comments like "I'm glad she's got a hobby to keep her busy"; "She *says* she's home writing all day, but *I* think she's napping"; "She's going to be so famous she won't need me any more"; and "While I'm out working all day, she's home writing," all show deep resentment and unspoken hostile feelings. This can be terribly destructive. Be alert for these and other signs that show your family may resent your time at the typewriter. Try to bring it into the open. Talk about their feelings and yours too. Sometimes (usually, actually) they may not even be aware of their resentment. But you need to clear the air and work out compromises that make everyone happy or, at least, comfortable.

Perhaps you can write only when everyone is in school and at the office, or for two hours after dinner. If home-baked desserts are as rich in emotion as they are in calories, teach one of the kids to do it, or agree to do it yourself, but trade off something else you've been doing that really doesn't matter as much to them. (Maybe you can pay a neighbor to bake for you and no one will be the wiser!)

Your family *can* scuttle your writing plans if they have a mind to. It's worth taking time to clear the mine field before you start moving.

How to Turn Family Fun and Folly Into Sales

Every housewife has moments of madness when she'd like to bolt out the door and run away from home. (In fact, many women have done just that.)

As long as you protect the privacy of your family (never mention them by name or embarrass them in any way) it's all right to use family situations in your writing. It's a good way to "run away from home" without hurting anyone or getting locked out. Everyone likes to read about how others have coped with similar problems. It's safe to assume that if something is a source of frustration for you and your family, it probably is to a great many potential readers as well.

I've used personal experiences in writing humorous articles as well as serious ones. "How we solved, coped, handled, or messed up" usually will find sympathetic readers. Our pets, problems, parties, and plants all have found their way into print.

Writing about family fun and follies has two definite advantages. Not only do you get paid for your problems, you also get the frustration out of your system. (It's a mild and therapeutic form of revenge.) And, after the story is published, you have the satisfaction of knowing that you're not alone, that others have the same frustrations you have.

Many times I've received letters from readers that said, "How did you know my family so well? I felt as though you were writing about us." People really are not all that different. In Chapter 8, you'll read more about how to get ideas from personal experiences.

Remember to Give Yourself a Vacation

Although writers always are absorbing something they can use for a character, article, etc., make certain you spend some time off with your family—and when you're wth them, BE with them, not half-thinking about that lead you're having trouble with. Listen to your husband when you're with him. Give him your full attention. You'd resent his replaying the Super Bowl in his mind while you're relating your run-in with an editor.

Other jobs (i.e., *real* work in offices) give vacation time off. You deserve it too. Take pictures for future stories, make notes (if, and because, you must), but break your writing schedule. You'll be more refreshed when you get back to it.

What to Do With the Baby

Combining a baby with a byline is probably the easiest of the mother-child stages for the housewife-writer-mother. Babies stay where you put them, they sleep a lot, and they eat when you feed them. I nursed all my babies so I didn't even have to worry about fixing formulas. (I also had an extra hand free while they nursed in case I wanted to jot down a note or two.)

But babies also cry a lot—and they can't tell you why they're crying. I found that extremely frustrating, especially with my first two when I was still feeling uncertain about my "natural instinct." By the third one you *sound* authoritative, although you don't know anymore than you did before.

I found it hard to write when they cried. I changed them, offered them more to eat, burped them, rocked them, firmly put them into the crib, and picked them up again when they cried. I remember days when we both cried as we rocked. *I* was tired and felt helpless. I never knew what made *them* cry.

Usually, however, the babies were "good," and when they took two naps a day, I wrote. When the baby was up, I did household chores with baby observing me from the wind-up swing, babyseat, or the blanket on the floor. I did a lot of "floor jobs"—wrote bills, planned menus, and cleaned drawers on the floor by the blanket so we were almost face-to-face. I talked to the baby (and aloud to myself). When baby went down for a nap, I went to work.

Before baby decided which finger to suck, I had dashed to my "office," a spot behind the couch in the family room. I worked two hours until baby woke for lunch. There was plenty of time for hugging and playing, then naptime again and more writing for me. I thought combining baby and byline was such a breeze that we had another baby—and another—and then Baby Number One became a toddler.

What to Do With the Toddler

Writing with toddlers toddling is a bit more difficult than with babies gurgling in the playpen. Toddlers are active and want to be with Mama, and there's little use trying to write in a room with the door shut and them on the other side. They'll just play the "Anvil Chrous" on the door until you let them in. You can't lick them, so you might as well join them.

I moved a card table and the typewriter into my toddlers' bedroom, and while they played with their modeling clay, crayons, and cars, I wrote. Because of the difficulty of concentrating with chaos around me, I changed my type of writing. Rather than working on detailed articles requiring extensive research, deep thought, and hundreds of reference index cards that attracted grubby little hands, I began to write verse for studio greeting cards, short inspirational and humorous articles, and nonfiction that required little research.

I used the little time there was when the children napped for doing research, phone interviews, final drafts, and outlines for future articles. My typing and busywork were scheduled for when they were up, around, and under foot.

There were many times when one would fall down, and while I was "kissing the hurt away," one of the others would climb up and do some additional "typing" on my manuscript. They spilled glue on the carpet, licked roll stamps and pasted them to the wall, and rubber-stamped my return address all over their sheets. But at least it was confined to one room.

When I tried working in the family room, the toddlers would roam the house. In the middle of my typing, the silence suddenly would shout at me. I'd dash around trying to locate the quiet ones and find them covered from head to toe with vaseline or flushing the wallpaper they had torn off the dining room wall down the toilet.

Sound funny? Not when you're living through it. It's great material for humorous articles—but not right at that moment when you're looking at the eggs they've scrambled for you in the dryer.

You need to accept the fact that even good little ones have fussy days—and some toddlers refuse to nap. It's vital to get help when and where you can find it. Rent a high-school sitter or a homebound mother who would like to earn a little extra spending money. If you can't afford to spend the money, see if you can exchange services—like typing the teenager's term papers or getting groceries for the homebound mother when you shop for yours. Take advantage of the story teller if your library has one. You can do some writing or research while the kids are hearing a story. Use your first check to pay for a good play school (for the kids, not you) even if it's only for one day a week. It's good for the kids and good for you too. There is a way, if you have the will.

With toddlers (as with life), the secret lies in remaining flexible. If there's absolutely no one around who can help you out when naptime is a total bust, try to teach yourself to work even with the youngsters under your feet. It's all in the way you concentrate and, although it's not my preferred choice, if it's the only way I can write, I'll take it. Some women manage to write romantic novels with their toddlers eating Play-Doh in a corner. Still others swear they could write humorous articles in the middle of a gang war. It's up to your personal desire, strength of concentration, and state of nerves. It also helps to have a few fantastic toys around that only are available when Mommy is working and some story-tapes even if you have to record them (with sound effects) yourself.

Although I wrote with my youngsters under foot when they were this age, I kept my supplies, files, and other "valuable" material behind my bedroom door, so they couldn't get to them. Having your toddler destroy your only copy of the article Reader's Digest seems to have mislaid and wants you to resend to them could prove hazardous to that child's health.

Try to accept that your kids are at a difficult stage for your career and soften this acceptance with the fact that they eventually will grow out of that stage. The next one may prove more difficult for you as a parent—but it sure is easier for the writer side of you.

What to Do With the Preteen-age Kids

At this age, kids really aren't too interested in getting into your supplies. They just want you to be around when they get home. I try to be through with most of my concentrated work so I can hear about their day and drive them to practice, haircuts, shoe store, etc. From 3 p.m. on, I try to be a housewife-mother and leave the writer in the study with the typewriter. That's not to say, of course, that as long as you have to wait at the orthodontist you can't bring a clipboard and do some writing. I've written entire articles as I sat waiting in the car or a doctor's waiting room. You really never should go anywhere without enough paper to keep you busy. (It's bad form, however, to edit while the ballgame's going on. Besides, you might miss out seeing your kid bat and have to wait through the whole lineup again.)

It is important to stress with children of this preteen age that although you're wearing your "Mom" hat for them, you're a byline to an editor somewhere who probably doesn't know (or really care) that you have a cast of thousands of kids running around at home. When the editor calls, it's to talk to a writer, not to someone who has to yell, "Hey, will you kids quiet down?"

Preteens feel their independence and want to do as much for themselves as possible. Often they don't quite achieve their desires, and they'll come running home to Mother. Expect interruptions that are loud with indignation about real or imagined hurts and frequent in number. Be patient, understanding, and ready to let go when they want to try it again.

What to Do About Teenagers

Much of the same advice goes for this age group too. They may have reports and themes to do and be more tempted to use your office. Make certain that you lay down the ground rules. May they use your typewriter? What about typing paper? Do they know where you keep things, and will they return them?

My teenagers respect my office for the most part. They do come in to use the phone for their "private" phone calls—but they make certain their doodling is on scratch paper and not on a manuscript. During exam week, they take turns studying in my office, but they ask my permission. They probably pop in with minor complaints and requests more frequently than they would call about those same things if I were in an office downtown, but I like being on hand.

They do borrow my reference books without asking and keep them in their rooms. I've had to run from room to room while they're at school, trying to locate the "P" *World Book* or my *Dictionary of Quotations*. It's maddening—but it's a fair trade-off. Half of what I write about is them!

Teenagers have split-second emotions. They can be giggling one moment—and drowning in tears the next. You may feel that these emotional peaks and valleys are your fault; if you weren't writing, they'd be "better adjusted." Sorry. You'll have to come up with a better excuse than that to leave the typewriter. My friends, who never write a word, report the same phenomenon at their houses. It's part of being a teen, not the result of being the child of a mother who writes.

Stay tuned-in to what's going on, though; not only for your youngster's sake, but also to know what to write about that's meaningful in their world. These young people are at their height of insecurity as they try their first tentative steps into the adult world, then scurry back to the safe world of children, then back out again. You never know exactly where they are, and they don't either. Listen to their worries. Usually they center on being liked, being handsome (or pretty), doing the "right thing" or at least the same thing the crowd is doing. You can do a lot of talking, but I think at this age listening's more important. Let them know their ideas are valued, that they're loved unconditionally, and that you're there—then keep your fingers crossed.

Use the concerns of your own teens to write for others. Tell teenage readers how to adjust to their parents' divorce, to be popular, how to say "no" to drugs without being a "goody-goody," etc., and you'll find loyal readers.

Listen to your children for ideas. Sometimes mine will be discussing something and turn to me and say, "Mom, why don't you write about this?" What better way to be fed ideas? It's a nice bridge over the so-called generation gap.

Sometimes your youngsters will bring problems home to you that they can't (or won't) discuss. Many women writers have taken their frustrations over a child's drug addiction, run-away habit, or pregnancy, and expressed it the only way they knew how—through their writing.

You also can use your teenagers as sample readers for articles of interest to their age group. They're blunt, but they're fair. But don't ask unless you really want an honest reaction. If they think it's lousy, they'll say so.

There are many additional family considerations, especially in today's changing world. You may have your husband's children by a former marriage visiting on weekends, and although it (you hope) doesn't throw the house into a turmoil, it does change your routine. Perhaps there are aged parents living with you, and every time you sit down to write his father comes in for conversation. How do you handle these "unusual" situations that are becoming more usual?

If the arangement is permanent, find ways to work around it.

Explain to the older couple that you need your privacy the same as they do. If they can't be left alone, get a competent teenager to come keep an eye on them a few times a week so you can write. Discuss your problems with your husband or a friend, preferably one who writes. Two heads often are better than one when it comes to solving puzzlers like this.

If weekends mean you have extra children in the house, try to work during the week or teach them to be as considerate as you hope yours are. Don't give up. There always is a way. You just may not have found it yet.

How does a housewife-writer cope with her family? With patience, love, and a sense of humor.

Escaping the Clutches (of Organizations, Friends, and Foes)

7.

Newton's Third Law of Motion says, in effect, that for every action there is an equal but opposite reaction. That happens as you begin to take your writing seriously. As you withdraw a little from the world around you in order to have some solitude for your writing, you'll suddenly find yourself in greater demand than ever before.

Friends who once shared hours of your time will be bewildered by your desire to spend so much of your time alone.

People you might once have considered friends will confide in others, "She always was a little secretive" (or "strange," "different," "stuck-up," etc.).

Organizations whose ranks you once helped fill may resent your withdrawal symptoms. Writers are valuable assets to any organization. Your talents can be utilized in writing publicity, newsletters, skits, and in organizing fund-raising campaigns. No wonder everyone wants your body—and the harder you resist, the more valuable you become.

Your greatest enemies are these distractors, people who help themselves to your time as if it were a bowl of big, red apples.

How can you get away, escape without hurting feelings or creating enemies, without letting other people down? The answer is that you can't. The trick, as Houdini must have said, is in making sure that you *do* escape.

Say "Good-bye" to Ladies' Luncheons

No one's asking you to become a hermit—just to utilize your time more wisely.

We all need friends, a change of pace, a time to relax. But meetings and luncheons (along with the telephone) tend to erode our time more than any other activity. Social luncheons never start or end on time. You eat (and drink) too much, and it's hard to get back to work.

I belong to a few groups, seldom go to their meetings, and have alerted the chairman to the specific tasks I am willing to do. I may miss out on some of the "fun" of belonging, but I'm published more now than when I tried to be an active member. Unless you produce fashion shows (or write about them), stay home and write. You couldn't? You adore fashion shows? Maybe you really don't want to write. You only want to be a writer. Remember that list of priorities? Only *you* can determine what goes where for you.

What to Say When People Complain, "You Never Call Me Anymore"

Friends (and relatives too) can feel very left out when you decide to take your writing time out of what used to be your "telephone hour." It seems as if you've dropped out of their world—and they usually take it very personally.

"It doesn't take that long to call," they may mumble when they see you, not realizing that fifteen minutes here and there add up to hours, hours when you could be writing.

Think about it. You spend about thirty minutes each day talking on the phone to your friend. Then there's another thirty minutes chatting to your mother, fifteen to thank a hostess for a lovely party . . . see how fast it builds up? You may be spending as much as two or three hours on the phone each day. That's enough time to get a great deal of writing done. People have written complete novels with no more daily allowance than that.

You can wait for others to call and interrupt you as you try to write. That will be frustrating to you and unrewarding to them, because all but the most obtuse will sense that you really don't want to talk.

Or, you can call them first, either before you begin work or during a break. In either case, set a timer so you don't go on talking into your work hours. In this way, you'll enjoy your brief conversations, make everyone happy, but stay in control by saying, "I have to go now" and then *hanging up*. I hate to tell you how old I was before I realized that *I* could hang the receiver up first and not wait for the other person to say, "good-bye." I happily pass this wisdom on to you in hope that you'll put it to good use.

I also have consciously weaned some of my friends away from daily telephone calls by saying, "I won't be able to talk tomorrow. I've got a heavy working schedule." A few I call every other day.

Some may become defensive when they call you and preface each call with, "I know you're probably busy. . . ." Don't let a guilt trip cause you to say, "Oh, no, I'm not busy. . . ." Say when you will be free and ask if you can call them, like around lunchtime or during a break. Staying in control of your time is vital if you're going to save up enough minutes to make writing hours.

Some calls can be eliminated altogether. Send thank-you notes to hostesses instead of calling. They'll be more appreciated anyway. (We all love to get mail.) Besides, notes will cost you only postage and a few minutes of your time. Make plans with friends on the first call so you don't have to call back to confirm.

If the phone still interrupts you, unplug it or turn it off, if you can. You always can put earplugs in so you don't hear when it rings. I have a second phone line for business calls and family emergencies. When I'm pressed for time, that's the only one I'll answer.

If you're *still* hearing bells, perhaps it's the doorbell. You can ignore it—or stick a wad of cotton in the clapper.

Coping With Friends

Friends are probably the most difficult to handle because you do sincerely care about them. You try to explain. They nod and say they understand. But you might as well be talking in Chimpanzenese. They hear you, but there's no comprehension.

I've had friends listen sympathetically as I bemoan the fact that my book's deadline is in just one week, and I'm expecting house guests this weekend. They'll shake their heads and agree it's really a problem—and, in the next breath, ask if I'll babysit their kids so they can go to a tennis tournament, or sign for a package and give the driver the one they're returning for the next size bigger in blue. Do you agree to help or refuse? No matter what you decide, you're in a bind.

Sometimes we allow people to freeload, because we can use their interruption as our excuse for not writing. "I had to drive Joan to the airport, so I really didn't have time to work on the chapter"; or, "Martha dropped in for coffee. I couldn't very well tell her to leave, could I? After all, she's my best friend!"

If we were working in an office, Joan would have found someone else to drive her to the airport. And Martha would not have come downtown for coffee. Would she drop in at the house even if you were firm about your writing hours? To be honest, yes, she might; but she might not do it the second time if you leveled with her and asked her to come during your lunch break instead. Speak up. This is not time for subtleties.

If you find yourself being "walked all over" by your friends, think about your unspoken message. Perhaps you're volunteering to be a doormat because you're afraid your writing's not good. But you'll never know unless you begin, will you?

When Friendships Fade

Accept the fact that some of your friends may become former friends. They'll be confused by your new set of priorities and be hurt that you "like to be alone with the typewriter more than me." It's lack of self-confidence and, perhaps, a little resentment on their part. They truly don't know what to make of you or who you are now.

Put yourself in their shoes long enough to realize that to some of your acquaintances, you have changed "overnight" from someone who could sit and listen to the neighborhood gossip, talk about babies, and trade recipes to someone who talks about first rights, deadlines, and speculation. You may know that you're the same person you've always been, but to them you're a little different, and that frightens them.

Trite as it may sound, friends who take you as you are end up being the ones worth keeping. Those who find you "weird" and try to keep you from your work, either through ridicule or impossible demands on your time, aren't worth giving up all you'd need to sacrifice in order to maintain that friendship.

Remember that, although most of your friends are amazed at your determination, they won't understand your need to write and probably won't even see or read your book or article. Enjoy their friendship—and listen to what they do with their day too. Don't be hurt if they aren't too interested in yours.

One woman, an articulate and successful novelist, said she was hurt by the reaction of some of her friends. "When my latest book came out, some of them didn't even mention it. They ignored my reviews in the *New York Times* and the *Washington Post* [which were good], and although I know they had seen me interviewed on a national talk show, pretended they hadn't. These are the same people who will say *I've* dropped them, but the truth is, I make them uncomfortable."

Are such former friends like these jealous? Awed? Self-conscious? Probably a combination of all three. But I've noticed that some of my friends who would never hurt my feelings by mentioning I had gained weight or was wearing an ugly dress think nothing of saying, "I read your article last week. I didn't think it was very good."

What can you answer? It may vary, depending on how you felt about the work. You can agree with them: "I didn't think it was my best work either." You may honestly feel it was one of your better pieces: "I liked it. I'm sorry you didn't," and change the subject. Don't try to pry "why" from them. If they're friends it may be upsetting to you both. If not, why should you care? Try to keep it from churning your stomach.

Be on guard for seemingly harmless comments that can undermine your confidence as a mother or wife. Comments like "Oh, your children have to make their own lunches?" . . . "Your husband drives the morning carpool? Oh!" . . . and "Well, maybe if you had taken the baby to the doctor sooner his cold wouldn't be so bad," show an underlying hostility. Don't think you're being neurotic if you sense a double meaning in them. But don't let them pierce your armor, either. You're not alone. Other working mothers hear that too, from people who feel they must be Guardians of the Guilt. Ignore this type of talk (and vow to include this character in your next novel, written up as a warty witch or black-caped villain).

As Evelyn Wilde Mayerson, author of *Sanjo*, said, "Writers are not reclusive. We need friends. Who else can you share the joys of the business with? Just don't expect instant adulation when you're successful."

How to Maintain Friendships With a Minimum of Free Time

This is a problem all working women face—and it's even more difficult when you're working at home and so available. How can you stay in touch with that small group of friends you're really close to? If you steal time for your writing, you've probably robbed it from leisure, ladies' luncheons, and gabbing on the phone.

But it need not be an all-or-nothing proposition. Like any other activity, you can plan for friendships by scheduling them as carefully as you do your working hours. Call friends for lunch. Just make certain that you've told them in advance that you have to get back to work at a certain time. If you don't set limits, lunchtime may eat up all afternoon.

If you don't feel you can control a phone call, send a note saying, "Thinking of you."

Sometimes you can mix business with pleasure. When I did some travel writing a few hours from home, I invited my friend to go with me. We hadn't had much time to visit, and this served a dual purpose. She read me map directions, pointed out attractions for me to notice, and even posed for some of my pictures. I enjoyed her company, found her notes valuable when it came time to write the articles, and didn't get lost!

If you write restaurant or play reviews, take your friends along. You'll have the benefit of their reactions and enjoy the companionship.

You might enlist a friend's help in doing research for you, or, if she's qualified, ask her to help edit your work. (I recommend this only if you have a great deal of respect for her judgment.)

Sometimes the only way to see a friend is to collaborate with her. I have a friend who also is a housewife-writer. We've coauthored three articles and a nonfiction book, and are "fooling around" with an idea for a mystery. We laugh a lot together, commiserate, and compare notes on writing. But we also work when we're together. If you're thinking about collaborating with a friend, discuss you goals and schedules to make sure you're on the same track *before you begin*. If you're dead serious about getting your section done and she's just dabbling at hers you're going to have problems, and these will spill over into your friendship.

Program Your Exercise

There's room (and need) in your life for exercise and fun. It relaxes you and helps you to be more creative. But if you play every day, make sure you leave time for your work too.

A tennis-playing friend of mine was upset that I wouldn't join a twice-weekly game of doubles.

"What you do is so isolated! You need to be out, with friends!"

I smiled and went back to my typewriter. I do play a little tennis, walk, and ride my bike. But a regularly scheduled game takes too much time for me. I'd rather use that time to write. Again, it's priorities. The purpose of exercise is to feel your best; but if you want to write your best, make sure the exercise program fits your writing schedule and not the other way around. Priorities!

How to Entertain Company So You All Enjoy It

You may not feel like giving dinner parties when you've been writing most of the day. And, if you spend all day cooking, you won't be writing. What's an author to do? Answer: Be creative.

1. Invite friends over for dessert and coffee (or cheese and fruit since people are more diet-conscious than they used to be).
2. Invite a few couples in for hamburgers, store-bought potato salad, and ice cream. It's friendship they're coming for, not food.
3. Ask a group of friends over for a buffet with everyone bringing one specified dish.
4. Invite the gang to a "happening." Have everyone bring something without saying what they're bringing. Once we had three Greek salads and six desserts. Another time we had a well-balanced and diversified meal. Both "happenings" were fun.
5. Go out for dinner and a movie, or come back home for a gab session after dinner.
6. If you miss your afternoon bridge game, have the ladies over one evening while the men go to a baseball or soccer game.

Don't worry about cleaning the house for friends. Make sure there's toilet paper in the bathroom, a clean bar of soap, and fresh towels. Pick up dramatic clutter, wipe off sticky doorknobs and light a few decorative candles in the living room and no one will notice the dust. If you spend all day cleaning for company, you'll be too tired to enjoy them—and you won't get any writing done.

If you feel you *must* give a dinner party (and sometimes there's no apparent way out), check with a caterer to see if you can buy the entree, or pop a roast or chicken in the oven and buy a fancy vegetable or rice dish.

There are many good recipes that you can make ahead, which leaves you part of the party day for writing. One of my favorite cookbooks is *Never In the Kitchen When Company Arrives* by Theresa A. Morse. Most of the food for my dinner parties takes less than thirty minutes to prepare. Forget sauces and fancy desserts. Hamburger and chicken can be fixed numerous ways that are delicious and don't require a great deal of time. Remember, the most important ingredient in any party is a relaxed hostess.

I've discovered that the best "camouflage" for lack of time to prepare for a fancy party is to be clever and plain. Let your decorations be creative. Kids have marvelous ideas and sometimes volunteer to do centerpieces and place cards. Use a bright tablecloth, colored dishes if you have them, and let fresh fruit be your centerpiece instead of flowers. It can be eaten for dessert. I also have made centerpieces out of children's toys (a Nerf football and helmet-shaped pencil sharpeners for a pre-football game dinner) and a castle made from blocks with Matchbox construction trucks when we entertained an architect. Unfortunately, my "turret" fell into the mashed potatoes. Luckily, our other guest was an insurance salesman and he said we were covered!

How to Answer When Someone Says, "Are You Still Writing?"

That's when it really hits you that others *still* aren't taking you seriously. It hurts.

You can express your frustration by answering, "Yes. Are you still practicing law (banking, medicine, etc.)?"

You can turn the other cheek and just say, "Yes." (You *could* add that you just won the Pulitzer Prize, but chances are that wouldn't impress them either.)

My answer usually is, "Yes. I'm doing it professionally now." But, realistically, I think I say that more to satisfy my ego than to get anything through to them—because with people like this, you never get through.

I have one friend (male) who keeps asking me if I'm "keeping busy?" It sounds as if I'm in occupational therapy. Maybe to him I am.

We all might as well accept the fact that *few* people think that:

1. Writing is work;
2. Anyone who works at home is "really" working; and
3. Women who write could really be professional writers.

To most people, housewife-writers are dabblers, hobbyists who keep busy and stay out of trouble by writing. It really doesn't matter one iota if you're published or not.

Accept it; develop a sense of humor about it, and DON'T LET IT INTERFERE WITH YOUR WRITING. Then, when someone asks, "Are you still writing?" you can answer, "Yes. Have you read my latest book?" or "article in _____ magazine?" Probably they won't have, but others will and you'll be glad you're "still writing."

How to Be Selective About Organizations

Organizations are a lot like the clothes in your closet. If you don't go through and weed them out occasionally, you won't be able to fit anything in. But it's difficult. We join organizations for a variety of reasons and with varying degrees of enthusiasm. Then, since we belong, we feel we should go to the meetings (which eat up large quantities of time) or we don't go and feel guilty about not going (which also wastes large quantities of time). If we wind up going to the meeting because it's the lesser of the evils, we find that club obligations erode even more time. The only answer then is to learn to be selective, even selfish, about the demands made upon you.

Ask yourself these questions about every organization in which you presently hold membership:

1. What is the purpose/purposes of this organization?
2. Am I interested in their activities?
3. Does this group really accomplish anything?
4. How often does this group meet? (Do I have time to belong?)
5. Do I enjoy being with the members?
6. What are the minimum requirements?
7. Why did I originally join?
8. Is my original reason for joining still valid?
9. Have I outgrown this particular organization?
10. What are the financial obligations?

Many of us join clubs without really knowing why or even understanding what the organization is all about. We join because our friend is an officer and she asked us to join, because the group is prestigious and we were flattered to be asked, or because it's something we like the sound of being a member of.

Sometimes we join a group whose purpose has nothing to do with our own beliefs. I knew someone who joined a women's group whose chief aim was support of the Equal Rights Amendment. She personally was confused about the issue and wasn't sure where she stood. Once in the organization, however, she was embarrassed to confess her conflict and remained a less-than-enthusiastic member.

I moved into a neighborhood where every woman was a member of the garden club. I was notified that two of my neighbors had nominated me for membership. I stayed in the group for a year, paying dues but never making it to a single meeting. Not only did I have little interest in gardening, I was writing full time by then, and the monthly meeting invariably fell on a day when I was completely engrossed in my work.

Finally, I faced the situation and called the president. I explained my position and mailed in my resignation. I felt relief for the first time all year. How much easier it would have been if I had just said, "Thank you. I appreciate your asking me, but I'm not interested," in the very beginning.

Perhaps you enjoy the activities of a particular organization but you really don't like the members or the numerous meetings. Ask yourself if you could accomplish the same goals outside the confines of the organization. If your interests are environmental, for example, could you write a booklet or newspaper article that would achieve the same ends, without requiring you to belong to an organized group?

Many groups whose aims we support, and whose members we enjoy, meet too often. If you find yourself without enough time for your writing, tell the president you'll come when you can, or resign because you can't (or don't want to) make all the meetings.

When I was writing part time, I found myself an officer in a group that had monthly executive board meetings, board meetings, and regular meetings. More than three days a month were fully occupied with meetings, not to mention occasional committee meetings. I still had two preschoolers at home, and the hours I spent sitting at the various meetings dragged like the days before my birthday when I was little. I finally decided that it wasn't a fair exchange and resigned.

Some organizations require very little from their members. Others have strict requirements and work-time obligations that must be fulfilled by service of some type. Think it over very carefully before taking on the latter type of commitment. If you're serious about this business of writing, can you handle the demands of clubwork too?

Some groups want you to sit on their board, even though they have an executive secretary who does all the work. The members of the board just approve everything and get their names on the letterhead. I guess if you want a lengthy obituary, that's fine. But even in organizations like this, board membership puts you on a phone list (which means you'll get more calls), a mailing list (more mail to sift through), and you'll still have a guilt feeling every time meeting days come around and you're not going.

Although I no longer sit on boards that do nothing, I pay dues to a number of organizations to which I've made it clear that my support is strictly financial and I prefer not being called or asked to work.

What about those others, though, the ones whose aims are yours, whose members you enjoy, and for whom you want to be active? How do you keep them from devouring your every spare moment? The answer is, with great difficulty, and by being always on your guard.

When You Want to Carry the Club

There are some groups you may feel you have to join: the PTA, a church or synagogue women's group, civic associations, etc. As mentioned in previous chapters, you can solve that problem by immediately volunteering for a one-time job so that you can feel you've been of service and have done something to justify your membership.

Professional groups are a little different, although you have to be discerning with these too. I've been in some marvelous professional groups where I enjoyed the members, felt myself being stretched and made more aware of life outside my own little world, and could support the purposes and aims of the organization 100 percent. Knowing other professional women as well as men and women in my own field has helped carry me over some rough spots in my career. But even in these groups, protect your time and strive to balance "outside activities" with your work.

Many writers belong to writer's clubs. These groups are found throughout the country under many different names. They usually are loosely formed organizations where writers may meet with other writers, exchange market information, and read their work aloud for critiquing by the members. These groups offer the beginning writer emotional support when it's badly needed.

The danger with writers' groups is that sometimes the members only talk about writing and don't do any. If you find yourself in such a group, look around for another whose membership is comprised of recently published writers.

How to Gain the Most from Meetings

Most meetings are time-wasters. Probably 90 percent of the meetings you go to start late, don't follow the agenda (if there *is* one), and accomplish little. You waste time getting there and back, indulging in idle chit-chat, and waiting for members to arrive. Anytime you can settle an organizational problem by phone, do so. It's better to spend one hour on the phone getting all your business done than three hours in a meeting.

If it's a meeting you're supposed to attend, look over the agenda, if any. If there's nothing really happening, if it's only a rehash of old business and no speaker (or one that doesn't interest you) stay home and work on those revisions for your book.

When you do go to meetings, make sure you know what's expected of you before you leave. Make the chairman clarify your instructions so they aren't so vague. Otherwise you'll waste more time later calling to find out what you're supposed to do.

Questions such as, "Now I'm supposed to get five volunteers and call you with their names, right?" and "When do you need these figures?" will force less-than-efficient leaders to be definite. You don't have time to waste with vagueness.

Think about going to meetings of organizations you don't belong to, if they have a speaker you'd like to hear or a special exhibit. Watch the newspaper for club announcements. Usually the group's president is listed and you can call, introduce yourself as a writer, and ask if you can come. Most meetings are open to the "interested" public, and chances are they'll be flattered you want to attend. Take notes and keep a file of those speakers. You may be able to use them and their expertise later for an article. Date the card, so you can call and say, "Miss R., I heard you speak at the Women's Club last May 4th. . . ."

Organizations are living things, and they change and grow, as you do. You may outgrow some of them, and feel that they no longer fill any need for you. A club that doesn't do much is like this. Originally you may have joined it to meet people, to make contacts, or because you believed in its goal. Now it's time to move on.

How to Keep from Writing Too Much for Free

I feel strongly that a writer should share her talents by contributing some of her efforts toward "good deed" projects. But you need to keep your voluntary writing in perspective to make certain it doesn't begin to occupy all your available time.

Your abilities are needed and will be welcomed by many groups. But if you don't protect your time, you'll be writing booklets, slide presentations, and fund-raising letters for every "good works" group in town and have no time left for your own writing.

Try to select one (two at the very most) groups you feel strongly about. Agree to write one specific project for them, never all their publicity. Meet with their public information officer once or twice to learn what they need and to gather information.

Never, never write with a committee. Professional collaborations are difficult enough without getting involved with amateurs who will delay, argue over every word, and use up precious minutes of your time.

Try to steer away from writing newsletters, skits for any type of organization, or any other type of writing where personalities become involved. I've learned from experience that the people whose names you inadvertently omitted or who think you wrote a "better part for her than you did for me" will make you sorry you ever began.

I prefer to spend most of my charitable (without pay) writing on brochures or booklets, something that I can write completely on my own and on my own schedule. I once spent two full weeks working on a slide presentation for an organization that needed it "immediately." I wrote the copy and even suggested what slides to use at each point. That was (at this writing) exactly thirteen months ago and the committee in charge still has not put it all together.

If you want to write professionally, you need to "give something back." But decide beforehand how much time you're willing to donate. Otherwise, without priorities, you'll discover that your work week is over and you haven't accomplished what you hoped you would.

Remember That Mother Said You Should Learn to Say "No"

How do you learn to take control of your writing life? By the simple (and difficult) technique of learning to say, "no."

One of the greatest boons to my writing career was the no-credit course I took in assertiveness training. I mentioned it before in Chapter 2. I don't think it can be mentioned too often. I strongly recommend it to any woman who is trying to be all things to all people and still save some time to be herself, a professional writer. We women are so used to being available, "on call" twenty-four hours a day, like a convenience store, that many of us always have trouble saying and meaning that little two-letter word: No!

You can add, "I'm busy," if you feel you need to explain (you don't); but don't add more or you'll get into trouble. Example:

Them: "I'd like you to write the publicity for the fund-raising dance."

You: "I can't."

Good so far. But then you blow it by adding, "I've got a deadline Friday."

Because now they can say, "Great! We don't need the publicity until a week from Thursday!"

You see? You should have stopped when you were ahead.

Learn to say, "No." If you have a problem with it, read some of the excellent assertiveness-training books or sign up for a course. And don't tell me, "No!"

More time can be saved by saying "no" than in almost any other way. It lets you do the writing you choose to write and keeps you from being talked into writing something else against your better judgment.

A few years ago I was asked to do some travel writing for a business organization. I was involved in many of my own writing projects and didn't really have the time. But my vanity made me say, "Yes."

The person in charge had very definite ideas about what he wanted. I rewrote my articles a couple of times according to his suggestions. He still wasn't satisfied. He was vague, yet definite; he couldn't tell me what was wrong with what I had written, but was sure I hadn't captured the essence of what he wanted. (I used to have clients just like that when I wrote radio commercials.)

The work I was doing for this man involved driving out of town (expenditure of both time and gas), and many hours of rewriting. I had foolishly agreed to a flat fee, rather than per-hour rate. At last it dawned on me that I never would be able to write it exactly as he had in his mind. It was time to throw in the towel. I suggested that he reimburse me for my mileage and we'd part friends. I learned a valuable lesson. Say "no" when you don't want to write (or do) something. It saves time, aggravation, and paper.

Sometimes your ego overwhelms your common sense and good judgment, and you find yourself in a situation where you "know better." I let myself be talked into working on a book query with another woman who is an expert in her field. I was flattered to be asked but knew that the book wasn't "right" for me. As proposed, it is heavily researched and documented nonfiction, a style I can write when pressed but find difficult to sustain at book length. To my surprise (and horror), the publisher liked our query and is considering giving us a contract. I find myself in the odd position of half hoping I get rejected!

That's why I can say without reservation that it pays to be assertive in your writing life. You'll take control. Things won't just "happen" to you anymore; people will stop taking advantage of you. The difference won't be them, it will be you. When you become assertive, you take responsibility. You become the person in charge. Believe in yourself and follow the leader you've become.

Ideas
(Keeping Them
Coming and
Going)

8.

"Poison Your Child!" . . . "Speakeasy" . . .
"Gawfnuddle!"

These are just a few of the key words posted on my bulletin board to
remind me of ideas for future articles and stories. Without ideas, a
writer is as lost as a teenager without a phone.

Ideas, like germs, are always around. It's just a matter of becoming
susceptible to them. They're there, like the Eiffel Tower; but like the
Parisian, you just don't see them.

Writers who also are housewives and mothers have a wealth of
ideas lurking under all the hats they wear. Think of it. In one day's
time you're a chauffeur, cook, seamstress, nurse/doctor, psychologist,
vet, painter, laundress, and carpenter.

Once you develop the habit of collecting ideas, you'll soon find
that, rather than having *nothing* to write about, you have acquired far
more ideas than you'll ever have time to write about.

Listen for Ideas

If you have children, you are doubly blessed. Because children, for all the aggravations, headaches, and pain they may cause, give great joy, comfort, tears of happiness, and good old belly-laughs. They also provide you with a wealth of material to use in your writing. With kids you have a continuous natural flow of good in-house ideas. Listen to them. What are they talking about? Dating? Drugs? Movies? School? What are their gripes? The drinking age? Competition for grades? Lack of "wheels"? What are their fears? Low SAT scores? Not being "normal"? Not being accepted by their peers? What questions do they ask—or not ask? What makes them laugh—and what makes you laugh about them?

My kids complain, "Everything we do, you write up for an article." They're smart, those kids. My career might be further along today if I hadn't had them all, but then what would I have written about?

I've listened to the kids as they talk to their friends. Concern over giving a speech in class led me to an article on how to do just that. Seventeen published "Speakeasy" in their Mini-Mag section.

One daughter's experiences getting her ears pierced (which led to my doing the same), and her later experiences with contact lenses gave me ideas for humorous articles. I've used many of their experiences as springboards for stories and articles, but I've never abused our relationship. I've laughed with them, not at them. When you have an abundance of children, as I do, it's better for all concerned to refer to them as "one of my sons," and not single any one of them out by name. Let people wonder which one needs to be threatened into the bathtub, which one tried smoking. Never embarrass your children when you write about them.

If you don't have children of your own, get to know your nieces and nephews, or the kids down the street. (On certain days, I'll gladly lend you one of mine!) Kids have a special way of looking at life that we seem to have lost. They're honest, direct, funny, and often very touching.

Listen to the rest of your family too. What's bothering your mother? Loneliness? Getting old? Poor health? Money worries? What about your sister? Your husband? What are they talking about? What makes them laugh—or cry? Their concerns, interests, and joys are probably shared by many others. If you can isolate them, develop them, make them meaningful, you've got a pretty good chance of putting together a salable article, story, or book.

While you're listening to your family, tune into your friends as well. What are they doing that's exciting or different? Do they

Ideas 127

surf-glide? Wrestle alligators? Transcribe books into braille? Provide a foster home for handicapped children?

Many times we take our friends for granted and listen to them without really hearing (as they do us). But if you'll start absorbing what they say, hear their gripes, plans, and concerns, you'll find an abundance of story ideas.

All this listening can lead to a little self-consciousness whenever you're around.

"I suppose you'll put that in one of your articles?" they'll ask when they've dropped a piece of barbecued chicken on someone's yellow velvet couch.

Just put it down to their being a little paranoid, smile, and dash off to the ladies' room so you can jot it down on a matchbook cover.

Don't be afraid to eavesdrop on strangers, either. It's part of the professional writer's stock in trade.

Irving Wallace said he got the idea for his best seller, *The Fan Club*, from overhearing some men joking around in the club car of a train.

But you can shop for ideas while you're doing the family marketing too. I overheard two women in the grocery talking about a forthcoming wedding.

"It's just going to be a simple wedding," said the mother of the bride.

That gave me an idea. I went home and wrote down all the horrendous stories I had heard concerning so-called "simple weddings" and sold the article to the *Tampa Tribune*.

In the shoe store I heard a woman talking about a camp her leukemic child would attend that summer. I introduced myself and asked about the camp. She told me about an exciting new program that gave children with cancer a chance to enjoy one of the normal joys of childhood, that of attending camp, as well as the names of other parents and camp officials to contact. The resulting article appeared in the *Floridian*. Without eavesdropping, I never would have known the camp existed.

Listen to what people are talking about; jot down their complaints, their pleasures, and what is making them laugh or cry. They'll trigger a world of ideas for you.

Store Up Sounds and Sentences

Sometimes you hear a phrase or sentence that "sounds good." You like the images it conjures up, it's pleasing to your ear, or you just like it for no logical reason. Save it—store them up. Eventually they'll all tie into something or give you an idea you can use. This is especially true if you write greeting cards or verse.

One Mother's Day, my kids offered to bring me breakfast in bed. "Just point us to the kitchen," one laughed.

I did—but I also wrote down the remark and sold it to Hallmark Cards. They've reprinted it, not only as a Mother's Day card, but also as a Mother's birthday card.

Kids have an uninhibited way of expressing themselves; old people do too. It's a lack of self-consciousness. If you listen for it, for the unique phrasing or tender way of expressing something, it can liven up your writing.

Many housewife-writers use their children's funny sayings. Others draw from daffy dealings in their lives. We housewife-writers have an easy time finding humor close at hand. (We'd go bananas if we took the absurdities too seriously.)

Talk to Strangers

Mother may have warned you against it, but you're a big girl now—so talk to strangers. Talk to everybody: neighbors, clerks in shops, people on the bus, etc. Most people like to talk about what's close to them; e.g., a hobby, their job, problems, dreams, etc.

My mother plays mah jongg, a game with tiles covered with colored dragons, flowers, and strange Chinese markings. She had played it for years, and I never thought much about it, other than enjoying playing with the tiles when I was sick as a child.

One day I was seated next to an older woman who mentioned that she too played mah jongg. Just to make conversation, I asked her how it was played. With great enthusiasm the woman told me about the history of the game, how it had changed over the centuries, and invited me to her weekly game. That led to an invitation to meet and interview a group of women from our local air base, who played a slightly different variation of the game. Then I interviewed, by phone, the head of the National Mah Jongg League in New York. My article, "Crack, Bam, It's Mah Jongg" paid well when it ran in *Florida Accent*. It was a story that had been under my nose since my childhood, but I had to listen to a stranger to get the idea.

My idea for an article on volcanic heating in Iceland came by overhearing a woman introduce someone with a name like "Saul Svenson" to a friend at a cocktail party. I hesitated—and then couldn't help myself. I walked over and blurted out, "You must forgive my rudeness, but I was interested in your name. It sounds so

Scandinavian—yet your first name sounds Jewish."

The gentleman smiled. "Yes, I am Jewish," he said. "I live in Iceland." He anticipated my next question. "Yes, there is a large Jewish population in Iceland."

I finally remembered my manners and introduced myself, adding that I was a writer, one who knew almost nothing about Iceland. He began talking about his homeland. By the time the evening was over, I had learned a great deal about Iceland, its people, and how they use volcanic steam for domestic heating. I also had made a friend who promised to send me more information as soon as he returned home.

When I was about fourteen, I visited Omaha for a youth organization conclave. The climax of the weekend was a dance and banquet, and I was treated by my parents to a spree at the beauty shop. I asked the beautician, "What's your work like?"

"Why?" she asked. "Do you want to be a beautician?"

"No," I answered. "I'm going to be a writer, but I may want to use a beautician in one of my articles."

I vividly remember her hesitating . . . and then she began to tell me some of the strange things that had happened in her work.

Everyone has a story to tell if you'll just listen to what that person has to say. The words, "I'm a writer and I'm interested in possibly doing an article about you," have turned on more people than a drug store full of uppers.

But the important words here are, "I'm interested in doing. . . . " Writers always are bombarded with, "Oh, you really should write an article/story about my grandfather who lived in Utah. . . . " Unless you become fascinated with your friend's story, suggest that she write it—and find your own idea.

Tune In to Yourself

Don't forget to listen to yourself. "I haven't done anything worth writing about,'" is your first reaction. But you have. We all have. Each of us is unique, yet each of us has much in common with our neighbor. It is this paradoxical combination that makes writing so fascinating. Doris Lund (Eric), Betty Rollin (First You Cry), and Nancy Friday (My Mother, Myself) all turned their personal experiences and emotions into best-selling books.

Think about it. What did you do today? It may not be as dramatic as the above stories, but that doesn't matter. Did you cope with an aging mother? Argue with your teenager? Have your beloved old dog put to sleep? These are typical experiences of life we all can relate to. If a reader can say, "That's exactly the way it was with me," you've touched her, made contact with her emotions.

Although each of us handles things differently, many of the same things are frustrating: timesaving equipment that doesn't work and/or save time, children who act like children, relatives who do too. Write it down before you explode. It's cheaper than paying a shrink and, as many writers have discovered, it may be profitable as well.

Keep a sense of humor and look for the funny side of life.

Think about what makes you laugh. Is it the red tape that's strangling all our lives? Conversations you've had with youngsters? Trying to train a pet? What makes you angry? Careless drivers? Repairmen who don't come on time? Toys that break the day they're bought? What makes you cry? Stories of sick children? Inhumane treatment of animals? Pollution? Your answers to these questions could be developed into a salable article or story.

People always are interested in reading how you handled a situation they also have experienced (or just enjoying a good laugh). We all are a little insecure, and it's comforting to know we're not alone.

Take something as simple (and dull) as getting kids ready for camp. As I was sewing 112 name tags on socks (fourteen pair for each of four children), I decided to laugh rather than cry and called the resulting humorous article, "Mother's Camp Count-Down Races."

Then I thought about it more seriously. After spending all the money, time, and effort to select the right camp, how could parents help to make certain that their child/children would enjoy it?

I compiled a questionnaire and mailed it to one hundred camp directors throughout the United States. They all belonged to the American Camping Association, but represented a cross-section of camps (private, Y-associated, specialty). I took some pictures of my kids "reading letters from home," etc., and sold the article to Lady's Circle.

Later, I updated the information, checked with additional camp directors, and sold "Prepare Your Child for Camp" to Family Weekly.

Mentally follow yourself around on a typical day. Ask yourself:
1. What have I done?
2. How did I do it?
3. Why did I do it?
4. When did I do it?
5. Where did I do it?
(You're right. It's the old "who, where, what, why, when, and how"

your high school English teacher talked about, but it works when you're trying to come up with ideas.)

Reminisce

Memory is a bubbling well of ideas. But sometimes you have to prime the pump.

Many writers take to their baths when they need to get ideas flowing. Others swear by solitary sailboat rides, walks in woods, or long car trips. But housewife-writers may find these mind-joggers difficult, and even impossible with small children. A car trip with kids shouting in the back seat is conducive to nothing more than a headache.

But you don't need to get away physically, if you learn to free your mind. Some say they get their best ideas from the television, that it trips a memory for them. I personally find both radio and TV a distraction. I have to sit in silence, which I found during nap time when the kids were small, in the bathroom when they were toddlers. Now most of my serious thinking is done while they're at school or when I'm fixing vegetables. To me there's something relaxing about the monotony of snipping tips off string beans, scraping carrots, or peeling potatoes. I get some of my best ideas then. Vacuuming is great for this too.

But whether you sit at your desk, staring into the vastness of the ocean beyond your window; or perch on the highest hill, waiting for inspiration, you need to be receptive. A blank mind usually results in a blank piece of paper in the typewriter. You must keep the idea button constantly on automatic. My husband always says your mind is like a magical computer, if you just let it work.

Let your subconscious work for you. It's one of the best ways to get ideas. Think about a scene from yesteryear and let it play for you. What did things look like? What were the smells and sounds? Why did things happen as they did?

Reminiscence is especially effective for writing about holidays and for scenes in books or stories, but it also can be used to trigger humorous and inspirational articles. Best of all, you don't have to research your memories; nor do you have to leave home.

One of my children complained I forgot to give him his allowance. That triggered the memory of my childhood, when I had the same complaint. My father said to my mother (who had forgotten too), "When I was a boy, my mother lined us up every Sunday afternoon by her desk and handed out the allowances." By the time I was through reminiscing, I also had completed a humorous, yet nostalgic, article called "Sometimes You Have to Make Allowances," which sold immediately.

Memories of what Valentine's Day meant to me as a child also furnished enough material for an article I sold to the same market.

Although many of my reminiscences have sold to newspapers and magazines as articles, I also have incorporated them in some of my fictional work. People from my past keep popping up as bits of characters I thought were straight out of my imagination. It's not unique with me, either.

In *Myself When Young*, Daphne du Maurier writes, "We are none of us isolated in time but are part of what we were once, and of what we are yet to become, so that these varied personalities merge and become one in creative thought, wearing, at times . . . the face and voice of someone observed at a distance and believed forgotten, or bearing the casual gesture of a friend."*

This is all the more reason we need to take notes of characteristics, speech patterns, scenes, and smells that strike our fancy. You never know when you might want to incorporate them into your work, or develop them into a full-blown idea for an article or story.

Confess

"I confess"—everyone moves closer, ears flapping. We all like to hear confessions. They're not only good for the soul, they're good for the pocketbook. These can be the confessions that sell to the confession-magazine market, but also stories and articles that say, "I was an Alcoholic Mother," "I was a Compulsive Shopper," etc. I've used this approach many times. It doesn't have to be your confession either. It can be someone else's or a subtle blending of many peoples experiences into one solid but first person narrative. Confessions give an immediacy and intimacy that stories told in the third person cannot. If you've done it well, the reader becomes involved.

The article, "Will you Poison Your Child?" is an example of one personal experience I wrote. I actually did poison my child—or, at least, contributed to it. I left a bottle of baby aspirin out on a high dresser in my two-year-old's room. She pulled a chair over to the dresser, pried off the bottle cap with her teeth (this was before the days of the safety cap, but I'd bet even money that she could still do it today), and devoured the entire contents. We had her stomasch pumped in time and left the hospital with a healthy child and some very shakey memories.

I turned those memories into an article; three articles, in fact.

The original article was a first-person story for my local paper, describing the accident, telling how the local poison control center functioned, and giving suggestions on how others could prevent similar accidental poisonings from occurring.

Later, I rewrote the experience with a national slant, using free information from the National Safety Council and including interviews I had conducted by phone with doctors from various sections of the country. I also included some details of our personal experience. This version sold to *Essence*.

A few years later, I visited England and discovered that accidental poisonings in children were a major problem there too. I researched the way their hospitals handled these cases and rewrote the story from a British viewpoint, using English expressions such as *cot* for crib, *garden* for yard and *mum* for mother. It was published in the English magazine, *Mother*.

I'm no expert in the handling of poisonings in young children, but my *personal experience*, supported by interviews with experts in the field and by research, gave me the expertise I needed to sell these articles.

Sometimes, however, you're the only expert that's needed. My qualifications as "mother" and "driver" gave credibility to my humorous article, "Carpools Drive Me Crazy"; and a series of low-budgeted costume parties my husband and I had given gave me all the authority I needed to sell "I Was a Party Smarty" to *Woman's Day*.

On days when you confess that you can't think of a thing to write about, your confession may be the answer!

How to . . .

You probably can think of twenty "how-to" titles in as many minutes. If you need help, check the covers of the popular women's magazines. Most of them have at least one how-to in every issue. It may be worded differently, ("Thirty-one ways to . . .") but it's the same mechanism.

In one month *Good Housekeeping, McCall's, Ladies' Home Journal, Ms., Better Homes and Gardens, Harper's Bazaar,* and *Mademoiselle* published these how-to articles: "How Parents Confuse Children About Sex," "Slim Down With Your New Year Diet," "Compromise for Love: How to Get What You Both Want," "Decorating: How to Make a Big Splash With Little Cash," "How to Rejuvenate Your Dejected House Plants," "Five Ways to Get the Best Out of Glasses, Out of Eyes," and "Yes, You Can Help Your Husband Be a Better Lover."

Ask yourself what you're an expert in. Don't be modest. Consider your skills, talents, and methods of doing things. You may be doing something—and taking it very much for granted—that most of us would be fascinated to read about and emulate.

Do you regularly cook for a family of twelve—or one? Do you teach babies to swim, or foreigners to speak English? Can you clean your house in one hour flat? (If so, I'd love to talk to you.) Do you know how to fix hamburger 144 ways?

Some of the most popular how-to ideas center around hobbies, crafts, and skills. Do you design your own needlepoint patterns, make table arrangements from dried leaves, paint birds on thimbles, or play a sixteenth-century instrument? If so, you literally have an article at your fingertips. If you know enough about your subject or area of expertise, you'll have a minimum of research.

Sometimes you can write about what you can't do! I can't sew, other than to make simple drawstring bags. I turned this singular talent into an article for The Woman, titled "Christmas Presents Even a Non-Sewer Can Make." I also used my lack of sewing ability as the central theme in a humorous article called "Sewing's Sew Sew."

You can do the same with your one recipe that never fails, how you escape from indulging in exercise of any kind, or ways you've devised to keep from dieting. When you're inventorying your talents for possible ideas, keep your mind open to your lackings as well. Where else can you make money by failing?

You can come up with how-to ideas by thinking in terms of what interests people. Anything that tells you how to make money, save money, live better, cheaper, more happily, be sexier, better liked, or raise pets, if researched and well-written, has a good chance to sell. Why? Because it appeals to people's interest in themselves, it pertains to them and how they live. Think about your day, your routine activities. Are you interested in knowing how to cut your housework in half? How to shop once a month and still eat well? How to amuse your kids without television so mommy can work? If you are, there are bound to be some other readers who are too.

Hobbies are another good source of story and article ideas, yours as well as others. I never considered my over two hundred hippos (metal and ceramic, not real ones) as a possible article idea until someone asked me how I started collecting them. I began wondering how many other people collected things and how they had begun. I started asking around. Soon the word circulated, and I was bombarded with friends and even strangers calling me up and stopping me in elevators to tell me about their collections. (One tip I followed up concerned a man who collected door knobs. When I phoned his home, his wife icily informed me that the collector had just walked out and left her—taking his door knobs with him!)

Read and Rip: Newspapers, Magazines, and Brochures

Another source of ideas is as close as your door, yard, or roof, wherever the delivery person throws your newspaper.

Newspapers, magazines, brochures, and other publications can furnish a wealth of ideas for articles, stories, and books. I know one full-time freelance writer who gets all of her ideas from the morning paper. Although you can't copy what already is published, you can get the idea, leads on experts to contact for quotes, and necessary background material.

Many writers make elaborate files, spending hours cross-indexing and making notations from these articles. Others let newspapers and magazines stack up to the ceiling and then waste hours burrowing through them trying to find a specific issue.

I tend to fall somewhere in-between. I clip stories that arouse my interest, write the date and source (page number if it's from a magazine) and throw them into a manila folder, marking the folder with the name of the subject.

Presently I have two drawers filled with files marked, "Drug Abuse," "Funny Names," "Time-Saving Ideas," "Teen Suicide," "Poetry Therapy," "Doll Houses," "Working Women," "Being Fired," "Clowns," "Left-Handed," "Theme Parks, " etc. Looking over the subject matter, you can get some idea of the type of article I'm interested in. Sometimes my subject matter overlaps. Then I either condense the files into one, or I don't. After all, they are my files. As long as I know what's there, it doesn't matter if anyone else does. The important thing is that when I'm ready to do an article, I can pull out a file and have a great deal of research material right at my fingertips. (This is especially important for housewife-writers with infants who have trouble getting to the library.)

Often, the newspaper story is almost all you need to do the article. One morning I was surprised to read that George Murray, the 1978 wheel-chair winner of the Boston Marathon, lived in my home town. I talked with him briefly to verify the facts, and wrote an article that same day, slanted to youngsters. It sold immediately to *Highlights for Children*.

Sometimes, my file of clippings is sufficient to complete a story. Usually, it gives me names of people to contact for additional information.

A one-column, three-line newspaper story about the local blood bank needing type A-positive blood not only moved me to donate a pint, it also inspired me to learn more about blood banks, what happens to the blood once it is collected, and who uses it. I sold that article, "The Medicine No Pharmacy Can Make," to the *Rotarian*.

But writing that article just whetted my interest. Learning that the clotting factor of whole blood often was removed and used for hemophiliacs, I began to interview patients with this disease, their parents, and doctors and developed another story on hemophiliacs.

Being a writer is very much like looking up something in the encyclopedia. You may start with *A*, but before you know it *balloon* catches your eye, which leads to *cockatoo* and *kelp* and finally, *Zuider Zee*. One idea gives birth to another until, like the gerbil cage, you're overflowing!

Sometimes, rather than turning a local story into a national one, it's just the reverse. Our local paper carried a book review of John T. Molloy's *The Woman's Dress for Success Book*. I read the review and found it interesting. It gave me an idea, so I interviewed local career women about their dress preferences and sold the article to the local paper.

Magazines also are a source of ideas. An article dealing with "Ten Ways to Entertain Children on a Rainy Day" could trigger an idea for "Ten Ways to Entertain House Guests," or "Ten Ways to Take a Vacation Right in Your Own Home." Try it with the titles of some of the articles listed on the front of magazines you have at home. How could you reverse or change those titles to come up with an idea for an article of your own?

Brochures also can stimulate the imagination if you give them the chance. A friend of mine picked up a travel folder explaining all the services available at the airport hotel in her home town: room movies, sauna, heated pool, shopping, gourmet dining room, etc. It sounded so intriguing that she and her husband spent the weekend there, just ten minutes from their home. Later she sold an article about it, which more than paid for their mini-vacation.

Ask your travel agency to give you some of their local and regional brochures. Think about the attractions within your own locale. (More about this later in this chapter.)

Pick up brochures wherever you go: the fire-prevention pamphlets handed out in the shopping center during Fire Prevention Week, the "How to Carve a Turkey" folder the butcher gives away at Thanksgiving, and the "How to Grow Roses" booklet available at your local nursery. The government has thousands of brochures available (free or for a small charge) on almost any subject. Just write to the Superintendent of Documents, Government Printing Office, Washington, D.C. 20402. Many magazines list brochures you can send away for; and companies like movers, drug stores, and furnitures stores often offer free brochures, yours for the asking. They're there. They've always been there. Now is the time to read them and let them stimulate some ideas.

Remember to keep your clipping system simple. If you spend too much time clipping, pasting, and cross-indexing, you won't have time to write.

Second-hand Books

I've always loved the smell of books, new or old. Maybe that's why second-hand book shops always put me on the scent of new ideas. For pennies you often can find reference material and idea stimulators— joke books, cookbooks, old pictures, and poetry—that sets your mind to clicking. One 1940 magazine I bought for five cents had a photo of two farm children standing by their pony. It reminded me of the kindergarten my children attended; a ranch with chickens, horses, and fence posts where the children learned to count by looking in the hens' nests for eggs and by figuring how many seeds to put into each hole in the garden.

I wrote up the history and success of this unusual kindergarten and sold it to *Early Years*. The idea had been under my nose for years, and it took an old magazine to make me see it.

Sometimes you find trade magazines at second-hand book stores. Often these are in the penny pile. I found one that showed a Christmas tree in a department store. A bell rang. A local store has featured a Talking Christmas Tree for years. My youngest carried on a running conversation with it all last December until they both were on a first-name basis. The store's promotional director was delighted to give me information concerning the tree's construction, how they cast the person who sat inside, reactions from the parents and children, and how he thought it affected the store's December profits. I sold the article, "Talking Tree Speaks of Profits," along with a picture of a child talking to the tree, to *Juvenile Merchandising*.

Let Travel Bring Ideas Home

Even if you never leave home, you can let travel create ideas for you, using geographic descriptions as a backdrop for your fiction or travel as a general theme. With more women in today's business world, there is a ready market for travel-oriented articles slanted towards women. Think about aspects of travel that concern, excite, or confuse you; find the solutions through research and interviews with travel experts; and write your articles.,

If you've done some travel, alone or with your family, you can draw on these experiences too. Most people are fascinated by travel of any kind—foreign, U.S., state, or even local. Tell them why it's different, exciting, fun, lonely, educational, cheap, or fantastically expensive, and they'll hungrily devour every word.

Look at your family vacation spot as a source of travel ideas. Why did you choose it? How did you get there, pack for it, like it? What guidelines could you draw up for enjoying a family vacation? What would you do the same? What would you do differently?

Study travel books available at the library; talk to travel agencies and friends who travel. Ask what problems may be created by different types of travel and what solutions they can suggest. What should one look for when traveling with the elderly? What happens if someone gets sick in a foreign country? How do you get a doctor? Should traveler's checks be in the husband's name only? What if a woman is traveling on business, and there's no lock on the door? What about eating alone in a strange town? Ask friends with small children how they amuse the kids on long trips. What do they do when the children get sick or hurt?

Look around your home town too. By driving no more than half an hour from my home, I can be in Ybor City, a Latin community with unique shops, Spanish-speaking people, and historical architecture; or I can be in the Greek community of Tarpon Springs, talking to sponge divers, sampling Greek food, and visiting Greek Orthodox churches. I can pick my own strawberries and tomatoes, visit Busch

Gardens and its collection of wild animals, see ocean-going tankers—the list is endless.

It doesn't matter how large or small your town is; it has something, many things, to give you ideas for your writing. But you must look with different eyes. Look for the historical, the unique, the beautiful, the ugly. Certainly you know your home town better than anyone else. Take a trip through it with your notebook and see how many ideas you get.

One of my favorite travel articles arose from taking a detour not far from my house. I drove past an antique shop and saw a woman standing outside by a bicycle. She was motionless and, as I drove past, I wondered if she were real. I drove around the corner and looked again. She looked real . . . but I thought she might be a mannequin. Once more around the block. I found a parking spot and went for a closer look. That was no lady; that was a dummy. I went into the shop and talked with the owner, who had been dressing his "lady" for years and putting her in rocking chairs, on bicycles, and once even had her "with child," pushing a buggy. His sense of humor was contagious, and I sold a humorous story called "The Lady's a Dummy" to *Florida Accent*. The only passport required for that article was a curious mind.

It really doesn't matter if you're flying a Concorde to London or driving a Ford down a side street in your town. If you allow yourself to be receptive, you'll find ideas.

Holidays

Holidays are a natural idea source because they always come around. "But," you say, "they've been so overdone it's hard to come up with a new approach." You can, though, if you just think about it. Your local paper is a good market because they have to run articles about most holidays and would be delighted for a different slant. It might as well be yours.

You can write about the holiday itself, how it originated, what symbols are associated with it, special foods, etc. List all the things the holiday conjures up in your mind. Sometimes, the holiday merely can serve as a convenient backdrop for a message you are trying to get across.

I used the holiday of Passover to demonstrate brotherhood to children in a story for *Highlights for Children*. Why Passover? Partially because it was more unusual a holiday than either Christmas or Thanksgiving; partially because I like its rich symbolism. The story, "The Missing Matzoh," was set in a small town (much like the one I grew up in). A non-Jewish family rescues a Jewish family from their burning house and proceeds to try to set up a Seder for them. The fact that the symbols of the Seder—the matzoh, etc.—were not available, proved to be far less important that the love these families feel for one another.

There are new things that can be said, or old things said in a fresh new way, if you think about them.

My offer to write a simple description about Chanukah didn't interest my local newspaper feature editor in the least. But when I suggested "Chanukah—from a Child's Point of View," I got the assignment.

A rabbi gave me permission to meet with the kindergarten class of his religious school. I took some pictures and talked with the youngsters, and ended up with some delightful and original thoughts about this Jewish holiday.

Think about your favorite holiday as a child. Was it Christmas? What traditions did you observe? How did they originate? Does your own family follow them today? If not, why did you let them drop? What food do you associate with Christmas? Dylan Thomas's marvelous piece "A Child's Christmas in Wales" is filled with magnificent description so vivid you can smell the food cooking and see the characters. Let your mind conjure up your personal scenes, unique to you alone.

Look at the holiday things your child makes at school. Can you improve on them? If so, write them up for a craft or children's magazine. Are you decorating the house or doing something special for Saint Patrick's Day? Father's Day? Halloween? Ask other people how they celebrate various holidays. If they're famous enough, you may be able to sell their answers to a national magazine. Think of the lesser-known holidays too, like Ground Hog Day, or National Pickle Day; and foreign holidays like Bastille Day and Swiss Independence Day. You might even try making up a few of your own! Remember to offer holiday-slanted articles to national magazines six to nine months in advance.

Clubs and Meetings

"You can't be advising me to go to club meetings!" you shout. "I'll never get any work done."

That's partially true; but by being selective about the meetings you *do* attend, you'll find additional ideas for articles and stories.

Most organizations have guest speakers. Some of them would make
complete articles as personalities. Sometimes what they have to say is
newsworthy. If it's an expert in some field, take notes and jot down the
speaker's name and date. You may want to contact him/her later, and
if you can say, "I heard you speak last October at the Audubon
Society," you'll have one foot in the door.

Last year I was in New York, attending a meeting for the American
Cancer Society. We saw a presentation about a creative antismoking
campaign aimed at teenage girls, a group whose smoking rate has
increased in the last ten years.

The campaign intrigued me. For weeks after I got home, I found
myself talking about it to anyone who would listen. Eventually it
dawned on me. This was an article idea that was pleading to be let into
my thick head!

I circulated my own questionnaire about smoking attitudes among
1,500 teenagers in my own area and to the youngsters of friends
scattered around the country. In addition, I contacted the people
involved in creating the original campaign. *Seventeen* bought the
completed article, one that I never would have written had I not
attended a meeting—and been receptive to an idea I found there.

What If

Remember those rainy days when your five-year-old kept saying,
"What if the lightning hits us? What if it never stops raining? What
if . . . " until you thought you'd scream? Hold off long enough to
think how effectively "what if . . . " can stimulate the imagination,
help catch the elusive idea. Let your mind play with fragments of
thoughts, expanding them to some conclusion by "What if . . . ."
Clive Cussler did it with his *Raise the Titanic*.

Some of my children were members of a local swim team, an
activity that is exciting to watch during the thirty seconds your kid's
event is taking place. The hours in-between, however, stretch out like
commercials on a TV special. I filled those endless hours by
daydreaming.

"What would happen," I thought one day, "if the star of a swim
relay team got hurt and the sub wasn't very good? What if the team
was winning until the sub took over? What if . . . ." I sold this
daydream about a loser who ends up a winner to *Jack and Jill*, as a
short story called, "Taking the Plunge."

It not only works in fiction, it helps with nonfiction too. One day I
was at the airport when I heard a shriek. A young boy had gotten his

sneaker caught in the escalator. The mother was screaming, "Don't cut it off! Don't cut it off!" I thought she meant the child's foot.

I watched the airport police stop the escalator and release the youngster, scared but unhurt.

"What if someone actually got hurt in the airport?" I thought. "What if one of these elderly people fell?" I talked with the airport police, who were delighted to tell about their magnificent Code 1-X rescue program. The story ran as the cover story of the local paper's Sunday supplement.

Let "What if . . . " find you ideas. What if the elevator in your highest office building got stuck between floors? What are the procedures for rescue? What if a child comes home from school and Mother isn't home? Think about it and write an article advising families to have a contingency plan. What if a mother fell and hurt herself? Does a child know how to call for help? What if company comes for dinner and you've no time to shop? "What if . . . " can give you a wealth of ideas.

"What if . . . " can be applied to all the other idea ticklers in this chapter. Let your imagination play with bits of conversation you've overheard, an article in the paper, or an experience you may have had.

Sometimes if the experiences don't come to you, you can make them happen. I love soccer. All my kids played soccer, but there didn't seem to be any leagues forming for women over thirty-five. I stopped wondering,"What if they ask me to play?" and took matters into my own hands. I talked one of the junior-high coaches into letting me join the team for awhile. I told him it was "for a story I'm working on," but the truth is, I wanted to play! The result? I had a terrific time and sold my expeiences "Mother Was a Soccer Player" to *Soccer America*. What's good for Mr. Plimpton is good for Ms. Plimpton too.

You also can make the fantasies work for you without going anywhere. Once, when I had four babies four and under, I felt swamped. The kids had been sick, it had rained for days as it can in sunny Florida, the dog had tracked mud in on the living room rug, and the car and washing machine simultaneously had expired.

"I'm going to run away!" I said to the pile of dirty clothes. "I'm going to disappear." And I took myself, not to the nunnery, but to my typewriter where I pounded out instructions on "How to Run Away from Home." (See, there's the "How to" again!) When I was through, I felt better, the sun was trying to shine, and I had an article ready to sell to *Baby Talk*.

To Have and to Hold (onto) Ideas

Hanging on to ideas is a trick in itself, rather like trying to pick up the dab of mercury that's fallen out of a broken thermometer. And like drops of rain, ideas often evaporate before they touch the ground. They need to be stored someplace safe for use in time of drought.

Even people who can rattle off their driver's license and social security numbers, who know what their third child weighed at seventeen months and the combination of the lock on their junior high locker, are likely to forget the (unforgettable) idea they had an hour ago. Often a lead sentence or a conclusion will pop into your head, when you're least expecting it. That's why you need to write down your idea no matter how fragmentary it might seem at the time. Write it down on your grocery list, checkbook cover, even the wallpaper if need be, but get it down.

Writers have been known to lose car keys, library books, and children (usually only in department stores), but we never lose our pencil and paper. Most of us keep them by the bed to record those wonderful words that creep up from our subconscious just before sleep. We load them into our purse and pocket and stack them by the telephone, in the car, kitchen, and, of course, the bathroom.

One author, who had struggled for months searching for a title for her book, reported success at last.

"The idea came to me in the bathtub," she said. "I should have known to look for it there. I wrote it with soap on the mirror so I wouldn't forget it."

Write notes to yourself anytime you have a sudden germ of an idea. (It's more accepted than talking to yourself, although most writers do that too.) And while it's all right to tell people what you're working on, don't talk out a story idea before you *write it down.*

It's especially important to write down things you hear. Kids have a delightful way of expressing things, and you'll never quite recapture it if you try to keep it in your head. You must write them down. But be sure to write enough down that it makes sense. Remember "gawfnuddle" at the beginning of this chapter? It was a great idea I had just before falling asleep one night, written down to jog my memory in the morning. I'm still trying to figure out what it means!

By writing ideas down, they multiply into others, in a sort of chain reaction. Sometimes it happens right away. Occasionally, the process is much slower.

For example, a friend of mine once casually mentioned that she had met an elderly woman who created beautiful original knitting patterns. My friend had written down the instructions as the woman knitted by "feel." Together they sold these to a yarn company. A non-knitter, I listened politely and forgot about it.

Two years later, I was doing an article for *Glamour* about ways to create your own job. Suddenly, that conversation came back to me. Luckily, my source was a friend, and I could call her for the pertinent details. Had she been a stranger, her story would have been forever lost.

Sometimes ideas have to sit awhile, like dough, giving the yeast a chance to rise. This book was one such idea. I originally came up with the idea in 1972, when my children were aged nine, eight, six, five and one. It was hard, if not impossible, finding time to write. I imagined other women were having the same problem. I queried some publishers but was told, " . . . we fail to see that the problems of women writers are that different from those of men." Perhaps not, I thought, wiping peanut butter and jelly off page 6 of my manuscript and redoing the outline as I sat in the waiting room of the pediatrician. I put my notes into a folder, adding to it over the years as I saw situations, problems, and concerns that predominantly affected women writers, especially those of us who are housewives and mothers. We *do* have unique problems and are learning to solve them creatively. But my ideas in 1972 were not well formed enough to turn them into a book.

What Do You Do With Ideas Once You've Got Them?

Love them! They're the seed from which you're going to harvest fields of first-rate crops.

Everyone develops her own system for the care and feeding of ideas. I store gereral ideas in large manila folders as I mentioned before. The ones I'm actively working on, I transfer to colored folders. I don't know why. Probably for the same reason I type each draft on a different-color paper. I like pretty things. But it also makes your active files stand out.

When I hear a phrase I like, or have an undeveloped idea, I jot down key words and the date on a 3 x 5 card and stick it to my bulletin board. Right now, some of my cards read: "Clown Face" (possible interview with one of the clowns at Ringling's Circus World near Orlando); "What's In a Name?" (idea about collecting strange names and the effect they have on their owners); and "Spice Is Nice" (idea for juvenile market about different spices, where they come from, possible picture angles, etc). These and other ideas I look at when I'm between articles and need to think about what to do next, put 'on hold' on the telephone, or when I'm stuck with what I'm working on. (I never use the expression, "writer's block." Somehow that sounds too immobile, too permanent.)

To expand your idea collection, take an idea and turn it around. See how it looks as a question, a statement, or a demand. "It Pays to Be Honest" didn't interest *Glamour*. It was too preachy. They did like and purchased "Does it Pay to Be Dishonest?" Try it both in positive and negative. "Why Some Women Make Good Mothers" is interesting. "Why Some Women *Don't* Make Good Mothers" is better.

If you think of a market possibility when you come up with an idea, jot it down beside your working title or the sentence that describes your idea. Often, by slanting the idea to a particular market, you can sell it more quickly. Others move around like gypsies before they find a home.

Ideas Are Everywhere

Ideas? Look around you. Listen to what people are talking about, fussing about, or wondering about. Be curious. If it interests you, it may interest someone else.

Ideas are everywhere, but the best idea in the world, badly written up, won't sell. Ideas need to be fleshed out with facts, anecdotes, quotes, etc. But, by keeping the flow of ideas constantly coming, by being receptive to what's around you, you'll find yourself more stimulated, more prepared to write, and more published.

How to Find Out (What You Always Wanted to Know)

9.

Research! The word has a musty ring, conjuring up visions of long library tables piled high with dusty volumes, stacks of index cards, and term papers soon-to-be overdue.

If you write greeting cards, humorous articles, or inspirational columns, chances are you'll need do little, if any, research. For these, it's merely a matter of letting memory come to the surface and flow over you, like bubbles in the bath.

Usually, however, you need to do some research to bolster even these memories, if only to make certain that the forsythia really *was* in bloom the day you said it was; or that the big fire was in 1956 and not in 1958.

The writing of most books and articles requires some degree of research. (You can call it "creative investigation" if that makes it sound less odious.)

Researching for an article or book is much like preparing for a dinner party. It's the preplanning: the arrangements, the gathering in of the foodstuffs and decorations, and the organization. Many parties fall flat because they're poorly planned and have little substance.

Many books and articles fail to sell for that same reason.

It's important not only to know where to find the information you need, but also how to store (or record) it efficiently so you can find it quickly, and to know when to use it.

Why You Need Research

The most basic reason for research is that it adds substance and validity to your work.

When I wrote "Seat Belts Save Lives," I could have just drawn upon my personal beliefs that seat belts in cars are an important safety factor. But, regardless how strongly I may feel on the subject, I doubt that anyone would have bought the article. Any editor worth his or her salt would have said, "Who's she? What does she know about seat belts?" And they would have been right. I'm not a car designer, medical specialist, or highway safety expert. Does that mean I couldn't write on the subject? Not at all. It just meant that I had to talk to these people, seek out statistics from the National Safety Council, and get case histories from the highway patrol to substantiate my opinions. Once I could prove, through research and fact, that seat belts actually *do* save lives, my article began to carry more weight. I now could write an authoritative article.

Research makes your work more believable in fiction too. It keeps you from making errors someone's bound to catch—such as having your heroine travel by commercial airline ten years before it was available. It also makes your reader nod her head and say, "That's right. That's exactly the way it was."

Because research makes your work more believable, it becomes more salable.

How to Begin

Usually you start with an idea, although sometimes I'll be researching for a different article and run across a fascinating bit of information. It piques my interest so I keep reading; and before I can help myself, I've trotted off on another track altogether. Most writers are curious by nature. It's a vocational quirk, like being drawn into a bookstore even though you have plenty to read.

Begin your research with yourself. How much do you already know about your subject? Sometimes it can be a great deal. Other times, you may know next to nothing, other than that the topic interests you.

I became fascinated with the subject of insect allergies after my husband suffered a serious reaction to the sting of a fire ant, an insect that has invaded most of the southern states and plagues farmers, field hands, and livestock as well as ruining expensive farm machinery. Until then, I had never realized how serious an allergy to insect bites and stings could be.

While he was being treated in the emergency room, I began talking with the nurses on duty and found that this type of allergy was not a rare one. I began to track down allergy experts. One doctor gave me the name of a colleague who specialized in treating people with this particular allergy. He, in turn, gave me the name of an entomologist who dealt exclusively with fire ants. And *that* expert gave me names of professionals in Washington and Atlanta to contact. I interviewed other victims of fire-ant stings, read every article I could get my hands on, and studied brochures published by the Department of Agriculture and other available materials.

When I paused for breath, I found I had accumulated a great deal of information on my subject. Reluctantly, I condensed my newly discovered knowledge and wrote (and sold) an article about fire ants to *Florida Accent*. My husband's personal experience with the fire ant probably wouldn't have found a market, but when supported by strong background material gained through solid research, it became salable.

A Writer's Best Friend Is Her Librarian

Most writers feel comfortable in a library; the stacks of books and card catalogues seem to provide some psychic comfort—perhaps a tangible proof that, indeed, some writers *do* make it into print.

I have loved libraries since the day I printed my name on my first library card in the children's room of the Fort Dodge (Iowa) Public Library. And, despite the fact that I wasn't allowed to use the adult section after I had devoured everything in the children's section, I still think librarians are a woman's best friend, especially if that woman is a writer.

It doesn't matter if yours is a small-town library or one in a major city. If you introduce yourself to the librarian as a writer and tell her you need information on a particular subject, chances are she'll be delighted to help you find it. Most librarians are far more familiar with the many source books available than a lay person is. If your library doesn't have a particular volume, they can get it for you through the Inter-Library Loan System, through which libraries borrow books from other libraries.

Start your formal research with the *Reader's Guide to Periodical Literature*. This guide is published twice monthly and lists approximately 175 magazines by article subject. It will give you an idea of what has been published on your subject in the past few years. Reading these articles, you'll get background information and names of experts you can contact for additional information. You can also learn if your topic is overworked and will be able to determine how to slant your article to make it different from what already has been published.

The card catalogue also is a tremendous help for locating books on your subject. Books are listed in three ways: by subject, title, and author.

Look in the library's vertical files too, for clippings, brochures, and pamphlets on your subject. Almanacs, encyclopedias, and biographies also are useful. This category includes such books as:

Subject Guide to Books in Print and *Forthcoming Books* (which will show you what books already have been written on the subject you're researching);

Who's Who (for names, addresses, and backgrounds of famous people);

The Writer's Resource Guide (a collection of almost two thousand sources for you to write or call to locate information. It tells you what *is* available as well as what isn't);

Famous First Facts, Kane: H. W. Wilson Co. (an especially important book if you write fiction. It keeps you from having your character use the radio distress signal in 1850 when it first was used November 22, 1906.)

Once you have gathered all the information you can, talk to the librarian. Tell her what you have discovered, and ask what suggestions she might have to help you uncover more.

Many housewife-writers let the kids help with research as soon as they are old enough. They can check the card file and list books for you, photocopy passages, and go through the *Reader's Guide* as well. It not only speeds up your research time, but also lets the kids feel involved. It aids them in their library skills, too. Not only will they be better able to locate material when they have reports to write, they'll also find the library an exciting place to visit.

If you can't park your little ones with the library story-teller, it's well worth the price of a baby sitter to have the peace and quiet you need at the library. The few times I've taken my little ones to the children's section to "read" while I go over to *my* area to work, I've found they make constant trips back and forth.

No sooner do I open the first reference book than they are by my side asking for a drink, the bathroom, or "Is it time to go now?" (Maybe the Fort Dodge Public Library knew what it was doing!)

In addition to your local public library, check out the many private and special libraries, art galleries, and museums. The men and women who work in these institutions usually are extremely well informed and are delighted to talk about their collections, especially to a writer.

If you have a college or university in your town, ask for permission to use their facilities. Our local state university requires special permits for nonstudent residents who want to check out books, but anyone can use their facilities.

Use Local Newspaper Files

Most newspapers record each edition of their paper on microfiche and microfilm, and maintain up-to-date clipping files (sometimes called morgues). Although these facilities often are not open to the general public, the authorities usually are most cooperative about extending "special permission" when writers have a project that could be aided through the use of this particular research tool.

By reading newspapers from the era about which you're writing, you can verify the cost of gas, milk, and eggs and accurately describe the style of clothing. Newspapers tell you the history of the day, who was in power, what was being read and talked about. You'll gain a sense of immediacy and be able to add depth and details to your work. What's more, the account will be accurate for things like the exact date of an event, such as a hurricane, so you won't write that it happened the following day. Some readers delight in finding errors such as these (they remember the date perfectly because it was on their birthday or the day their mother ran off with the diaper-service man) and will report your mistakes gleefully to your publisher—who will wonder why you weren't more accurate in your work and will continue to wonder when contemplating the publication of your next book.

Talk About What You Need to Know

Once you begin to work on a story, article, or book, talk to others about what you're doing. Don't talk out the story line; keep it fresh for the typewriter. But if you mention what you're working on, someone is bound to know someone else who's an expert in that very thing, or have something in their possession that can help tremendously.

A friend of mine was working on an article about things people found in their attics: old phonographs, grandmother's wedding dress, etc. She mentioned it at a luncheon, just in passing.

"Oh," said one of our mutual friends. "I found a stack of my great-grandmother's letters to her mother. It was all about her experiences moving west."

You could have heard a paper napkin drop. My writer friend looked at her greedily. Not only were those letters invaluable for her article, but she also is using them as a major source for a novel.

I had a similar experience with an article about people who collect things. I found one woman who collected objects with an owl motif. She knew a lady who collected miniature shoes. That lady knew someone else who . . . well, you get the idea. Everyone, it seemed, knew someone who collected something and before long, I had more than enough examples to use in my article. (People are still coming up to me to see if I'll do another article and include them and their collection!)

Anytime you interview one person for your article, always ask if he or she knows of anyone else who could help you. Your interviewee usually will give you one or two more names, or refer you to specific books or magazine articles. One antique dealer gave me a book to use, and each time I've offered to return it she says, "Keep it. You may do another article. I know you have it if I want it."

One doctor did more than recommend names to me. He picked up the phone, dialed a colleague in another city, and handed me the receiver. "Here," he said. "Ask him what he thinks."

Sometimes information comes to you in such waves that you feel you *have* to jump on it just to take advantage of it.

Jack McClintock, a Florida freelancer, went into a bar to interview someone for an article he planned to write. A dart game in process caught his attention. He became so fascinated with it that he forgot about the original article he was researching and began to seek out people who were experts at dart playing. One person referred him to a handful of others. He dug out background material and the history of darts. He wrote two articles on the subject and had so much information left over that he wrote a book, *Book of Darts*.

Check the Telephone Directory

Your local phone book and those of other cities (which you can find at the library or in the lobbies of some larger hotels) can be of great help when you're researching. Most businesses are affiliated with national organizations or associations that have staffs available to disseminate information to people like us. If you're not sure how to get in touch with them or whether or not a particular industry has such an organization, call one of the local businessmen and ask him how to contact his national association. Many times he'll even be able to tell you whom to ask for.

The American Red Cross, National Association of Home Builders, and National Secretaries Association are just three examples of such organizations. Most of these groups have local and/or regional, district, and state divisions as well, so check your phone book. A local article would probably use information and statistics from the local branch, but if you're doing an article for a national magazine, you'll need to zero in on the national office to get the larger view.

In writing an article about secretaries, I not only requested and received cooperation from the national office of NSA, but they also were helpful in giving me names, addresses, and phone numbers of the presidents of local chapters to contact in order to ensure a geographic distribution.

By checking your local yellow-page classifications, you'll find a valuable collection of local experts. We all tend to take the telephone directory for granted because it's always around. But, when used as a research tool, it can provide a vast amount of information.

Check With Colleges and Universities

If your area has any type of institution for higher learning, you have professional experts right at hand. Psychologists, historians, and scientists are just a few of the authorities you can talk to when doing research for a book or article. Not only can they give you the names of other experts in the field, but they often have a wealth of material from their professional sources that you might not otherwise be privy to. I've had medical people loan me slides to illustrate my articles that were far better than I could have come up with on my own.

Educators delight in sharing their knowledge and experience with others. I've found that the problem is not in getting these professionals to talk to you, it's getting them to stop when you've absorbed all you need for your article! Their specialty is their life (that's why they chose it) and usually they're most helpful.

If there's no college or university in your area, don't despair. Ask your librarians to help you track down experts at schools elsewhere, and write to them or call.

Ask the Experts

People don't have to be educators to love to talk about their favorite subject. I've found that most experts in their field—regardless of whether it's loggerhead turtles, leisure time, or historic preservation—are extremely willing to share their enthusiasms.

Naturally, you give them the courtesy of arranging for an appointment and requesting the amount of time you'll need. If you have a definite commitment from a publication, it helps. But otherwise, just say you're collecting data for an article you plan to write, sound sincere, and you'll get some time. (More about interviewing in Chapter 10).

In the few cases when I've been turned down by my first choice of an expert, he/she has always given me the name of someone else who may have a freer schedule. Experts are merely people, just like you and me. They love what they do or know and like to talk about it.

Remember, however, that being human, experts can (and often do) disagree. Listen to more than one opinion so you can offer a balanced report. You can draw your own conclusions, of course, although you should identify them as such.

Most medical writing needs to be balanced in this way, as I have seldom seen two doctors who agree on everything. If you mention a treatment, for example, you can say that this is often the standard treatment. If you say that it's the only proper treatment, you're leaving yourself wide open for comments from a confused and upset reader who didn't get that particular treatment from her doctor, and from the hostile and irate doctor who doesn't use that as standard treatment and doesn't appreciate your playing doctor.

If you're writing about medical subjects, quote your medical expert, not yourself (i.e., Dr. Slicer says, "It's better to begin with clean instruments because . . .").

Another good source for expert information is a public relations firm. PR people are paid to get their clients' names in print, so it stands to reason that they'll be cooperative, well-informed, and considerate of beginners. After all, everyone has to start somewhere, and maybe you'll go on to write about their client in national magazines.

Don't expect them to do your work, however. Know what type of information you want. Be specific. Don't just ask for "pictures," for example, but rather, "black-and-white glossies showing your product being used."

Always remember that the PR firm is being paid to make its client look good. Don't take everything you're told as "fact." Do a little research on your own, in addition to what you've been spoon-fed by the public relations people. If nothing else, it will confirm what they told you. And if it doesn't, you'll be able to write a more balanced and more professional piece.

Let Government Agencies Help You

As a taxpayer, you've been helping to support the government for a long time. Now, as a writer, you can get something back.

There are virtually thousands of governmental agencies on local, state, and federal levels that can aid your research greatly. It sometimes takes patience to find the proper person or authority, but once you're there, it's worth the struggle.

These agencies usually have publications, statistics, and case histories that will give your work the validity it needs. The people there want to help. Besides, they're on *your* payroll, so you might as well keep them busy. They often can refer you to other sources too.

Write to or call the particular department that you think may be of help. You might begin with the local or regional federal office or start at the top, in Washington.

To get on the government mailing list so you can see what publications are available, write to: The Superintendent of Documents, Government Printing Office, Washington, D.C. 20402. Many of the publications are yours free for the asking, although some may require a small fee. If there is a particular topic you're interested in, tell them that too. You'll be inundated with material!

Contact State Departments of Tourism, Chambers of Commerce, AAA, and Travel Agencies

If your writing interests are travel-oriented, or if you're writing fiction that requires strong geographic support, let the specialists at state departments of tourism, chambers of commerce, AAA, commerical travel agencies, or foreign travel bureaus help you. These people all are professionals. They're trained to know their area and can give you interesting backgrounds, history, or tell you about points of interest.

If you need to know where the "wrong side of the tracks" are in a particular city, or where the hero would have taken THE GIRL for dinner to impress her, ask one of these experts. They'll take on the challenge with great gusto, expend great effort to give you whatever information you need for your factual article or fictional piece, and if they don't know the answer, they'll track it down. Travel people have to love adventure to be in their line of work. What better adventure than helping a writer?

Not only will these sources furnish you with an abundance of written material about their area, they'll often have photographs. If you're lucky, they'll suggest other ideas you might use when writing about their area.

Eavesdrop

This can be a "fun" way of doing research. If you're writing about inflation and want some feedback on what people really think about the price of groceries, go to a few stores and listen. Do the same if you're writing about young people's attitudes on drinking, drugs, or dating. You can question them too, but by eavesdropping you'll hear what people are saying, not what they particularly want you to hear.

Often the most revealing comments in an article come from listening to conversations that really weren't meant for your ears: tuning in on a bus, department store or tennis court such as this conversation overheard between two young women in the lobby of a theater during intermission.

"Well? What do you think?" asked the first girl.

The other girl hesitated. "I think," she said, "that it's the kind of play I like to say I've seen . . . more than actually seeing it."

Isn't that a perfect lead to a commentary on today's theater scene! Would it have come out the same if I had asked, "What do you think?" I don't think so.

So go ahead and eavesdrop. I know you mother said it wasn't polite, and it embarrasses your husband, but it's fun and helpful to your writing too.

Interview

(See Chapter 10)

Filing Your Facts

At this point you are inundated by stacks of index cards; file boxes; scraps of paper with important ideas scribbled on both sides; and notebooks filled with quotes, dates, and data. But it won't do you a bit of good if you can't find a piece of information when you need it. Knowing how to control your data is every bit as important as knowing how to find it.

Eventually you'll devise your own "system" for handling and filing information. What works well for one writer is confusing and burdensome for another. I'll tell you what works for me and you can try it—or develop something better and let me know.

I use a notebook and record each source, assigning a number to each. For example, Daphne Du Maurier's book, *Myself When Young,* is source number one for this book. I use index cards for all the information I want to remember, one idea per card. In this case, it was a quote I liked. I headed the index card "#1-65" and wrote the quote out on the card. The "#1" refers to the book (it could be an article, interview, or brochure as well) that the material comes from. The "65" refers to the page on which the quote appeared.

My interview with writer Jack McClintock originally was done a few years ago for an article I wrote on freelance writers. This card is numbered "#42-5." Translated, "#42" is my interview with Jack, and the "5" is the particular information I used.

Working with cards this way you are free to shuffle the order, reorganize and redo the index cards without disturbing the source listing so you forget who originally said what. Another advantage is that it prevents your using the same anecdote more than once. It also aids in compiling the index for a book and gives you great flexibility when revising.

I previously used notebook pages for all my notes, cutting off pieces of quotes and facts when I needed them and pasting them in whatever order they fit best. But I kept losing the little bits of paper, and I couldn't remember where the material had originated. Thus my present system was born. It works for me. It may not work for you, or you may use it and improve on it.

Record Sources

Always record your source along with the information used from it. Editors (or their research assistants) have a strange way of asking, "Where did you get this information?"

My mind always goes blank at that point and I become extremely defensive. I have no idea where I found it, so I usually blurt out, "I *know* I found it somewhere!" (Perhaps it was under the couch with last year's Christmas bell I just discovered.)

You'll sound more professional and less hysterical if you can pull out that quote or statistic from your notes (providing you can find your notes) and locate the source neatly listed beside it. I date my notes from interviews for the same reason. It makes life much less stressful for you and for your editor . . . and for the harried research assistant who spends all day on the phone tracking down information like this.

Photocopy

Sometimes I'll find an article with a great deal of information in it.

Rather than taking copious notes, I'll photocopy these pages. It saves time . . . and also gives the quotes within their context. Make certain you write down the name of the magazine, issue, and page number. Many magazines don't print their name or the date of each issue on their pages, and months later it's often impossible to remember when or where a particularly useful article was published.

Be Receptive to Titles as You Research

Often, in your reading, you'll come across a phrase that could be used or paraphrased into a good title for your work. It seldom is a conscious thing, at least not on my part. But to capture the idea if and when it comes, I keep a blue index card available so I can jot down title possibilities as they "hit" me. Sometimes they're useless, but often a quote or a phrase winds up as a title.

Be Accurate

Take pride in your accuracy. Even a minor error can make your veracity suspect. If your statistics are based on a five-year-old report, someone is bound to expose you. There's almost always someone who can give you the up-to-date answers you need. You just need to keep searching to find that person.

Each time an editor has asked me to include some special information and I wail, "I'll never be able to discover that!" I'm always embarrassed because I DO find it and it never was as hard as I thought it would be. You have to let your mind wander a bit; you have to ask around, dig a little, play detective. But in the long run, it does make the story better than before, because now it's supported by fact.

Research Reminders

1. Use quotation marks when lifting material intact. If you quote material from another source, you must put it into quotation marks and credit that source. If it's a great deal of material, you need to write for permission from the publisher. Tell them what you want to use the material for, exactly what you want to quote, and how it will be used. Usually, they'll grant you permission. Sometimes they may require a small fee.

   If you're only quoting a sentence, it's all right to use it, providing you credit the source and use quotation marks. If you omit material, use ellipsis points to show you haven't used the entire quote.

   Always put quotation marks around a quote when you're taking notes to remind yourself that you are quoting someone else's work.

2. Don't copy someone else's errors. Be careful when you copy down "facts." You may be passing along incorrect information. I often

have discovered errors in dates, inaccurate statistics and false quotes. Try to get as much verified as you can. Usually, but not always, dates in reputable encyclopedias and almanacs are correct. If you can't take the quote back to the original source, then at least attribute it to the author and admit you are presenting it second (or third) hand.

3. Authenticate your quotes. When you find an expert named in one of your research sources, try to get your own fresh and original quotes. Usually an article will say something like, "Dr. Ocelot from Zoology Department of Cage University says. . . ." All you have to do is write (or call) Dr. Ocelot, mention the article you read concerning his theory of mating leopards with ostriches. He may reveal to your ears alone that now he's onto shortening giraffe necks and you've got a totally different slant to your article. More important, you've got fresh material from an expert, rather than copying some tired facts from another author.

It surprises me how often an expert will complain that she was misquoted in a previous article and will then go on to give the correct version to me. This allows you to set the record straight and prove to your editor that you are a careful writer who has respect for facts, even in your fiction.

4. Give yourself a deadline. It helps to have a deadline for the completion of your book or article (even if you have to impose it on yourself). You should create a cut-off time for doing research too.

Having a deadline makes it easier to work with others who are sending you information. It creates a sense of urgency. (Be sure to set the deadline a little earlier than it actually needs to be, so many people only remember to fill your request the day you said you need it.) By saying, "I need this information by May 1," it sounds as though you are efficient and professional. Isn't that the type of image you're trying to maintain?

Sometimes you need to impress yourself as well, and having some type of deadline will prevent your continuing to research forever and never writing at all. It forces you to be selective, reading only the best of what you have uncovered and only contacting those people who are most likely to be of value to you and your work.

5. Don't make your notes too perfect. Because we writers are experts in the fine art of procrastination, it's a temptation to perfect complex forms of note-taking, transferring dates on charts and graphs, recopying information on different color index cards and using a variety of file folders. Like carefully showing everyone how to squeeze toothpaste from the bottom of the tube, not the middle, this process is a lesson in futility. It keeps us from our main business, which is writing, not becoming professional note-takers.

You *do* need a system that works for you, of course, and sometimes it takes a while to figure out your own system. But stay alert for time-wasting activities.

6. Don't over-research. I think I dislike research, yet it grows on me. I get immersed in checking on "one more" source, calling "one more" expert. When do you have enough? When do you call it quits? Obviously, when you have enough to write your book or article. When is that? Sorry. There's no definite point. You have to sense it and be alert for it. When you finally sit down to write your article or book and find that you'd rather continue researching because it's the easier of the two, you probably have enough material to begin. We all know so-called writers who have been "researching my book" for ten years. Chances are that's all they'll ever do. Fear of failure has kept many a would-be writer from even beginning.

Research can be a frustration and a chore—or it can be a fascination and a delight. The secret is in using it as one of many steps in writing and not letting it become a resting place.

How to Interview (Without Sounding Like a Housewife)

10.

Most of us get nervous when it comes to interviewing. We're afraid we won't know how to get an interview and even worse, won't know what to do if we *do* get it. We're afraid our years of keeping company with Captains Kangaroo and Crunch will show.

"It's easier not to do it," sighed one housewife who writes fillers that are nostalgic and humorous and come from *her* experience alone, no interviews needed, thank you.

Why Interview

But there are three very sound reasons why you need to learn how to conduct an interview, regardless of whether you write fiction or nonfiction.

    1. *It makes you more expert.*

        Arthur Hailey, author of *Hotel*, *Airport*, *Overload*, and many other novels, interviews numerous experts to make his fiction realistic. He researches his topic too, but the interviews bring his books to life.

        I wrote a booklet for the Florida Division of the American Cancer Society called "Living In a Strange World" for parents who had just learned that their child had cancer. Before writing it, I interviewed parents who were trying to cope with daily life and a terminally ill child. They gave me background and insights that no reference material ever could have.

Regardless how well you may write, national magazines want to know that you've contacted "experts" on whatever subject you're covering. It could be a local veterinarian or your child's physical education teacher, but a quote from someone other than yourself adds credibility to your book or article. It lets the editor know that you haven't written it off the top of your head—and that you've done more than copied from reference material in the library.

2. *It gives you quotes.*

Sometimes your interviewee says something better than you ever could have. Their natural phrasing gives life to your writing.

I interviewed a man who had been arrested for fishing illegally in waters of a foreign nation. He was not a commercial fisherman, but was thrown into jail for four days with all those who were.

His quote: "I felt as though I had been thrown into a Grade B movie and the director quit," was much more effective than if I had written, "He said he felt lost."

3. *Your interviewee is the subject of your article.*

Often we interview someone for an article that stands on its own, such as an inspirational article on how a person has overcome a problem; a "how to," when someone describes how she/he turned a hobby into a money-making business; a personality story, as with an entertainment star or sports figure.

Many articles for local newspapers and regional magazines are no more than interviews with interesting local people.

There's really no getting around it. Unless you write strictly greeting cards, self-originating nostalgia, or humor, someday you'll have to interview someone.

How to Arrange for an Interview

First of all, you'll have to decide *who* you want to interview. To add weight to an article on communication, for example, think about whom you might contact. It could be a communication expert from a local or state university; someone in the business world who teaches communication to executives; a psychologist; or an author who has written books on the subject.

Begin by calling a public relations firm, university, or a public company. Give your name, say that you're a writer who's doing an article on commnication. Tell them you'd like to talk with someone who is an expert in that field. Explain the slant of your story. (Are you trying to show families how to communicate more effectively or are you dealing with more efficient communication between manager and worker?) If you already have the "okay" from an editor, say so. Never try to fake it by saying that you have an assignment when you don't. The person you're talking to may be the editor's brother-in-law, and if he finds out you've lied, you'll ruin your credibility as a writer.

If you have no assignment and the person asks who you're writing it for, say "I plan to submit it to X and Y magazines." You don't need to add that it's on speculation or that this is the first article you've tried to write.

If your experts are local, call them, say what you're writing, and ask for a personal interview. Business people usually have secretaries who screen their calls, so explain what you need. She may put you through to her executive, or she may ask that you put your request in writing. I prefer making the phone contact first. Executives get so many letters that yours easily can be overlooked.

Occasionally, your expert will say she is busy and ask you to conduct the interview over the phone. If you aren't prepared at that point, say so. Don't waste both your time by asking unimportant questions. Tell the expert that you'll call back at a time convenient to you both.

If you have a friend who knows someone who's an authority, ask her to alert the expert to your call. That way your call won't be out of the blue and you'll be more likely to get through.

Often, however, our experts are too far away or we're afraid we can't get through by phone. Then write a letter, saying you'd like to call and interview them by phone, or asking for an appointment for a personal interview.

You also can send your questions, along with a stamped, self-addressed envelope, and hope your expert will answer them. I've interviewed by questionnaire many times. Its expensive, sometimes more than phoning because you have printing and postage costs. Usually you have to send out many more questionnaires than you get back. It's very useful, however, when you need many opinions or a geographic distribution.

Regardless of how you arrange for an interview, there are a few points you need to remember:

1. Give your name. Spell it if it's a difficult one.
2. Say that you're a a writer and give your credits, if any.
3. If you have a definite assignment for a publication, say so.
4. Give some idea what type of information you want. "I'd like to interview you" is much less likely to get you an interview than "I'm

doing an article on women who created their own business and would like to talk with you to learn how you began yours.'' People are somewhat leery about talking to writers. They'll feel more comfortable if you give them some idea what information you're looking for. If your subject is controversial, couch your remarks by saying, "I'd like to hear your views of the problems involved with abortion," than "Why are you against abortion?''; or "Why do you think the drinking age should be changed?" rather than "Why are you against eighteen-year-olds drinking?''

5. Give some idea how much time you need. If thirty minutes could do it, say so. Chances are you'll end up with an hour anyway. But if you think you'll need more time, ask for it.

6. If someone has recommended this particular expert to you, say so. It may be the key that unlocks the door for your interview.

7. If you make your original contact by phone, do it at a time when things are quiet at home and you sound professional. A writer who calls for an interview with kids fighting in the background, dogs barking, and a baby crying may not be taken too seriously.

Remember that most people enjoy being interviewed. They're glad someone is interested in their opinions. Out of over one hundred questionnaires I recently received back from secretaries for an article for *Glamour*, only two asked not to be quoted. And remember, they still returned the questionnaire!

When a friend and I began interviewing women for a book we wrote (yet unpublished) on middle-aged women, we found most of them extremely vocal. Some actually came up to us at parties and began relating experiences without waiting for our questions!

Research Your Subject Before the Interview

Once you've make the appointment for an interview, it's time to get to work. Do as much research as you can. If you're interviewing someone for an article on sailing, become familiar with nautical terms and types of sailboats. You'll only have a limited amount of time for your interview, so don't waste time by asking, "What do you mean by 'starboard?' '' He'll think you're a total landlubber and won't tell you about safety factors one should look for in a boat, a harrowing experience at sea, etc. Reading up on your subject also prevents the embarrassment of saying, "How did you become vice-president so quickly?" to the man who married the boss's daughter; or asking an actress what it's like to be married to her famous husband when they've just gotten divorced.

When you're interviewing someone about his experiences, read as much as you can about the person ahead of time. Don't ask where your subject was born, went to high school, etc. You already should know.

When singer/actress Dorothy Collins and comedienne Dody Goodman came to my area in dinner theaters, I arranged to interview them both. Before I met them, I read everything I could find about how they received their training and theatrical experience, what TV and/or Broadway shows they had done, and what work they were best known for. At the actual interview I was able to concentrate on questions like "Can a woman successfully combine a theatrical career with any semblance of 'normal' life? Is there any prejudice against women performers? What was it like working with _____?"

If you're interviewing someone who has written a book, try to read it first. If there's no time for that, at least read a few chapters and look over the table of contents.

No one, especially a well-known personality, likes to be asked trite questions that could have been found in any "Who's Who" or bio-sketch. To do so marks you as a rank amateur who doesn't do her homework.

Have Some Specific Questions

If you go into an interview without preparation and say, "Tell me all about your nuclear plant," you'll probably be ushered out or handed a printed booklet very quickly. You need to have some idea of the information you want in order to ask the proper questions.

Know the slant of your article. Are you trying to write about how people adjust to a nuclear plant in their neighborhood? The safety factors built into the plant? The type of people who go into this line of work?

In your interview you probably would get answers to these and many more questions, but if you have no idea what information you want, you may end up afterward at the typewriter with nothing to say.

Plan a few major questions to be answered regardless of what direction the interview takes. I usually have about ten such questions. Sometimes I never get around to using them all because the interview has taken a different track, one that I like better than my original plan. That's why you must listen to what's being said. If it isn't what you want to know, be prepared to gently lead your expert back to where you want to go. If you like the new direction, however, be flexible enough to adjust your questions accordingly.

Word your questions so you ask for your expert's opinion, feeling, and experience. That's why you make the interview with him and not the expert next door. Ask "Why did you . . . ?" "How did you . . . ?" All of us are flattered by attention. If your expert keeps talking about "The company thought . . ." ask what his contribution was.

Arrange Your Schedule So You Don't Have to Dash Off to a Carpool

Sometimes things click between a writer and the person she's interviewing and you're talking like old friends. Nothing shouts "Housewife Hobbyist" as much as your suddenly looking at your watch, saying "Oh, my goodness, it's time for the carpool," and dashing out. Not only will your interviewee kick herself for giving you the time of day (not to mention an hour), but you'll ruin it for the rest of us who are housewives and professional writers.

Always allow at least an hour extra in your schedule when you have an interview. Your subject might offer to show you the vaults or a secret diary. If you have flexibility in your schedule, you can take advantage of the unexpected.

If the only time available for the interview makes timing tight for you, call upon a friend or relative to do the carpool or arranage for your child to visit a friend until you get through with your work. Plan ahead—so you don't get flustered at the last minute in front of your expert. You might want to interview her again sometime.

You'll find that you'll be more relaxed during an interview if you don't have a tight schedule. If you're relaxed, your subject will be too. Keep an eye on the time so you don't wear out your welcome, but be ready to stay if she encourages you to and if you're getting usable information.

How to Look Professional

It doesn't matter what you wear when you work (my usual outfit is jeans, my faded college sweatshirt, and sneakers), but when you're out meeting the public, what you wear does make a difference.

There's no shame in combining being a housewife with being a professional writer. There really are very few full-time free-lance writers, so most of us are something else! But it's important to look like a professional writer, not housewife, when you interview someone.

Unless you're interviewing someone in a coal mine or on a ski lift, don't wear jeans or casual sportswear. I personally wear my "business suit" for most interviews. It consists of a skirt, jacket, and tailored blouse. Business executives identify with it; so do doctors, lawyers, educators, and almost everyone else I've interviewed. It's what professional businesswomen wear, and that's what we housewife-writers are!

There are exceptions, of course. When I interviewed my "fire ant expert" and traipsed across fields littered with fire ant mounds, I wore a pantsuit and walking shoes. When I interview young people I usually wear pantsuits, too.

Make certain that you're comfortable in your clothes. A skirt that's too short and needs constant tugging to keep it over the knees is very distracting to someone who's trying to answer your questions. The same is true of a blouse that's too tight across the bust or too transparent, as well as dangling necklaces and bracelets or long hair you have to keep brushing out of your eyes.

Forget the heavy eye shadow, the strong perfume, and the revealing neckline. You're there to get an interview, not a date. Never wear curlers unless you conduct your interviews in bed.

Never chew gum when you're interviewing (I can't work at the typewriter without it), and you're better off not smoking. Your interviewee may not like smoke, may not like women who smoke, and may be more interested in observing how you can hold a pencil, notepad, and cigarette all at the same time without dropping one of them than with what he is saying.

Empty Your Handbag

This really is part of looking more professional; but I think it is so important that I've put it in a section by itself. It's another aspect of splitting your personality, dividing the "housewife you" from the "professional writer you."

Your handbag needs to fit in with the professional image you're trying to create. If it's a tote bag crammed with food coupons, a fancy light bulb that needs to be matched, and an extra T-shirt for your son whom you are picking up as soon as school is out, you're going to have a hard time convincing Mr. Busy Executive that it was worth giving you an hour for an interview. Either the tote bag will topple over, revealing your "other life" to God and everyone, or you'll have to dig around zipping and unzipping compartments as you look for a pencil, muttering all the while, "I *know* it's in here somewhere!"

Before you go off for your interview, find the smallest, most tailored handbag in your closet. That means leaving your football-shaped bag with the autographs of the entire Tampa Bay Buccaneers defensive team at home next to the purse with the names of all of your children embroidered on little red felt apples. Many women just use their briefcase, slipping their billfold and comb in at the bottom.

Whichever you carry, make certain you include:

1. A handkerchief or tissue. (That's my grandmother's influence. She was certain no lady went anywhere without one.)
2. Two sharpened pencils and/or a pen *with ink*. (Don't laugh. I once tried to cover a story and found that my felt-tip had dried out. Rather than admit I had no replacement and borrow one, I tried to memorize everything that was said. The resulting story was short and rather flat.
3. A notepad or folded paper that's large enough to write on, but small enough not to distract your subject. A steno notebook works best for me, but everyone has to go through trial and error to see what works best for her.
4. Your business card (so your expert can send you any important pictures, information, or just call to add one or two more anecdotes). It also helps add to your "professional image."
5. Only what other "purse" supplies that are vital, such as your driver's license, comb, keys, money, or nitroglycerin tablets if you take them.

Arrive On Time

Once you have set a time for the interview, be prepared to get there on time. It shows professionalism and that you're aware of the other person's time. That means you must take into account the traffic, finding a parking place, that last-minute dash to the ladies' room, etc. Certainly, if the entire Swiss train system can run on time, one freelance writer can too! (Note: If the phone rings as you're leaving the house, don't answer it. One minute later and you wouldn't have heard it anyway.)

Being on time (or even a little early), gives you a chance to catch your breath and pull yourself together before walking into an office. It keeps you from dropping in with pencils flying and sweat streaming down your face, as you pant your name to the receptionist.

If you get there too early, go to the ladies' room and check for gray eyebrows or poppy seeds in your teeth. Or go into the office, smile, and say "I know I'm a little early." Then sit down quietly and go over your notes. But don't get there *too* early. They'll think it's the only thing you have to do that day, and that's not the illusion you're trying to create.

If you are late, through some unforeseen happening, call and say, "I'll be _____ minutes late." Cancel entirely *only* if you don't know when you can get away because there's been somethings quite traumatic, like an accident or sudden illness. These things do come up, you know, and most people usually are quite understanding. If you arrive only a few minutes late, apologize *once* and get on with the interview.

Smile

When you walk into your subject's office, smile, shake hands, and say your name clearly. Often, when we're nervous, we become very intense. This, in turn, makes your subject nervous. By looking as though you're enjoying your meeting, you'll relax and so will your interviewee.

Obviously you don't ask bereaved parents how it feels to lose a child with a smile plastered all over your face, but a sympathetic smile will go further toward getting insights and confidences than spitting questions out as though you were a prosecuting attorney.

Exude Confidence

"How?" you wail. "I don't have any!" You don't need to. If you *look* as though you are confident and *act* as though you are confident, people will think you are, and to your surprise, somewhere along the way (when you stop thinking about how scared you are), you'll find that you, indeed, *feel* confident.

Everyone discovers her own system. I take a couple of deep breaths, enter a room, and shake hands. Touching the other person helps me to remember that this is a human being just like me, even if it happens to be someone whose face is instantly recognized by millions.

Often you'll be offered a cup of coffee. If there's a table handy nearby so you don't have to hold it all the time, go ahead, It's a good way to relax (providing your hand isn't shaking so that you spill the coffee all over your business suit) and gives you a chance to informally warm up to your subject. But if there's no place to put it, you're going to have to juggle the mug (or worse, the cup and saucer) as you take notes. Also, coffee may stimulate your kidneys. It can be hard to pick up on an interview after you've had to take a timeout for a bathroom visit.

Remember that most people are delighted to talk about themselves or a subject close to their heart. Let your conversation be your only stimulant. Refuse an alcoholic beverage. Say with a smile, "I never drink on duty," or if pressed, take it, take one sip and put it down. You need your wits about you. Forget what you've heard about hard-drinking writers. They're a stereotype like the "dingbat housewife." You don't need to pretend to be either.

Be a Lady—but Make Them Treat You Like a Pro

You may find a male chauvinist who will grant you an interview, then spoonfeed you what *he* wants you to know. Don't be afraid to ask hard questions, the difficult ones.

Without losing your temper or your ladylike poise, you can say, "Let me be the devil's advocate . . ." or "Some people say that you're . . ." If pressed for your sources, you can smile gently and say, "You know writers don't reveal their sources, Mr. Price-Fixer."

When I interviewed Peter Falk, he asked if I'd be satisfied with an autographed picture of him! I said, "No, I want to interview you." He seemed amused but agreed—until I began.

"Wait a minute," he said. "I thought you just wanted to be able to say you had met me and then would write up what everyone else does."

I smiled back at him (still thinking he's one of the sexiest men I've ever met) and said I didn't work that way. I wouldn't write up an interview unless I actually *had* interviewed the person. He waved me to a chair and talked for forty-fives minutes—until I finally said he had spent enough of his time with me, thanked him, and left. He was most gracious, once I had stood firmly by my guns.

Once my determination to get a story almost backfired. I was interviewing a security guard for a large building. He kept skirting the issue of what procedures actually went into effect if someone were found trespassing. I kept trying to bring him back to my question. Finally, he paused and looked at me. In a flash, he had his gun out and leveled at me.

"I tell them to stop or I'll shoot," he said.

Ignoring the fact that my heart had stopped, I managed to swallow, smile, and say, "Yes, and then what happens?"

To Tape or Not to Tape

This is another personal decision. The advantage of taping an interview is that you don't have to take notes, although some writers do take a few from time to time. It *does* free you to listen and interact directly with the person you're interviewing. You also get a sense of the rhythm of individual speech. Many people feel that they'll be quoted more accurately if the interview is on tape, and you have proof of what actually was said if your subject says he's been misquoted.

Others, however, close up like a nervous turtle as soon as you push the "record" button. I've had subjects who chattered constantly—welcomed me with open arms, plied me with coffee and jelly doughnuts, bubbled over with anecdotes and statistics—until the tape began to move. Then they sat, like a freshman before a senior discipline committee, and either mumbled, answered so softly I could't hear or said nothing. A few felt the situation called for a speech and began pontificating, and talked around my questions.

I don't like recording interviews. Invariably, I've found that my brand-new batteries have a tendency to die right about the time my subject says, "Then I hid the money in. . . ." While I'm leaning back, passively listening to the conversation, my tape recorder is sleeping.

The last time I used a tape for an interview, it took three reels. Three times I had to interrupt to change reels. I carefully put them "someplace safe" so I wouldn't lose them—and so the kids wouldn't tape "The Grease Spots Sing the Blues" over them. To date I haven't found the tapes, although I know they're secure wherever they are! Fortunately, I also took a few notes, but the natural mood and rhythm of the speaker is forever lost, at least until I find the missing tapes!

How to Take Notes

I prefer taking notes because I can add information about the speaker's clothes, mannerisms, gestures, and voice, and she'll never know. Like most writers, I've developed my personal brand of shorthand. Part of it comes from a speedwriting course I sent in for a long time ago and never finished, and part of it has evolved through experience.

Here are a few tips you might consider when taking notes during an interview:

1. Abbreviate words, use symbols for commonly used ones, and omit the unimportant ones. As long as you can understand what you've written, don't worry about your technique.
2. Write down the important facts only. Look at your subject and react to what she's saying.
3. Repeat figures to make certain you're accurate. "Thirteen thousand units a day? That's amazing. . . ." With luck, your subject might add, "That's nothing. Next month we add our new X-963 machine. . .," and you'll have information you otherwise might never have heard.
4. Date the notes. Later, if you need to check anything, you can say, "On November 13 when we met. . . ."
5. Listen for good quotes and jot them down accurately.
6. If your subject seems reluctant to talk, put your pencil down and ask

conversationally, "What made you decide you wanted to leave your former company and go out on your own?" or "How did you become interested in sports?" Barbara Walters's book, *How to Talk With Practically Anybody About Practically Anything*, gives numerous suggestions on how to open even the most reluctant clam.

7. Make notes on mannerisms, speech patterns, physical appearance, and clothes. It adds color to your story and makes your interviewee more three-dimensional.

8. As soon as you leave, quickly sit down and fill in any other information you want to remember. You'll find you almost have total recall.

Learn to Listen

That seems obvious, but often writers get so carried away by taking down what's being said and thinking about *their* next question, that they forget to listen.

How a person talks sometimes is as important as what he says. For example, if an ad man says, "The client said he wanted . . ." and he's busy doodling, you'll learn that: (1) the ad man disagreed with the client, and/or (2) isn't too enthusiastic about the campaign.

Be alert for your interviewee couching his comments with "They felt," "The company decided," rather than being direct by saying "I decided," "I changed our direction by . . . ."

Make sure you're getting answers to you questions rather than getting a "snow job" from the public relations department, prepared pap that *they* want you to hear.

Let your expert talk, interrupting only when you have to—to get back on the right track or to clarify a statement.

A pause can be most effectives. Don't feel you have to fill the void. Smile and look at your speaker, and chances are he'll begin to talk once again. Often I get the best quotes from an interview by listening to these "void fillers."

Listen for Character

People have a unique way of expressing themselves. You can learn a lot by the words they select and the way they put them together.

Some company managers talk as though they're quoting from a company brochure when they describe their employees and business procedures. You get a far different impression when a manager says, "Oh, we've grown up together, sort of like a large family. Old Wendell Wesslinkee, why he's been here twenty-five years. Started in the mailroom and now he's head of the broken bottle division. His kid,

Wendell Jr., is working in the mailroom now."

I've interviewed businesswomen who used off-color language to show me they're tough and businesslike. There have been executives who sprinkled *me, I,* and *mine* throughout their conversation to emphasize how singlehandedly they have achieved their success. And there have been actors who used *beautiful, darling,* and *dear* so frequently that these words were stripped of meaning.

Good quotes add interest and authenticity to an article. Listen for those that:

1. Sparkle by describing something in a unique way ("Her skin was as smooth as an onion.")
2. Tell something about the speaker ("I've never been a lazy man. Work is what we were put here on earth to do.")
3. Give facts or statistics in an interesting way ("We make enough shirts here in one week to clothe every man in the state of Rhode Island.")

Like anecdotes, good quotes just happen, like a beautiful setting sun. If you ask someone to give you a good quote, she'll just look at you in panic. But listen, and you'll find them. Sometimes the best quotes come when you've put your pen away and are walking to the door.

"I'm glad you're doing this story," said the head of a blood bank. "We always are in need of donations. It's the medicine no pharmacy can make!"

I used his last sentence as my title for an article on donating blood for the *Rotarian.*

Don't Talk About Yourself or Your Children

We all love to talk about ourselves, and there's nothing wrong with answering a few friendly questions about why you want the interview and how you became a writer. Just remember that you are the interviewer, not the interviewee.

Once I left an interview thinking how friendly my subject had been. It wasn't until I started to drive home that I realized that he knew a great deal more about me than I did about him.

Reluctant interviewees often try to reverse the order of things. Be on guard. If necessary, say, "Enough about me. Let me ask what *you* think about . . . ."

Never, never, never talk about your children. It takes you out of the "professional" category and marks you a "housewife hobbyist." Men can get by with it. Women can't. It's unfair, but so is much of life. If Mr.

Executive pulls out snapshots of his brood beginning with when they were six months old, admire them, "ooh" and "ahh" if you wish—and then get back to business. If he asks if you have children, you can answer "yes" or even add, "We have sixteen between the ages of two weeks and five years," but stop there or you'll never discover how he made billions by adding a string to the tea bag.

Watch Your Subject as You Listen

This is one reason tape enthusiasts prefer their machines. It frees them to watch their speaker. But if you take notes properly—enough to help you remember and not too much to prevent eye contact, you can jot down many things you see as well as hear.

Does your speaker refer to notes when quoting figures? Does he stare off into space? Sign letters as he talks? Forget?

I once interviewed a woman accountant who "touched up" her nails as she talked. Later I discovered she had "touched up" her books as well.

A man who constantly checks his watch, tidies up the papers on his desk, and lines his pencils up so all the erasers point due north is bound to be a little more rigid and compulsive than the one who shuffles through scattered folders, bits of paper, and memos written on the back of envelopes looking for a statistic you wanted—and then finds it scrawled on the inside of a match book in his suit pocket.

Observing your speaker will help you when you write your story—and tell you much about him as well.

Quote Accurately

If you're trying to be professional in your writing, you'll want to be known for your accuracy.

Check the figures you hear. It's better to say, "You said five million tons of refuse?" than to write "five tons." Your expert will be pleased you're careful and may give you more privileged data as well.

If you are quoting someone on a controversial issue make certain you're accurate. Don't quote someone as saying, "I'm vehemently for . . ." if what she really said was, "No one could say I'm vehemently for. . . ." If you aren't certain you've recorded the quote accurately, repeat it. Writers often are accused of being sloppy with quotes. Make it your business to prove that's not so.

I always read back quotes that include unusual language, medical terms, legal definitions, and scientific jargon. You'll lose the service of your expert (and any of her friends) for future stories if you misquote.

Sometimes, if it's a complicated or highly technical manuscript, I'll send a copy of the entire work to be checked for accuracy. In these cases, I *always* include the request, "Please check for *accuracy* only, not writing style." A few frustrated "editors" make creative changes anyway, but I ignore them. Always send a stamped, self-addressed envelope to make it easy for your expert to return the manuscript, and give a deadline when you need it back.

Learn to Say Good-Bye

Business people and professional people are busy and are use to working on a tight schedule. If your time is up, don't sit around chatting until they ring for help from their secretary. When you've got all the information you need, get up and go. Only if your expert begs you to stay for one more anecdote should you remain. Otherwise, make a graceful exit. Say "thank you," shake hands, and don't dawdle in the doorway. If you haven't already given him your business card, do so just in case he forgets who you are—or wants to send you pictures, more information, etc. A business card adds to your credibililty as a professonal writer.

I usually hand my card at the end of the interview and say, "In case you think of anything else I should know, here's where I can be reached." (I do *not* add that I can be reached there night or day because it's home!)

Conducting the Mail Interview

You can conduct an interview through the mails too, if your experts live far away. It's harder than a face-to-face interview because you don't have that rapport and you learn nothing of the person's personality, mannerisms, etc.

It's also easy for them to throw your letter away without answering it, so do everything you can to make it more likely you'll get a response.

1. Always send a stamped, self-addressed envelope along with your letter. Most people can't bear to throw away a stamped envelope, especially with the price of postage today.
2. Try to address your letter to someone specifically by name. If you don't know any name, zero in on the department you want by creating your own title, such as "Director of Management Testing" or "Director of Designing, Perfume Bottle Division."
3. Introduce yourself as a professional writer.
4. If you have some writing credits, list them so he knows he's dealing with a professional.

5. Include name of publication if you have a definite assignment.
6. Explain what type of story you're writing and what specfic information you need.

   When I was writing a story about one of West Point's famous graduates, I wrote to the Press Relations Officer of the Academy and said I needed specifics on how Beast Week was run, what the dining hall looked like and how many it served, and what buildings were around when my "hero" was there. The response was rapid and overwhelming. They disregarded my stamped, self-addressed envelope and filled their own manila envelope full of answers to my questions, clippings, photographs, and even a copy of the yearbook pages where my subject was listed. I have always found all governmental agencies to be extremely helpful once they know what you are looking for—and once you discover exactly where to write.

7. Give some deadline for when you need the imformation. Otherwise your letter rests indefinitely in the "to-be-answered" basket.
8. Don't expect essay-type answers. You may get them, but don't ask "What do you think about the younger generation?" Ask specifics, like "How has television affected today's young people?" "What are young people's attitudes towards marriage? Dating? Drugs? Dropping-out?"
9. Ask if you may quote him by name.
10. Write a thank-you note to everyone who responds.
11. Send a copy of the article when it is published.
12. If you send out questionnaires, expect a low response. One psychologist told me she sent out 600 questionnaires to professional women. She received 375 responses. Most of them came back the first few days. "That's a high response," she admitted. "Normal is 30 to 40 percent.

How to Interview By Phone

It's expensive, but when you need answers fast, it's often very effective. Some people are more likely to consent to a telephone interview than a face-to-face one.

To get the most for your money, write out your questions in advance. Some people prefer to send a letter first, to introduce themselves. Others just call, hoping to find the person in—and available.

Always introduce yourself by your first and last name, not as Mrs. John Smith. The former sounds professional; tha latter sounds like a housewife, and she doesn't get interviews.

Only begin a telephone interview when you know you won't be

disturbed (when the baby is in the crib, the toddler being watched by someone, or the kids are at school). If you have to tell a scientist to "hold it" while you put Patsy on the potty , you may return to a dull disconnect hum on the phone. Even people who are extremely family-oriented have litte tolerance for children when they're "tuned in" for business. This definitely is one time when you must wear your professional hat—even if it means going to your mother's house to use the phone.

Ask for the correct spelling anytime you're in doubt.

Repeat statistics and quotes to make certain you've quoted your source accurately.

As with all interviews, send a thank-you note.

Also, send a copy of the article when it's published.

Keep your sources happy. You may want to contact the same person again for another story. If you've been thoughtful, you'll stand out.

Making Things Click (So You Like What Develops)

11.

"Have you thought about taking your own pictures?"

This innocent question from my newspaper editor threw me into hysterics. You would have thought he was asking me to rewire a computer.

"Take my own pictures? With everything else I have to do? I'm a writer, not a photographer. Each is hard enough without. . . ."

"Just thought I'd ask."

In the years that followed, I thought about his question every time I lost a sale because I had no photographs to go with my article.

There's no doubt people have become more picture-oriented. Television has trained us all to look for quick, easy-to-digest information, and that often means pictures.

A Picture's Worth a Thousand Words—and Sometimes Pays More

It's a fact of life. Not only do editors usually pay extra for photos to illustrate a nonfiction article, they often pay more for the picture than they do for our sparkling copy. As someone who is predominately a writer, I resent that. But, as a realist, I accept it (and the extra checks that go with it). Strong pictures have saved articles that may have been a little weak, and occasionally I've lost the sale of a strong article because I had no pictures!

I interviewed a retired fireman who had a vast collection of fire-fighting paraphernalia: helmets, patches, uniforms, etc. The editor of *Collector's World* liked my article and wanted to buy it, but he asked for illustrations. I didn't have any. The old man had died shortly after the interview, and his daughter ignored my request to photograph his collection. The editor was disappointed (not as much as I was) but said he couldn't buy the story without pictures. If I had taken my camera with me, I would have made that sale.

Think of pictures you remember, like the Marines raising the flag at Iwo Jima, the astronauts landing on the moon, or little "John John" Kennedy saluting at his father's funeral. Pictures have power. They do speak loudly.

Of course, you have to understand what a picture's trying to say for it to be effective.

A picture used to illustrate an article needs to be eye-catching, easily understood, and supportive of the written material. It should complement the flavor of the copy (humorous, dramatic, technical, etc.), and should make the viewer want to read the article.

To get all this into one picture, you need to take many shots. Never be stingy with film. It's cheap when you compare its cost against the increased payment for your illustrated article—or with the fee you'll lose if the sale falls through for lack of a picture.

Always buy enough film and shoot a variety of shots—horizontals and verticals, close-ups and long-shots—so you're sure to have a few that are "just right."

What Equipment Do You Need?

You *can* get by with the minimum. I know one writer who has successfully illustrated her articles with photos shot with a Kodak Instamatic. Don't use the kind that takes 110 film, though. The negatives are too small to be blown up into 8 x 10 prints, which is the size most newspapers and magazines prefer.

I use an Olympus OM1 single-lens reflex camera, loaded with either Tri-X or Plus-X film. Both are black-and-white films, as most of my markets use black-and-white glossies. The Plus-X is used when you think you have plenty of natural light; the Tri-X when you don't expect a great deal of natural light. Someday I plan to buy a second

35mm camera and keep it loaded with film for color slides so that I can offer either to my editors.

I seldom use a flash attachment because the high speed of Tri-X does not require it (except in very dim light) and because *not* using flash makes the photographs look more natural.

There are many brands of single-lens reflex cameras. Just a few include Konica, Canon, Pentax, Nikon, Olympus, Minolta, Mamiya, Leica, and Fujica. They are reasonably light to carry, use interchangeable lenses, let you see the picture you're actually shooting, fit a small hand and, if you're short as I am, let you shoot over shoulders and heads and still hope to get in the picture.

How "good" does your camera need to be? Good enough for you to take professional-looking pictures; good enough for you to understand how to work it; good enough to still be of value as you begin to learn and understand more about photography. It shouldn't be the most expensive, most complicated camera on the market. That will only frighten you away and keep you from experimenting and pushing yourself to learn.

Most newspaper want ads list used photographic equipment separately, and you often can get a good buy from someone who has lost his enthusiasm for picture-taking or has moved up to a more complex camera. Always take someone with you who is knowledgeable in cameras, and only buy with the condition that you may return it if your first test roll doesn't turn out.

I also have a twin-lens reflex, which was my first "professional" camera. It's the rectangular kind you hold about waist height, look down into, and shoot. I like it because it takes oversize negatives, which are very clear when blown up, and it's good for taking pictures of nonmoving objects like flowers, buildings, etc. But I found it was too heavy for me to carry and was too bulky to feel comfortable in my hands. Many pros use it, though, so if you have access to one, try it. Mine is a Yashica, but there are Minoltas, Rolleiflexes, Mamiyas and other brands as well.

The twin-lens reflex doesn't give the flexibility of interchangeable lenses the way the single-lens does. That can be an important difference. Having the right lens for a job is important too. I now use a 35mm (wide angle) lens and a 135mm (telephoto) lens. This latter purchase came about after I lost a sale, not because I had the wrong camera, but because I had the wrong lens.

A few years ago my husband and I were on a well-known cruise ship. There was a bomb-threat phoned into the ship and the vessel stopped, mid-Atlantic. There we waited for the Royal Air Force bomb-disposal crew to parachute into the icy waters off our stern. They were to be picked up by the ship's launch and brought aboard to search for the bomb (which turned out to be a hoax).

All the passengers and most of the crew lined the railing of our ship, trying to catch sight of our rescuers. I took pictures with my normal lens (50mm) and, when we landed, offered my film to the BBC representative who wanted to buy some photos of the RAF crew jumping into the ocean. I had great hopes of selling mine. But, without a telephoto lens, my pictures only showed three tiny black dots against dark clouds. I was very disappointed—and equally determined not to let the wrong lens mess up a possible sale again.

There is a vast array of other lenses you could use, depending on your particular needs. Many people get by just fine with only the 50mm or normal lens. But, if you want to do extreme close-up work like photographing insects on plants or threads in cloth, you can buy a special lens for that. The "fisheye" lens takes a curved picture, almost a circular image. The effect is artistic and interesting, but its use is limited.

Before you buy a lens, check with a friend who is a "camera bug," a reliable camera shop, or some of the photography magazines on the newsstand.

How to Care for Your Camera

With a minimum of care, you should be able to keep your camera for years, until you're ready to "trade up" to a more complex model with a myriad of dials, buttons, and numbers.

Keep it in its case when you're not using it. When you are, carry it by the strap. I replaced the tiny, thin strap on mine with a wide, colorful one. It makes my camera easy to pick out if it gets mixed up with any others, but more important, the wider strap doesn't cut into my shoulder as much. Even a light camera gets heavy when you're carrying it all day. When I travel, I have a shoulder bag filled with film, lenses, billfold, glasses, and everything my husband can't carry in his pockets. With that load it's imperative that my camera be as comfortable as possible.

Don't carry your camera in your purse or handbag, no matter how large your purse is. It could be dropped, scratched by your comb, smeared with eyeshadow, flooded with contact lens solution, etc. Some people carry camera bags fitted with special places for the camera, lenses, film, etc. I find these to be as heavy as my purse! When I use a bag for all that equipment, I prefer a lightweight flight bag.

Most camera shops carry a small accessory that has saved me a great deal of aggravation and my lense from damage. I was losing the lens cover constantly until a salesman showed me a gadget with a sticky circle at one end and elastic at the other. The elastic fits around the lens and is connected to the sticky circle that you put on the cover. The cover dangles when you're taking a picture, and you don't have to wonder where you've put it. Before I found these treasures, I tramped through snowdrifts, pulled pockets inside-out, and tore up the house all for the sake of a lost lens cover.

Three dangers to your camera itself are heat, dust, and dampness. Never keep your camera (or film) inside a locked car or glove compartment. The heat builds up and can ruin both your camera and the film.

Always keep the camera in its case when not in use, and keep the cover on the lens. Dust can scratch this delicate glass and all your pictures will have lines on them. You can buy a special soft brush at the camera store to gently dust the lens. Do *not* use a toothbrush, Kleenex, eyebrow brush, or feather duster!

Dampness also poses a threat to your camera. If you have to take pictures in the rain, have someone hold an umbrella over you or create your own awning with your plastic raincoat. If you're taking pictures at the seashore, keep the camera covered in plastic when you're not using it and be careful of the salt spray.

I learned the hard way that a camera's batteries need to be replaced from time to time. It was my husband's *special* birthday. To celebrate, we invited some close friends for dinner and, as a surprise, I outfitted the children as French maids and waiters with black ties. I took pictures all evening—as the "butler" let our guests in, the headwaiter opened the bottle of champagne, and the two French maids with their frilly white aprons and headpieces sat on my husband's knee. Not a one of the pictures turned out because the camera's batteries were too old!

Have your camera checked once a year by a reputable camera-service shop. They'll give it a thorough going-over, and you won't be out pictures too precious to lose. Occasionally you can clean the batteries and the battery box yourself with a Q-tip dipped in alcohol (just so it's damp, not dripping). But this doesn't take the place of an annual check-up.

Never let your camera out of your sight. Little ones will jam the shutter if they don't drop it first; and the older ones will leave it in somebody's car, loan it to a friend, or lose it if they don't drop it first. If it's a tool of your trade, make it your business to keep it close at hand. It's worth it to buy the kids an Instamatic of their own, or a second-hand "good" camera, to keep their mitts off yours.

Let me reassure you that I am not an expert photographer. Far from it. My camera is semiautomatic, which means I turn the shutter speed to 125 or 250. Then, with the aid of the electric eye in the camera, I line up a little pointer that lines up the f-stop (opening) for me.

I've taken two photography courses. The first was for hobbyists and explained what the parts of the camera were and what they did (which I didn't and still don't understand too well). The second course was a university course in photojournalism. At this I learned, among other things, how to develop my own pictures. Even more important, I learned how to crop a photo when taking it so the view finder is filled only with what is truly important; with no trees growing out of people's heads, no unnecessary figures cluttering up the picture, no dogs in the background to distract the eye. I also learned to crop the picture at the enlarger, so you can blow up (enlarge) the main point of your picture and omit what you don't want. That course also taught me the vocabulary I need in order to talk to a printer who develops my pictures and to know what can be done with a picture.

It's important for nonphotographers who are trying to look good (or rather, make their pictures look good) to learn to "bracket" your shots; "hedge your shots" is another way to put it. You shoot the same picture at different settings so that if one doesn't come out sharp enough, another may.

If your local Y, church group, adult education department, or college offers a course in photography, consider taking it if you're just a beginner. It's a legitimate business expense. If no course is available, ask in your bookstore for a good basic and reasonably simple book on beginning photography.

Although my credentials as a photographer are only fair, I've learned to take sharp, strong, and interesting pictures that are in focus. That's really all you need. My sales to newspapers and magazines have increased noticeably since I've begun to submit my own photos along with my manuscripts.

Try to be as original in your pictures as you are in your writing.

Don't take stereotyped photos of women pouring tea, someone holding a plaque in one hand and shaking someone else's with the other, or a line-up of smiling faces squinting into the sun. Try to close in on two faces, or even one: the young girl holding the heavy teapot in both hands, her mouth tensing with effort, or a little boy staring in awe at his high-school hero's stack of trophies.

The best way to determine what type of picture you'll need for your article is to study samples in your intended market. If the editor uses pictures with people, chances are photos of "things" won't sell. Some editors prefer formal shots, others candid or casual shots. Basically though, most editors want pictures with human interest, action, or something that is unusual or important. A picture of a marching band isn't too different, but one of a tiny girl pounding the big drum is. Don't always focus on the child catching the ball. Look for the one who misses it. Capture emotion—and nine times out of ten, you'll have a good picture.

In addition to selling pictures in conjunction with your articles, you can sell pictures by themselves to house organs, newspapers, and magazines. As more magazines (especially regional ones) adopt the photo-essay format, a writer's creativity in the fields of both writing and photography can give her a definite edge in the marketplace.

Another growing market for pictures is that of greeting cards. Although many card companies still are dominated by cartoon-type illustrations and drawings, many others have turned to the use of photographs, especially for their Christmas lines and more romantic or emotional cards.

Calendar companies, advertising agencies, and other businesses also buy color slides (transparencies) and black-and-white glossies. You'll find a multitude of markets, their requirements and payment schedule in *Writer's Market* and *Photographer's Market*.

How to Package Your Pictures

Be sure to package your pictures so they arrive at their destination in good shape.

Have a small rubber stamp made with the words, "Credit [your name] & return to [your address]." Stamp the back of all glossies you send out. You may not get them all back, but it certainly will improve your chances of getting a byline with your picture.

Each picture should have a caption on it which tells what the picture shows. Don't repeat anything from your article, but tell who the people are (if that's important) and where the event takes place.

Type the caption on the *bottom* of a sheet of white paper. Tape the top of the paper to the back of your photo, so that someone can look at the picture and read the caption at the same time. Then fold the paper up over the photo.

Some writers tape their captions to the back of their pictures. This is dangerous because there is the possibility of the picture being damaged when the caption is torn off.

Another system is to number the picture on the back and then send an accompanying sheet with the captions listed.

The inherent weakness in this method is that you're giving the editor another piece of paper to keep track of. By keeping photo and caption together, you increase the chances of its staying that way until it finds its way into print.

Sandwich the picture between two sheets of strong cardboard to keep the photo from being bent. The back of a tablet really isn't strong enough. You need something firmer, like cardboard cut from a grocery carton.

Put the picture (without paper clips) and the manuscript into a large manila envelope.

Be sure to include a return envelope big enough to hold the photo and hope that the editor will package it carefully if he must return your work.

Some writers won't send their printed photos. Instead, they offer the editor a contact sheet, which is negative-size versions of all your shots printed on one sheet. That way an editor can select whatever she wants, and you don't have the expense of printing 8 x 10 glossies that aren't used.

Don't Be Afraid to Ask for a Handout (or a Hand)

When I began freelancing in 1961, I often "helped" editors by including suggestions that might be useful when they illustrated my articles. If the story was for a local market, I even worked with the staff photographers, describing ideas for the picture arrangement, getting models, and showing what angle the photo should be shot, from a closeup of a marzipan city with its "creator" looking on, to a shot looking up as in a child's view of a department store, etc.

It wasn't until ten years later that I included a "handout" photo with my story on Viking ships for the local newspaper. I had gotten the picture from the Scandinavian Tourist Bureau. To my surprise, I received more for that story because I had included the photograph, even though I hadn't actually taken it.

Nobody has to hit me over the head! I immediately began to think of ways to include pictures with many of my nonfiction articles.

There are numerous places to get these "handouts." *Writer's Market* contains thirty pages of sources for photographs, some of which are free for the asking. Photos also are available from news services, newspapers, tourist bureaus, governmental agencies, industry, chambers of commerce, and public relations offices. But, although these sources will give you suitable illustrations for your story package, the photos often don't convey the exact meaning you need or would like for your article

I received some beautiful (and free) black-and-white glossies and color shots from the United States Marine Corps Barracks in Washington for an article I did on their famous Friday night parade. For this travel-oriented article, these photos worked perfectly. But for my second story, one slanted to a children's market, my own shot of a child being escorted to her seat by a tall, handsome Marine in his dress blues was far more expressive.

If you don't want to bother taking the pictures yourself, you may want to team up with a freelance photographer. You do the writing and pay her either a flat fee or a percentage of the article payment for taking the necessary pictures. I don't use this method because I find it hard enough to work around my own busy schedule, without trying to incorporate someone else's as well. Also, I know what feeling I want to express in my articles, so I know what I want my pictures to say. Someone else doesn't.

A good compromise in this situation can be to make use of your husband's good nature *and* photographic skills. He can take the necessary pictures while you take notes. He's probably your travel companion on trips anyway, so why not mix business with pleasure?

I've also enlisted my eldest son, having him take shots needed for rush jobs. It gives him good exposure—plus the photographer's cut of the fee and a photo credit.

Pay for Your Vacation with Pictures

As long as you're going somewhere, you might as well be paid for it—by selling the pictures you take. And it really doesn't matter much where you go. I've been paid for pictures of sculpture I found while vacationing in Oslo, Norway, and for those of sea oats found a few miles from my home. I've captured scenes of people at work and at play both here and abroad, scenes typical of the area I'm visiting as well as unusual and/or historical attractions.

Sometimes I write about only one aspect of the vacation, using my photographs to illustrate it. Occasionally, I'll use pictures from various trips to show similarities or contrasts. I usually don't make enough to pay for the entire trip, but enough so it covers part of it and definitely covers the cost of the mementos I buy there.

Taking pictures when you travel, even if it's only to the neighborhood park and back, gives you more to write about, adds color and depth to fiction, and makes you more versatile (and therefore more valuable) to your editors.

Use Your Camera for Note-Taking

But there are more uses for a camera than just taking pictures for resale purposes. In addition to illustrating an article, the camera can aid the freelance writer in many other ways, such as taking notes.

On one trip to Colonial Williamsburg, I took a picture of a plaque near the Capitol Building. It was faster than copying all the information down and came in very handy for reference when I wrote the article.

I also took many pictures of an unusual outdoor restaurant on an island in the Lake Como region of Italy. The photo gave me all the descriptive information I needed, reminding me of the cobblestones, colored umbrellas, and checkered tablecloths when I sat down to write about it two years later. Because of my photographs, I could give the article a feeling of immediacy and realism.

Almost all the photos I take while traveling are planned with eventual pubilcation in mind. But they also serve to remind me of details I might have overlooked while taking notes or, sometimes, actually not seen at all. Often a person or thing in the background of your photo is more interesting than what you originally were photographing.

For example, say you have taken a picture of a tourist attraction and don't realize, until looking at the prints, that in the background is a person in a wheelchair being pushed up a ramp. That gets you thinking—how well do the tourist attractions in your area serve the handicapped? That story might be far more interesting than the one you originally were planning to do—in fact, I may write it up myself!

Use your camera often, and let its objectivity suggest article ideas to you.

Let the Camera Do Your Outline

Photography also can be exremely helpful when you have to

organize material. I took a series of photos showing the steps in making peppermint lollipops at the candy factory in Disney World's Buena Vista Shopping Center. I didn't realize, until I got the pictures back, that I was holding a ready-made outline for the article.

I arranged all the pictures in front of me on the floor (nobody eats off my floor, but I do work better on it) and numbered them in order. It was easy to then write the article, simply by following my "pictorial outline," and then to illustrate the article with those same pictures.

Anytime you're writing a "how-to-make" type article, take pictures of each step. It prevents your jumping to Step Five from Step Three, and makes illustrating your article a breeze.

A Picture Can Be a Creative Turn-On

Sometimes I take pictures of things just because they interest me. I put them in a folder and let them simmer, hoping they'll stimulate my imagination. I have pictures of a bicycle up in a tree, a cat and dog asleep by a fish tank, a forlorn little boy in a ragged shirt standing by a garbage can, a toddler peering out of a gate with a sign saying, "Beware of Dog," etc.

A photo of a tree entangled by its own limbs taken on the grounds of Sarasota's Ringling Museum might be used one day to describe a forest surrounding a witch's village in a children's book of fantasy, or as the place to conceal a body in an adult mystery. The shadowy figure of a woman standing on a beach, staring out into the Gulf, fascinates me. Who is she? Why is she looking into the sea? Has she lost a child? A lover? Is she planning to disappear into the gloomy water? Perhaps someday I'll know; but right now, the picture keeps my subconscious fermenting. I can turn to this folder anytime my imagination fails me and use these same pictures in any way I care to interpret them.

For the past years I've photographed unique and interesting signs for my own amusement. Now it's turned into a possibly profitable venture, as I'm putting together an article on "creative signing" for an advertising magazine.

Let your imagination run wild with pictures you've taken "just because. . . ." Film is cheap when you consider how valuable it can become, and how many uses photographs can have for an active writer. It's like having "instant replay" at your fingertips. Get into the habit of taking your camera with you, even if you're just going to the grocery. You never know what you may find waiting for you.

"What about me?" you say. "I write fiction. Why should I take pictures?"

While it's true that fiction writers don't need to illustrate their work, many women say they use pictures to help them capture moods, remember descriptions of the way people dress, details in furniture, cities, etc. If you're writing a period piece, pictures from a museum showing that era could be most helpful, as could photos of the way houses and streets looked then. It's the little details that make fiction come alive, and often a camera can serve as your magic wand.

Use Your Home-Bred Models

The beauty of being a photographer when you have children is that you can record each period of their lives for posterity. The beauty of having children when you're a photographer is that you have a ready supply of models, and you don't need a model release when they're yours.

I've illustrated many of my articles with pictures of my own kids. They've climbed under sinks to show "How to Prevent Your Child from Being Poisoned," looked forlorn as they read a letter from home in "How to Help Your Child Adjust to Camp," fed chickens, climbed trees, and worked a one-hundred-year-old loom, all for the benefit of my camera.

Once, for a photo-essay on "The Making of a Lady," I enlisted two of my kids. My daughter didn't mind posing with a baseball and cap, reading a book on the facts of life with the catcher's mitt on her lap, or even primping in front of a mirror. (She did rebel a little when I suggested she hold hands with her brother and look adoringly into his eyes.)

For the most part, the kids are born hams and love posing for me. I enjoy working with them, and my editors seem to like the relaxed pictures that accompany my articles.

If you have to "borrow" the neighbor's kids, remember to get written permission from the parents. Such permission is called a "model release," and some publications won't use a picture unless this permission form comes with it. It doesn't have to be a legal-sounding document. Just something like:

[Your Name Here] has my permission to use the photograph of [my child, Horace; my guinea pig, Nina], for whatever use she sees fit."

Date:

Signed:

This way you can sell the picture with your article to a magazine or sell it alone for advertising purposes. If you know your intended market, tell the person, and be sure to give them a copy of it when it's published! They'll think you're fantastic, smart, talented, etc.

Perfect your technique by taking pictures of what's around you, what you know best and feel most comfortable with. Use the children, pets, room arrangements, your parents, and your spouse, if he's willing. Take pictures at birthday parties, and try out various shots: active group shots during Pin the Tail on the Donkey, single close-ups when the birthday boy or girl blows out the candles, and pictures that tell a story—a youngster who couldn't find a chair when the music stopped. Zero in on faces and hands, the most expressive parts of our bodies.

Should You Have a Darkroom?

There's absolutely no doubt about it, it's a lot more fun working in a darkroom and seeing your picture come up in the developer than sitting at your typewriter, struggling to put words into an order that makes sense.

But it's hard enough finding time to be a writer when you're a housewife and mother without trying to make time to be a professional photographer as well. The freelance writer needs to know how pictures are developed, enlarged, cropped, etc., but you need to decide whether you are primarily a writer or a photographer. You probably won't be able to make time for both the typewriter and the darkroom too.

I prefer to use a custom lab and let their experts work the darkroom magic. I now know what can be done to get the most from a photograph and can talk to the experts in their language (albeit haltingly), but I think my writing time and photo-taking time would be drastically reduced if I also processed my own pictures.

Learning to take good, sharp pictures is becoming as important for a writer as how to type or put a sentence together effectively. The pictures you take are uniquely yours, showing your particular interpretation of an event, and your own creativity.

The time you spend learning to take pictures is well spent because it makes your product more marketable and gives you an edge in the marketplace. It means you'll sell more, and you'll often get more for what you sell. And, many times you'll sell pictures you would have taken anyway, just for fun.

Making It
Your Business
(to be
Businesslike)

12.
A businesslike attitude toward your writing is vital
if you're going to be successful. You'll be able to achieve more during
those precious moments when you have time to write, be less frazzled
when chaos is all about you, and be better able to "roll with the
punches" when unforeseen circumstances (like five "snow days" in a
row) arise.

By acting businesslike, you'll soon begin to think that way.
Thinking *is* believing, just as they say.

Think of Yourself as a Writer

This means a number of things—such as turning down things you
really don't want to do so you can write. And turning down things you
really want to do so you can write. It means practicing self-discipline.

I never say, "learn self-discipline," because that is something we all
have to constantly work at. Like Weight Watchers and Alcoholics
Anonymous, we writers must take one day at a time. With us, the
challenge is to make time for our writing. The temptations to
procrastinate, to go play, or to sit down and read a good book are
always around us. Our friends and loved ones beckon us away from

our typewriters with, "Come on. You've worked hard enough today. Give yourself a break." Do we weaken—or can we remain steadfast and dedicated?

Unfortunately, sitting at a typewriter, looking out the window or at your cluttered bulletin board doesn't resemble "work" as many people know it.

"I didn't think you *looked* busy," is what most people say when they barge in on me unannounced. If they catch me typing, it goes something like this: "Oh, good. You're only typing."

But, if you consider yourself a businesswoman, a writer, you'll make yourself say, "I can't talk now. I'm working."

It's contagious—although it sometimes moves as slowly as the last month of pregnancy. If you keep at it long enough, your family will begin to think of you as a business person; and then, like ripples on a smooth lake, the realization bounces against your friends. Realistically, it doesn't necessarily mean that they'll respect your time, but it does mean they'll realize and accept what you're doing.

Once you've set your writing hours, stick to them. As I've said earlier, don't make social calls during the hours you've designated as your business hours. Don't cook or clean either. Write! Whatever schedule you set, follow it as rigidly as if you were punching in and out on a time clock. It's better to start with only one hour a day and stick to it than to try for four hours each day and be frustrated when it doesn't work out.

Always be alert for ways you can save time and put it to better use on your work. Condition yourself to have an alarm that goes off in your head anytime you think some procedure is taking longer than it should. Ask yourself, how would a businesswoman handle this? Then follow your own good advice, because that's just what you are.

Business Stationery Means Business

A friend just set up her own business at home. She really hadn't gotten the project off the ground. She wasn't thinking of herself as a "businesswoman" yet.

"Have you ordered your business stationery yet?" I asked. "Business cards?"

She seemed surprised. "No, I didn't even think of that."

How can you run a business without at least having business stationery? Of course you could type your name, address and phone number on each sheet. But that not only is a waste of time, it also is much less professional looking. You needn't spend a lot for stationery either. In my area you can have one hundred letterheads printed at a quick-print service for just under five dollars. Number-ten envelopes with your return address run under ten dollars. That's not too much to look businesslike, is it?

As long as you're at the printer's, consider having business cards made up. They should include your name, address, phone number, and, if you want, the words: "freelance writer." Many people today are reluctant to talk with strangers. If you hand them your card, they feel you must be "legitimate." It was my business card that persuaded a suspicious usher to let me backstage in a New York theater the night I interviewed Peter Falk. It makes you look like you might be "somebody"—and it makes you feel you are!

Be careful about being too "cute" with your cards or stationery. This is not the place for "Ramblings from Ruthie" or clever cartoon figures. Watch those "personalized touches" so you don't end up looking amateurish.

Be Accurate

As a writer, you're part of "the media," an active participant in the communication field. As such you have a responsibility to your readers to be accurate. Most people have a strong belief in the "power of the press." If they read something in print, it must be so. Don't abuse that confidence by sloppy writing. Take pride in your accuracy. Professionals do.

Check out your facts, then check again. Try not to copy what someone else reported that political leader, I. Emma Hacque, said. Call or write Ms. Hacque and find out for yourself. If you can't get firsthand information, then identify it as hearsay.

After you type an article, check it over before mailing it. With medical articles I always send one copy to a doctor who specializes in that field to make certain I have spelled medical terms correctly and am accurate in every detail.

Sometimes, even with the best intentions, you goof! I once wrote an article about a regional theater. It was an impressive complex incorporating three different theaters under one roof. I mentioned the seating of each theater—and neglected to double-check my notes. (Do as I say, not as I sometimes do!)

When the article appeared, I was horrified to read that the largest theater (which actually seats 685) "seats 285." At first I blamed the newspaper. (It's always easiest to blame someone else.) Then I pulled my copy (always keep at least one carbon of your work) and saw that somehow I had typed a 2 instead of a 6. Who knew about it? Possibly someone visiting from that area who happened to read my article. But more likely, no one. I doubt that my editor even caught the error. But I know and it embarrassed me. I've always been proud of being a writer who is always careful to check her facts.

I've been super-cautious ever since.

Keep Deadlines; Be Dependable

Once you've promised an editor that your article will be ready by a specific date, move heaven and earth if you must, but get it there on time.

Be realistic about the deadlines you set or agree upon. Children do get sick, and I've heard that occcasionally mothers do too! Give yourself a few days' leeway to cope with an afternoon sitting at a school health assembly to watch your son play "Mr. Eyeball." (He blinked and was gone, and so was your writing time.)

Don't masochistically plan a major rewrite for the two weeks you're at Martha's Vineyard with the family; or during Christmas week when it's your turn to have the relatives for dinner; or when (God forbid) your husband is home sick with the flu.

Treat your deadlines seriously and schedule those dates intelligently.

If you find, however, that the dates that you thought were perfectly reasonable have suddenly been clouded by unexpected illness, because the electricity got turned off so you can't use the typewriter, or your fingers got stuck together with Krazy Glue, call your editor and explain the problem. Usually she'll grant you an extension and will appreciate your businesslike attitude.

Be dependable if you're asked for additional material or corrections too. Schedule it on your work calendar so you don't forget it or let it get buried under the book you're now writing.

Once you've queried an editor on a subject and gotten a go-ahead, write the article. If you've changed your mind about doing it or can't find enough information, let him know. He may be planning to run your article, or may say no to another writer because he thought you were going to do it.

Writing is a serious game. It's fun, but if you're going to play it like a professional, you've got to follow the rules. Maintaining a businesslike attitude is one of those rules.

Train the Family to be Businesslike With Your Calls

This is about as easy as training your children to hang up their clothes, but it can be done. It just takes a lot of patience and yelling. Remind them that they must:

1. Take your messages seriously, as you do (or should) theirs.

   I once received a verbal aside, "Oh, Mom. I forgot to tell you. Somebody from the Digest called yesterday. You're suppose to call back."

   "The Digest? *Writer's Digest? Reader's Digest? Science Digest?*"

   The child (the one I always considered so bright and so mature) shrugged. "I forget. Does it matter?"

   No, I didn't hang that child from the pegboard—although I felt like it. I did make sure, however, that since then, they all became more reliable with my calls, repeating and spelling names and numbers to make certain they have them correctly. They also have learned not to go through the mail first and inadvertently take *my* letters with them to school. It's called "mutual respect." It's an important commodity in any household, but even more so if you're a housewife-writer working at home. It gives a poor impression if you return a call and ask for Miss Dinsman and the editor's name is Mr. Glinden. Even if he has kids of his own, he'll wonder if your writing's confused too.

2. Give you the message. This may sound academic, but I used to find important messages lying in the bathroom, under piles of toys in the playroom, and once, scribbled on the entertainment section of the newspaper. (If I hadn't wanted to see a movie that night I never would have found it.) Now we have a spindle in the kitchen for "Mother's messsages" and any person or persons not spindling a message will be folded, spindled, and mutilated.

3. Keep QUIET when you're on the phone. This is probably the most difficult "must" for the kids to follow. Invariably, fights break out in that split second between the time the phone rings and you say "hello." If you can, calmly discuss the fact that screaming, "Shut up, you guys," into your editor's ear makes you sound very unprofessional.

   If you have children of playpen age (no, it is *not* reasonable to put seven-year-olds in a playpen!) keep the playpen away from the phone. My kids used to play quietly, amusing themselves with the dust balls that floated between the playpen bars, until the phone rang. As soon as they realized I had my business voice on, they'd start screaming.

How to Handle Mail—Once

Mail delivery is slow, but our own processing of it often is even slower.

When you bring in the mail, sort it into piles. Put the children's mail in a *specific* spot where they'll know to look for it. I bought a cute old-fashioned mailbox with cubby holes for each child's mail. It was ideal but they never looked for their mail there. Now I just leave it on the kitchen counter, and that's the first place they head when they come home from school.

Sort the mail over the wastebasket. Any flyers or junk mail you don't want should go into the wastebasket immediately. Bills go in your bill box or a special spot allotted to them (although you should open and check them over quickly to make certain the store hasn't make an error).

Your personal mail should go on your desk or wherever you answer it. If it's an invitation or other "social" mail that you want your husband to see, put it in the spot you both have agreed should be the mail drop. I've tried wicker baskets, silver trays, and dresser tops, but once again am back to dumping it on the bed so he can't miss it.

All of your business mail—acceptances, rejections, and business magazines—should go in your office basket so you can process it immediately. Rejected manuscripts should be checked to see if they need retyping. Otherwise send them out again that same day. Acceptances should be noted in your card file or on the carbon, and interest in queries posted on your bulletin board. Mail has a dreadful way of piling up like snowdrifts if it isn't removed or at least shoveled aside. Magazines and catalogues you can't bear to throw away can go in your bathroom for john or tub reading, or by your bed. You might find an early Christmas present you can order in one of them.

Don't keep shuffling mail from one spot to another. You're bound to lose something that could be important. Businesses have learned that it's more efficient to have the mailroom sort and distribute the mail immediately rather than have everyone paw over the stack, pulling out their own. You're a business now, so take a tip from the experts and handle your mail—once.

Do You Know Where Your Manuscripts Are?

If you're striving for professionalism, you'll soon have more than one manuscript in the mail. You never should stand by the mailbox waiting for an editor to respond. Not only is it a good way to catch pneumonia or get sunstroke, it also shows your neighbors that you're not working on anything new.

There's another advantage of having more than one project in the works. You finish one and mail it off with hope and a hug, but then you've got to go back and get the others in shape. You don't have time to worry how your first offspring is doing.

Most writers develop their own system or systems for keeping track of their manuscripts. Whatever you decide upon, don't let your system keep you. A schedule can become so complex that it consumes all your time.

My first system was beautiful in an artistic sense. It involved a rainbow of different-colored pencils. (Felt tips weren't "in" then.) By the time I had sharpened all the pencils and lined them up just so, marked the sheet in all the different colors corresponding with what was "in the works," what was out, and what was back, etc., it was time to start dinner. I stuck the pencils in pots for my plants to lean against and started over.

Now I use 4 x 6 index cards. I began, optimistically, with 3 x 5s, but found that I needed more space as some of my articles kept "coming home to mother." If I haven't sold a manuscript by the time I've filled my 4 x 6 card, I take a second long look and usually either rewrite it or scrap it altogether.

I put the title on the top of the card and the market down the side along with the date it went out. If it's returned, I mark that date and add any remarks the editor might have made.

When an article is purchased, I'll mark the card "sold" and write down the amount and date of the check. Then the card gets moved to the back of the box where "sold" cards live. (You don't need to buy an expensive file box for these cards. A shoe box works fine.)

I also keep a list beside the telephone of all manuscripts, who has them, and when they were mailed. This list came about when the umpteenth editor called to talk about a particular article and I couldn't remember what I had sent to her. Now I can clear my throat, glance up at my list and sound intelligent,or at least reasonably well informed.

Most editors keep manuscripts longer than they say they will. If the information listed beside the name of a magazine in a market guide says, "Replies in two weeks," add two weeks more before you start getting nervous. Do not, however, let publishers keep your work indefinitely.

Recently I received a manuscript back after more than a year. It had been submitted in April after receiving a go-ahead from the editor. In July, I returned it with some changes she had requested. I wrote in September, November, and January to see what decision had been made and received no reply. In March I called and asked for the manuscript to be returned, which it was—in May! Now I'm trying to get the pictures back.

I had written for this publication previously and found the association to be a pleasant one. What's going on? I don't know. Would I write for her again? Never!

Luckily, most editors aren't like this. Most are overworked and struggle under stacks of manuscripts. But they *do* reply, or at least drop a line to say they're behind schedule.

With the mails being less than dependable, there's always the concern that your manuscript never was received; that it's stashed in the basement of a mailman who's gone haywire or lying in a swamp because some pilot chose that particular mailbag to lighten the load. You can free your mind by including with your manuscript a self-addressed postcard that says, [Your Title Goes Here] was received in our office on [Date]. It also makes you feel good because you can tell your scoffing friends, "I've already heard from the editor about my manuscript."

Keep Track of Your Expenses

I use a ledger to jot down expenses that I can write off; such as parking, reference books, duplicating costs, supplies, etc.

Be sure to date each entry and get a receipt whenever possible. Sometimes it's important to get information immediately, so rather than write a letter, I use the phone. As I place the call, I write down the date, phone number, and purpose of the call so that when our phone bill comes I can extract that amount and mark it in my ledger.

Keep Records of Your Sales

You may think that you could record your sales on the head of a pin. But before you know it, you'll need good records of all your sales for yourself and for the IRS. You might as well be businesslike from the beginning.

I use my index cards (the ones used to keep track of the manuscripts) to record checks as they come in. Once an article has sold, I move the card to the front of the file box. I keep it there until the check comes in. (Occasionally it doesn't, and you'll have to remind the editor about your payment. By having the card in the front, it serves as a reminder to me as well.) When my check comes, I mark the date paid and the amount on the card. Then I put it in the back of the box, the Gold Medal division. (I review this collection of "winners" to encourage me on days when I've been flooded with rejections and everything comes back, including the letter to mother because I forgot to stamp it.) When the article is published, I record the date it ran and under what title.

I also record each check in a master ledger, listing the company issuing the check, the name of the publication (they often are different, as some companies like Condé Nast publish many magazines: *Glamour, Mademoiselle, Vogue*, etc.), the amount of the check, the date the check was issued, and the check number. The latter is important in case you have correspondence with a publisher about your check. I also record the name of the article. If a different title was used from my original one (which often is the case) I list both.

Keep Your Notes

In addition to dating notes from interviews and phone calls for future use, you also should keep your old notes. They may come in handy for other articles, or you'll need to refer back to them when checking facts. Often an editor's assistant will call to ask, "What issue of *Time* was your quote taken from?" or "When did General Custer give you those statistics?" If you can pull out your notes and give an authoritative answer, you'll be acting like a "pro."

How to Handle Your Money

Isn't this a nice problem to have!

Most women writers put their earnings into a separate checking account. That way they can pay for their business expenses out of that account and not get it confused with the grocery money—unless that money *is* the grocery money. Some guard it jealously and use it for buying "special" things they wouldn't have purchased otherwise.

By having a separate writing account, it's easier to tabulate your expenses and keep track of your progress. When you buy a new lens for your camera or sign up for a writing seminar out of the money you've earned, you'll feel you've come a long way—and you have.

Many people, including parents, husbands, and childhood friends, really don't take housewife-writers seriously UNTIL you can wave a check in front of them. Once they realize that someone is actually paying you for this stuff you've been writing, they'll begin to look at you in a new light. It's a sad commentary on the power of the almighty dollar.

Virginia Woolf said it in her book, *A Room of One's Own*: "Money dignifies what is frivolous if unpaid for."

Making It Pay (More)

13.

Recently, a manuscript I thought completed—well-researched, documented, and carefully written—reappeared in my mailbox with a memo from the editor.

"Run this through the typewriter again."

Frustrated as I was, I couldn't help smiling at the pictures it conjured up: my paper whipping through a magician's mimeograph machine—or, me in a flowered housedress *Spray and Washing* the manuscript and running it through the permanent press cycle again to get rid of the "ring around the copy."

I wish it were that easy. The only way I know to write (and to rewrite) is through hard work. I write, crumple up wads of rejected thoughts and sentence fragments, and write some more. My wastebasket fills like a popcorn popper at movie time. Finally, when I think I'm close, I read my work aloud. If it "sounds" right, I'll let it stay.

Every writer develops her own tricks for turning plain paper into greenbacks. But there still are a few basics to remember. Knowing them will give you a better chance to sell your work. Without them you still might be published, but it's like trying to wash your hands with one tied behind your back.

Study Your Markets

Every businessperson knows the importance of market research. If he's to sell a product, there has to be someone willing to buy it—a market. How do they know this? Certainly not through intuition alone. They spend vast sums of money for research, zeroing in on their intended market, so they can offer a product their buyers want.

Writers need to study their markets as well. It sounds logical enough, yet every editor has received manuscripts totally unsuited to his or her publication.

There's no use sending *Bride's* an article on travel, for example. The staff handles that. Nor should you send *Highlights for Children* a story about teenage pregnancy. Their readership age-range is two to twelve. You'll find this type of information in *Literary Market Place* and *Writer's Market*. The latter, published annually, contains thousands of possible outlets for your work, including the type of material each market is looking for, where to send it, the name of the editor, and what pay scale you can expect. When you get a copy, read it like a novel, from beginning to end. If it's your own copy, mark the pages that sound interesting to you. If you're using the library's copy, jot down possible markets on index cards, noting precisely what each market buys, length needed, etc.

I never had heard of *Juvenile Merchandising*, *Today's Catholic Teacher*, *Soccer America*, or *Early Years* before I found them listed in *Writer's Market*. But because I did, I was able to slant articles for them and sold to each of them.

Some magazines aren't listed in these market sources. They either don't buy freelance material, don't update their listing annually, prefer not being listed, or are too new to have been included. You'll find them in friends' homes, waiting rooms, and hotel lobbies. Develop the habit of leafing through them. If you find any that interest you, ask for a few old copies. After you've read a few issues, you'll have a better idea what that particular editor buys.

Also look through magazines on newsstands. Study what type of article is being published, preferred length and style, and whether or not pictures are used. Then, if you want to supply pictures to illustrate your article, you'll know what has been accepted in the past.

Postal rates are too high today to waste money sending the wrong type of article to markets that will just pop your manuscript back to you in the stamped, self-addressed envelope. This type of carelessness also tends to make editors think about closing their doors to newcomers.

What Do You Want to Write?

As you study the markets, think about the type of writing you enjoy—and the practical aspects of it. Some writers like variety. They enjoy doing a little nonfiction for magazines, writing biographies for children, and mysteries for adults. Others prefer to specialize. Sometimes you have to try a little of everything, like a smorgasbord, in order to discover what you enjoy most and what you do best.

Throughout my years of writing, I have tried many types of writing trying to "find myself." Some I have liked better than others. I don't care much for heavily documented political or scientific articles; yet I have written and sold them. I am not terribly keen on straight factual news stories—yet I have sold these too. Each has been a learning experience and a valuable lesson in self-discipline.

In the long run, though, it's probably best to do the type of writing you enjoy most. Why? Because it's fun; because you probably will do it better; and because writing is hard enough without going out of your way to make it harder.

Many times your lifestyle has a great deal to do with your decision of what type of writing to tackle. If you need money, you may prefer to turn out short articles that you know you can sell quickly in a local market. They may pay less, but they buy more and buy more often. You may have to postpone writing poetry until you need money less and have more time to write for "copies" or a small fee.

Novels may tie you up for a year or years, with no income coming in. But, when they sell, you may hit it big. TV scripts and Broadway plays are difficult to sell without an agent; but if you have access to an experimental, regional, university, or community theater, you may be able to see it performed and sell it right from your own back yard.

Mothers with young children often find that the short story and brief articles are best for them while the children are still home and very much underfoot. They can stop to give a hug, stop a fight, or wipe a nose without interrupting their thought process much. Later, when all the youngsters are finally of school age, they can branch out into gothics, lengthy novels, or major articles.

Other women prefer the longer work from the beginning. They break it into workable segments to blend with their concentrated writing time. I discovered that the type of writing I did fluctuated greatly with the number of and ages of my children. Invariably, with each new baby came an increased production in humorous articles under a thousand words; brief articles based on personal experience, memory and/or minimal research; and greeting-card verse. As the children grew, so did the lengths of my manuscripts (more on this subject in Chapter 6).

How to Write a Query

A query is an inquiry, usually in letter form, to a particular editor. It describes your proposed article and asks if he or she would be interested in seeing it. It serves as your introduction, writing sample, and sales pitch and, as such, is an important selling tool. Because of this triple function, you need to give it a great deal of thought before sending it on its way. Writing a query is a lot like flirting: Have some idea how far you want to go *before* you begin! Are you sure you really want to write it (and have time to) if you get an "okay"?

I usually start my queries with an opening paragraph designed to capture the editor's interest. Often it's an anecdote, quote, or unusual statistic. About 75 percent of the time, that first paragraph becomes my lead in the article itself.

The next one or two paragraphs describe the scope of my proposed article and give details on what I intend to include in the way of interviews, statistics, research, etc. I don't reveal all my information; just enough to show that I've given some thought to the article and have done some preliminary investigation.

If *Reader's Guide* shows that there have been a few articles published recently on my subject, I mention it and then go on to say how my proposed article will be different.

The query also should mention the tone of your proposed article, whether it will be light and fun or deep and factual. Be specific too. Don't say you'd like to write about dogs; say your idea is how dogs are trained for use in industry such as protection dogs, those used in smelling out explosives, drugs, etc.

It's also important to be realistic. Make sure you know whether there's enough information on your subject to make a good article or book. Don't promise the moon—or that you'll include quotes from the Royal Family, President of the United States, and the Pope. When you find that these people are inaccessible, you'll probably end up dropping the project.

Meanwhile, back at the publisher's, another writer (probably me) will be turned down on her query for that assignment because the editor thought you were doing it. Also, the editor may schedule your article for the November issue because you said you'd have it completed in time and she thought you'd come through.

Include in your query whatever expertise you may have for doing a particular article. In my article on preventing accidental poisoning in young children, my major qualification was that I inadvertently had poisoned my child and had to have her stomach pumped. My account of this experience, of course, had to be supported by solid research and interviews with experts. For the article on teenage attitudes on smoking my expertise was contacts with various experts plus a survey I offered to conduct in my own area.

You may have access to information no one else has—like an interview with an eighty-year-old who just swam Lake Michigan or your own experience painting the exterior of your four-story house without a ladder. If so, mention the exclusivity of your information.

List only those writing credits and qualifications that are pertinent to the proposed article. The fact that you've sold a story to *Motor Trend* won't impress an editor you're trying to interest in an article on child abuse. The fact that you've been president of your garden club won't help you get an assignment for a story on shoplifting, but it might help you get one on "Ten Ways to Grow Tulips." If you have some writing credits in a different field and you want to let the editor know, just say, "I have sold articles to other publications," and let it go at that. There are two views on this: Some people feel you should mention any professional credits, regardless of what market they were in, in order to "show" the editor that someone thought your work was good enough to buy. I feel that there's no purpose in telling a nationally known women's magazine that you've sold to *Wee Willie's Bedtime Tales*. It certainly doesn't show that you're capable of slanting an article to the women's market. But, as with many things, you must decide this question for yourself.

Never say you're a housewife unless that information is absolutely intrinsic to the article. You're selling yourself as a writer. Once you're successful, you can reveal that you get your best ideas while picking melted chewing gum out of blue-jean pockets.

If your article requires pictures, tell the editor that you can furnish them (only if you think you can). If you take your own photos, mention that too.

I always include a working title in my query. It's a psychological trick; it makes me feel as though the article is less of an idea and more of an actuality, and gives the editor something to refer to when she thinks about my idea. I like to think of it as the article's "maiden name," although sometimes it's the same one the article finally is published under.

Despite all the things you need to include in a query, you still should aim to keep it short—one page, two if absolutely necessary. A book query usually is longer. It should include a brief synopsis, an outline of chapters, and perhaps one or two sample chapters so the editor can get an idea of your writing style.

Because the letter of query usually is your first contact with an editor, it's important to make a "nice" impression. Be careful with your typing. *Always* check your spelling and facts before mailing your letter.

Two years ago I queried the editor of a regional magazine about an article I wanted to do on theater "angels" (backers or investors in plays). The mother of one of our state officials dabbled in this type of investment and I mentioned this fact in my query, adding that I thought I could get an interview with her.

The editor wrote back that she was interested in my proposed article; but as I had called this particular official by the wrong title, she was concerned about the accuracy of my work!

Was my face red! I wrote back, assuring her that my faux pas had been the fault of temporary insanity due to sniffing rubber cement. She gave me the benefit of the doubt and a "go-ahead" on the article. I learned my lesson; I was super careful and double-checked everything after that.

Check with *Writer's Market*, *Literary Market Place*, or the magazine's masthead for the name (and correct spelling) of the editor to whom you'll send the query. Be sure to include a self-addressed, stamped envelope too.

By using the query as a selling tool, you'll make the best use of your writing time because you'll write only what you know an editor has expressed an interest in seeing. Sometimes he'll give you tips on how to write it so he can use it: "I like the idea, but try slanting it along the lines of. . . ." This doesn't guarantee that he'll buy the article when you're finished, but it does mean that you'll be more on the right track.

When an editor writes, "I'll be happy to see your finished article on speculation," make certain that you follow your query exactly. I once got the "go-ahead" to do an article on speculation for *Today's Health*. Knowing that "on speculation" meant they would buy it if they liked it, I began to add details and ideas to make sure they'd like it. I wandered far astray from my original query. The editor returned my article with a personal note, "Sorry, we can't use."

About six months later they ran an article on the same subject as mine had been. Upset, I wrote to the editor and asked her why she had rejected mine.

"Your query had interested us," she said. "That's why we asked you to write the article. But you didn't do what you said you would so we couldn't use it."

Moral? Follow your query. You've given time and thought to it, the editor has expressed an interest in it, so why not write what you said you were going to?

As you begin to sell more articles, particularly to the same market, you may be able to stop writing on speculation and get definite assignments. This should be your goal, because then you know you have a firm commitment. If your article doesn't work out, or the editor who gave your the "go-ahead" leaves to study belly dancing and the new editor detests your brand of humor, you'll still get some type of "kill fee." This is only a small percentage of what you'd get if the publication had bought the article, but as least you recoup something for your time and effort. I always offer to try to rewrite first, but sometimes it just doesn't jell or the magazine has changed its image and there's no way to salvage the article. Then it's comforting to have the "kill fee," and you're free to try to sell the article elsewhere

Although some writers send a query to more than one editor at a time, I don't recommend it. You'd have a problem if two editors like your proposal, and if it's as good as you think it is, they might.

Face Your Editor So She Knows Yours

Beginning writers often are frightened by visions of the editor, this faceless, unknown monster with supreme power to accept or reject. It helps to dispel this image if you can meet at least one face-to-face.

Begin with your local markets. If you want to write for the newspaper or Sunday supplement, call the editor. Explain that you're a writer and would like to meet for a few minutes to discuss what type of material she's looking for.

If you're feeling flush, invite her for lunch. Later when you're one of her writers, she'll treat you.

Once you're a face, not just a name on a manuscript, you'll be able to write more informal queries, or call to "get a reaction" before writing a query. This doesn't mean you can get by with sloppy writing: quite the reverse. I find that I try even harder than usual to please an editor once we've met.

As you get to know certain editors more personally, you'll learn more about their likes and dislikes, what they want in an article, how they react to humor, how they feel about use of first-person stories, etc. I've had editors suggest ideas to me too, over lunch or coffee. Editors are people; some are housewife-mother-editors. A few have become good friends. That's one more "perk" (benefit) that comes with being a writer.

If you're able to visit New York, Chicago, Boston, etc., where one of the magazines you'd like to write for is published, call for an appointment with the editor. They're busy people, but usually are willing to take a little time off to meet a prospective new writer. They like to have writers from areas other than "the big city" because it gives more variety and interest to their magazine. Don't expect a full afternoon of her time, though, and don't take it personally if she can't meet with you. There always are unexpected crises in the publishing business, and she truly may be swamped.

Prepare for your meeting by reading back issues of the magazine and have some new ideas for proposed articles. Prepare a résumé of your writing credits, if any, and list subjects that you're especially well suited to write about (and why). We all have favorite issues, and one of yours may be exactly what they were discussing in the editorial meeting that morning. Even if nothing specific comes out of your meeting, you'll be more than just a name on a slip of paper when your next query crosses that editor's desk.

You also can "meet" and get to know an editor over the phone. I've always tried to relax and be myself whenever a new editor calls, even though my heart may be pounding. It helps to take off your shoes (if they're not already off), put your feet up on the desk, and pretend it's someone you've known for years.

You don't have the advantage of seeing "body language," of course, so don't be afraid to ask questions if you don't know exactly what the editor means. Repeat what you think your instructions are, just to verify them. Subtleties (and humor) can get lost over Ma Bell.

But what if you would like to write for a national magazine, can't get to the editorial office, and have no legitimate reason to chat with the editor over the phone? Then you're more the rule than the exception. Let the qualilty of your work be your calling card. You'll find that after writing for the same editor a few times, this pen-pal closeness usually develops naturally anyway.

Be Speedy—but Take Your Time
This may seem like a contradiction, but it isn't. Suppose you get the "go-ahead" from an editor. She likes your proposal and wants you to write it up, "on speculation."

Obviously, the first thing you do is call your husband and your best friend and tell them, and then corner the mailman, warning him to be prepared to carry your manuscript with the utmost care and concern, and buy a new outfit in case the editor wants you to appear on the Today Show. Then it's time to settle down and go to work.

The onus is now on you. You have to put your money where your mouth is, sink or swim, fish or cut bait, and all those other trite expressions. You have one foot in the door, and it's up to you to push the rest of yourself in—on the weight of a carefully written manuscript.

This is the point at which I usually get an anxiety attack, eat a hot-fudge sundae (or butterscotch sundae, depending on which diet I currently am breaking), and ask myself what a nice girl like me is doing in a place like this. Then I begin writing.

Start by writing the editor, thanking her for her great wisdom in recognizing the value of your proposal. In professional lingo it goes something like, "I'm pleased that you're interested in seeing my manuscript, 'Ten Ways to Build a Couch with Conch Shells!' I should have it in your hands by. . . ." At this point you need to realistically evaluate how long it will take you to complete the article.

You've done, it is hoped, a great deal of preliminary work in order to write the query. You know how many shells its takes to build a couch with conch, how long it takes, how to make conch cushions, what to do when the conch couch crumbles (or gets clammy), and where to find natural springs. You need to line up interviews with conch couch craftsmen, take step-by-step photos, etc. Determine a realistic deadline leaving you room for family situations that may (and usually do) arise. Make it far enough away to give you time for a good job, but close enough to ensure that the editor doesn't leave for a different magazine, that the magazine doesn't lose interest in do-it-yourself articles, and that environmentalists don't make conch collecting not only passe, but subversive as well.

Almost every writer has lost out on the sale of an article (or book) because he or she took too long to complete it. Manuscripts are like soufflés: if you rush them, they fall flat. But if you let them sit too long, they're ruined as well.

Once you commit yourself to a deadline, do everything in your power to keep it. The editor may be planning to include your article in the issue featuring a sponge cot and an eel end table, and if you ruin her "Furniture From the Sea" issue, she'll probably scratch you from her list of professional writers.

Musts to Remember

There are many technical points to remember in preparing your manuscript for an editor.

You need to learn how to present your work in a professional manner. The editor doesn't know or care that you're a housewife who works in faded gym shorts and an old "I Like Ike" T-shirt. She'll judge your work as professional as long as it's well done and appears in professional form.

Always type your manuscrpt. It doesn't matter if you've always gotten A in penmanship or you just received your Ph.D. in Italic writing. If you want your manuscript read—and that's why you wrote it—type it. If you can't type, get someone to do it for you. Use pica, rather than elite, and use a roman face, never script or any of those "cute" type styles. Use black ribbon, preferably a reasonably new one. If you long to use a violet, chartreuse, or plaid ribbon, save it for letters to your fans. If you use it for your manuscripts, you'll never get published and won't have any fans.

Always type your manuscripts on white paper and on one side of the paper, leaving one- to one-and-a-half-inch borders. Don't use onionskin paper or the easily erasable stock because your type will smear and no one will take the time to guess what it was you were trying to say. Unless you are Alexandre Dumas, who wrote his magazine articles on pink paper, his poetry on yellow, and his novels on blue, save colored paper for drafts on carbon copies.

Always keep a carbon copy of your manuscript. Manuscripts have a way of being lost in the mail, mauled by the editor's malamute, or inadvertently shredded for a New Year's celebration. If you can whip out your carbon, you'll save yourself a great deal of heartache.

Another good reason for keeping a carbon or Xerox of your manuscript is that your editor may call and ask you to rewrite pages 26-28. If you have a carbon copy, you'll know what she's talking about. Of course, if you're one of those people who can rattle off her social security number and driver's license number, you've already memorized your manuscript.

With long manuscripts, such as a book, it's a good idea to have two carbons of everything you write and keep them in separate places. My secretary thought I was being paranoid when I asked her to keep a copy of this manuscript "in case anything happens to my copy."

I *was* paranoid about it—but with good reason, as it turned out. I had an air-conditioning leak in my study when about half the draft was completed. I woke up one Sunday morning and discovered my manuscsript soaking in about a quarter-inch of water. Naturally I did what any writer would have done. I became hysterical. It didn't matter that the wallpaper was peeling, the rug was sopping, the ceiling was turning green with mold—all I had eyes for was the thick soggy mass that had been the focus of my life for more days than I cared to remember.

Luckily, we had made an extra copy of it and I was spared a major rewriting job. I strongly recommend that you give a copy of any lengthy manuscript to your husband to store in his office, to a friend with a dry basement or an attic, or to your mother to keep along with your booties and first lock of hair. You never know when *your* air conditioner will leak!

Once you've typed the final draft of your article or manuscript, read it over carefully for typing errors. You may be sick of it by this time, but appearances do count. Although you want your manuscript to be more than just a pretty face (and if you've researched and written it carefully it will be), even the best manuscript with spelling errors, typing mistakes, and too many handwritten corrections can disturb an editor. You've worked hard and professionally this far; don't let down now.

Once you've checked the manuscript over carefully, it's time to send it on its way. Be sure to include a self-addressed, stamped envelope—one that the manuscript can fit into for its return, should the editor suffer from a momentary lapse of good judgment and reject it. (Omitting this courtesy will *not* keep your manuscript from being rejected. It just will prevent it from being returned to you.)

What about cover letters? Many writers say you don't need to send a cover letter, that the manuscript will speak for itself. This is probably true when you send an article in cold, without querying first. But when I have queried an editor and gotten an expression of interest on her part, I usually include a short note, reminding her that I had queried her on the idea, received a "go-ahead," and, therefore, am submitting the article as suggested. Editors are extremely busy people. Although I'd love to think that I'm the only writer who really counts with them, I know that's not true. If they're even half as forgetful as I am, I think they'd appreciate being reminded that they originally had liked my proposal and that I'm not just sending the manuscript in cold.

Don't add in the note that you hope she'll buy the article because you want to prove to your husband that you haven't been wasting your time, or that you need a sale in order to get an A in the creative-writing course you're taking, or that you need the money to repair your husband's baby spoon (that got "eaten" by the garbage disposal) before your mother-in-law comes to visit. I haven't tried those ploys, but those who have admit they didn't work.

Time Is Money

If you're like most of us who combine writing with home and family, you have a limited amount of time. Constantly be aware that time is money. There's a reason lawyers keep a timer by their phone. They know their time is valuable and they charge their clients accordingly.

You need to apply the same principle. The more time you save, the more time you'll have to devote to your writing. The more writing you do, the more you'll sell (you hope) and the more money you'll make.

Always be alert for ways you can save time, through time management, better organization, and a businesslike attitude.

Use postcards, when possible, rather than typing formal letters.

Never retype letters because you've make one mistake. Use your own judgment on this. If your corrections make your letter messy and illegible, then by all means redo it. But I've received many letters from editors with a correction or two done in longhand.

Try to keep your supplies and papers organized without spending all your time dividing and subdividing your filing system. Everyone's filing needs are different. But the purpose of filing is to keep things safe until you need them and to make it easy for you to put your hands on them quickly. I have one file cabinet for published work and one for unpublished articles. Brochures, notes, and booklets are filed under major headings, like: "Contact lenses," "Depression," "England." My individual article files are arranged in groupings, with headings such as: "Women's Interests," "Travel," "Humor," etc. Then each file is arranged alphabetically. If "Misc." gets too fat, I subdivide it. Published articles are filed according to my title, not the published one. That may not be the best way, but it works for me as I never can remember someone else's title.

Have a supply drawer (or box, basket, or bin). If you have to spend two hours looking for a new ribbon or carbon, you won't have much time left for writing.

When you plan a proposed article or book, remember to figure not only the cost of your supplies, but what your time is worth as well.

Stories requiring numerous interviews, travel, and/or extensive research must pay more or you're losing money. I have some regular markets that don't pay much, but they buy consistently. I try to keep my hourly rate down on these by never attempting to begin an article that I think will cost me more in expenses and my time than I can hope to see in payment. If one that I've promised to such a market begins to get out of hand, I'll look for a secondary market where I can send a different version of basically the same idea, to make it pay. Sound too commercial? Too crass? Perhaps, but remember that Samuel Johnson said, "Anyone who won't write for money is a fool!"

Sometimes, when you're beginning, it's worth investing in yourself and doing an article for a national magazine even though you know you'll come out short when the bills are paid. In that case, consider the writing credit as part of your pay—but don't be so eager to see your byline that you work for free forever.

How To Determine the "Cost" of an Article

I've already explained why you need to know the approximate cost of an article. It's no different from a shoemaker estimating his costs to determine the price of his shoes. Unfortunately, most of us writers are not in the position where we can put a price tag on our goods, so we have to work the other way and keep costs down.

If an article is going to involve questionnaires, consider the cost of duplicating them, postage, and the time you spend tabulating them.

Interviews also can be costly: babysitting fees, parking costs, and the time spent on the interview. Time is money. If you've only earned one hundred dollars so far this year, your writing time is worth less than if you earn one thousand dollars or more an article. When you're beginning you often have to expend more time and energy putting an article or story together, but once you begin to sell, you need to keep your unit costs in line.

If you have to travel for your article or take pictures, try to spread the information out for other articles as well. When you travel, remember to consider the cost of food and gas along with your time expenditure.

Do you do your own typing? Or must you pay someone else to do it?

If you have a typist, be sure to include his or her salary when figuring your article costs.

Multiple Sales: How to Get More Mileage from One Manuscript

Don't rest on your laurels (and respend the same check five times) after you've sold an article to a magazine. There are many magazines that buy reprints. You'll find them listed in *Writer's Market*. Get permission from your original publisher, and submit proof of publication, along with when and where the manuscript was published to the reprint publisher.

Many newspapers and Sunday supplements are willing to buy an article published elsewhere, providing it was in a noncompeting market. Don't try to sell the same feature to two papers whose circulation areas overlap.

If you have an article that has appeal to different trade publications, you often can sell the same material to both of them. An article dealing with ways to use sewing-machine parts to fix bicycles, for instance, might be accepted by both a home economics publication and a hobby magazine. If in doubt, it might pay you to ask.

Once you have done major research for an article, don't file it away. Rewrite the material for different markets. This is different from selling reprint rights, because in this situation you actually rewrite: changing the slant, the contents, and the organization of your material to fit a new market.

For example, the subject of time management is of interest to many people—and would be of interest to markets with widely different, non-overlapping readership. Take the original research you did for your article on organization for businessmen and write a second article, this one slanted toward homemakers, telling them how they can apply those same proven theories in their homes to get more out of their working day.

Without doing a great deal more research, you could seek out successsful women who are homemakers and also working in offices or in volunteer jobs, using them as your examples.

Youngsters also can benefit from learning efficient use of their time. Every teenager would be interested in ways to expand her after-school hours to make time for homework, sports, part-time job, dinner, TV, and social life. By using the same principles as in the other articles, you could write another article, this one showing teens how to take control of their lives.

In each case, slant your writing for your particular audience. It could be farmers; theater students; doctors who want to see more patients yet still keep up with their medical journals, spend time with their families, relax, and play a little golf. You need different examples, peer interviews, and statistics to interest each publication, but the basic information doesn't change. Just answer your audience's question—"Why should I care about this?"—and you can recycle the same information into checks for you.

Expand Your Productivity

Try to have more than one article in the works at all times—or one article and a book. Each can be at a different stage; first draft of one and final for another. As long as you don't get confused, it's a good way to expand your efforts. You could be writing about horseshoe crabs for a scientific magazine, for example, and as long as all of your research is handy and fresh in your mind, also do another version for a lay audience and/or a children's market.

At present, I'm working on this book, have just completed a 2,500-word article for *Glamour*, am reworking a children's picture book, writing a column for a weekly newspaper, and producing three 750-word articles for local markets.,

If you're just beginning to write, it's probably best to concentrate on only one thing at a time. But as soon as you begin selling, consider expanding your productivity.

The master of this type of writing, of course, is Isaac Asimov, who has written more than 200 books, 1,200 articles, and 250 short stories. We'll probably never even come close to this record, but then he doesn't take his kids to soccer practice, cook dinner for seven (four of whom are picky eaters), or have six loads of dirty clothes lining the kitchen floor, waiting to be washed as soon as the machine's fixed. At least, I don't think he does.

Once you know a subject, specialize. It's fine to be all things to everyone; but when you know a subject well, put that expertise to work for you over and over again.

I have a friend and writing colleague who has written numerous articles about interior decorating for homes and offices. Now she knows all the experts by their first names. She's made all the important contacts. She'd be crazy not to milk her subject. Right now editors are calling her with *their* ideas for her to write. That's what happens when you become known as a good writer in any specialized field.

Draw Upon Your Own Experience

Anything you learn or experience while being a volunteer in any type of charitable organization may be recycled for possible use in future articles or books. Naturally, you don't use actual names or situations without permission.

Research gained from writing brochures or radio spots for the American Heart Association, for example, could be included in articles demonstrating the importance of exercise, how heart patients can become active again and lead normal lives, or what to do when someone has a heart attack.

Be aware of your emotions too, using them and experience gained through volunteer work with crippled children, the elderly, or the visually handicapped as background material for fiction, or as the central focus on an article or book.

These experiences, gained through the charitable side of you as a writer, are no different from other experiences that may be used as ideas for your work. Yet many writers forget about them when trying to come up with "something to write about."

Pulitzer Prize-winner Henry Brooks Adams wrote, "All experience is an arch to build upon." He was right. And it's especially true when you're a writer.

What About Subsidy Presses?

Sounds as though it takes a lot of work and a great deal of time to get into print, doesn't it? The truth is, it does. And finding a publisher who wants to print your book usually takes even longer than for a magazine article.

Many writers take a short cut and pay publishers to have their books printed. These are subsidy publishers, nicknamed "vanity" presses. They run ads in local papers, saying that they're publishers in search of authors. They are, of course. And it's doubtful that they'll reject your manuscript. But rather than paying the writer for the privilege of printing her book (a percentage of the sales, called "royalties"), these subsidy presses charge the writer for printing it.

Does it really matter? Isn't the important thing just "getting published"? It depends on why you want your book published. If it's to prove to everyone that you finally had a book published, and you can afford the five thousand dollars or more that it costs to have it printed, go ahead. But it's doubtful that your book will get any publicity. It probably won't get reviewed either. Most reviewers won't review a book from a subsidy press—and libraries won't buy them, bookstores won't stock them, and, after your mother, favorite aunt, and best friend buy a copy (or get one free), no one else will touch them. You'll find yourself with wall-to-wall copies of *The Fascinating Story of My Life*.

Most subsidy press salesmen will disagree, of course. They'll point with pride to famous authors like O. Henry and Thoreau who published their own material. That may have been true. But that was a different era, before books were promoted in magazines, newspapers, and on television talk shows. If your book is good, if you write well, and if there's a market for your book, find a publisher that pays you. Most of us housewife-writers work too hard to make time for our writing to waste it (and our money) by paying for publication. We've all got enough books around the house to dust.

Self-publication is a little different, though. For example, many times a a woman will create and collect so many speciality recipes that her friends will urge her to "publish" them. This often is true with special cookbooks; cooking for children with cancer or diabetes, ethnic cooking, etc.

The writer gives her manuscript directly to a printer. There's no middleman involved. The writer is responsible for distribution of the book after it's printed. Sometimes, if she's lucky, the book sells well and attracts the interest of a commercial publisher. Vicki Lansky's *Taming the C.A.N.D.Y. Monster* began this way.

Many housewife-writers have successfully published books that were guides of their home towns, "what to do on a rainy day" for children, specialized sewing hints, inspirational messages, arts and crafts, hobbies, etc.

If you choose this route, remember that you may be so busy checking stock in bookstores, filling orders, proofing editions, etc., that you don't leave yourself time to write.

Speak Up When You Get the Chance

Don't think I'm recommending that you buttonhole everyone in the elevator and ask if they've read your article in January's *Mad Mama's Mumblings*. Nor do I think that you necessarily should take copies of your latest book door-to-door and sell them along with your daughter's Girl Scout cookies, although I might change my mind.

Once you begin to feel good about your work—and confident in your ability as a a writer, you'll begin to think of ways to promote yourself and your writing.

Accept speaking dates when they're offered. As difficult as it may be to speak before an audience, do it. The more exposure you get, the more readers will look for your byline. People enjoy reading something written by someone they've actually met. It will help create an interest in your work and should persuade editors to publish your work because they know you "have a following." That's why book publishers try to get dates for their authors on national television talk shows. They know people are more likely to buy a book when they've seen and heard the author.

Be sure to give the program chairman a list of your writing credits before you speak to a group. This is no time to be modest. You may know that you were paid in copies, but that's probably more pay for writing than most (or any) of your audience has received.

Never lie about your credits or say that you've sold something to a magazine when, in truth, it was a letter to the editor that was published (although even a letter to the editor is better than not being published at all).

There's a fine line between bragging and acknowledging success. But this field is a hard one, and there are far more people wanting to write and be published than those who do and are! So if you've earned the "warm fuzzies," enjoy them.

One word of warning, though. Don't get so carried away with speaking engagements that you forget that you're a writer. Sometimes it's difficult, because it's much more fun to talk to people about writing than getting back to doing it. But as Alex Haley, author of Roots, discovered, you can be so busy speaking about what you've already written that you don't have time to write anything new.

Like so many other things, this requires proper balance. Keep your writing in its order of priority in your life. Coordinate other things, like speaking engagements, to support, not dominate, your writing. It is the gravy, not the meat and potatoes.

Think of additional ways to use your published work to get other assignments. If you've done an article on "Ways to Stretch Your Food Dollars," for example, have it reprinted (you need to get permission from the publisher) and offer it to the grocery stores in your area. Do the same with suitable material for nursery schools, camps, banks, laundries, etc. They may contract you to write for them sometime in the future.

I once received free publicity assistance from the subject of one of my articles. I had written about the owner of a quick-print shop who also was an artist and did his own artwork. In addition to interviewing him, I took some pictures and submitted the entire package to one of the printing industry's small publications. They bought it. The owner was pleased with the published article, reprinted it, and included it with all of his completed orders. I still hear from people who read my byline on the article he enclosed with their stationery, flyers, etc.

Am I embarrassed with the extra publicity? Not at all. And neither should you be. If you get even one extra assignment because of an article you wrote, or as a result of publicity you received because of your writing, you're that much further ahead on your writing career.

So, if the society editor calls from the paper and wants to do a feature about you and how you manage to write, entertain one hundred for a sit-down Chinese dinner, and teach concert violin to your eight preschool-age children, say "yes."

Remember what Hillel said in the Talmud:

"If I am not for myself, who will be for me? If I am only for myself, what am I? If not now, when?"

Persistence=Published

Determination, persistence, stick-to-itiveness. Whatever word you choose, it amounts to the same thing. Given the same amount of ability, the main difference between a selling writer professional— and a hobbyist is that the professional didn't give up.

How persistent are you? Your "PL" (persistence level) often can be the key to success. How well do you score on this "PL" quiz?

1. Do you have a regular routine for your writing?
2. Do you study market requirements?
3. Do you rework your first draft to make it better?
4. Do you proof your final draft?
5. Do you begin something new as soon as you mail off your completed manuscript?
6. Do you look over a rejected manuscript to see where it might be improved?
7. Do you send a rejected manuscript back out to a second possible market shortly after it's been returned from the first?
8. Do you rewrite and resubmit when requested by an editor?
9. Do you keep queries flowing?
10. Do you ignore comments like, "Why don't you give up? You'll never sell anything"; or "Come bowling with us. You've been tied to that typewriter long enough"?

If you can answer eight to ten questions "yes," you have a high persistence level. If you only answered five to seven questions in the affirmative, you might reconsider your motivations for wanting to become a writer. If you answered fewer than five questions with a "yes," you probably are more interested in talking about being a writer than being one.

Luckily, your "PL" can be raised, and you're the one who can do it.

Putting Something Back: Sharing Your "Gift"

Writing for charity has many dividends. The first one is obvious: you are contributing a valuable service to that organization. It is every bit as important as contributing money, stuffing envelopes, or answering phones.

The secondary advantages are a bit more personal, more selfish. (Selfish isn't a bad word anymore, you know.) This type of work gives you additional experience, lets more people know the quality of writing you're capable of, and, if you're a beginning writer, gives you additional credits.

In offering your services as a writer, be certain to communicate exactly what you are willing to do. If you don't want to write publicity for newspapers, but would be willing to write a brochure that could be used for fund raising, say so. If you enjoy writing occasional features or news releases, but don't want the ongoing responsibility of a monthly newsletter, tell them.

No one can read your mind. By volunteering for exactly what you'd like to do, your services will be readily accepted 99.8 percent of the time. (A Shimberg Instant Statistic, but one that I think would hold up under scrutiny.)

You'll probably feel relaxed about your voluntary writing assignments because they're free from stress. You *know* they'll be accepted. This can help you develop self-confidence in your work. Transfer this feeling over to your writing-for-fee work as well. After all, few organizations would use your writing if it were lousy, even if it were free!

Get Credit for Your Work

Theologian Nathaniel Emmons wrote, "Make no display of your talents or attainments; for everyone will clearly see, admire and acknowledge them so long as you cover them with the beautiful veil of modesty."

I disagree. An overly modest writer loses valuable recognition that can be gained through bylines, listing of proper credit when due her, as well as publicity that could lead to additional writing assignments.

Recently, I completed a booklet for the American Cancer Society,

Florida Division. It took me many weeks to write, involved some travel and a great deal of emotional outlay. When the Division's staff suggested that my name be listed as author, I demurred.

They persisted, and I reconsidered. I finally agreed because I realized that the byline was fairly earned, that anyone disagreeing with me or questioning what I had written certainly had the right to know who had been the author, and that it would be a credit to add to my list of medically oriented writings.

Does that sound mercenary? Not when you consider that I am a professional writer. I always am receptive to offers to write for payment. Just as the architect uses a building he has just designed as a "sample" of what he is capable of in order to get additional jobs, so must the writer use her work as an ongoing sample case. If someone likes the quality and the style of writing found in the work I did as a volunteer for the American Cancer Society, they may contact me to write something for them, for pay.

That's not why I did it—but it's a nice extra. Call it free publicity or just a "perk" (extra benefit) of doing volunteer work. Don't feel guilty about it either. Many women today are using their volunteer efforts as a springboard for future paid employment. You, as a writer, can do the same with your volunteer contributions. Just make certion that your new "boss" doesn't want you to work for free too!

I'm active in a local university theater support group. For two years, another writer and I edited the quarterly newsletter, a tongue-in-cheek, fun-oriented publication with silly clip-art, shameless puns, and news of what's happening in the theater department.

Recently, I complained to the dean of the theater department that we had received no feedback; no one had mentioned that they either loved or hated our efforts.

"I don't think anyone bothers to read it," I complained.

She smiled. "Do you think the problem could be that you never said who the editors were?"

We hadn't even thought about that. In the next issue, we printed our names as "Editors due to circumstances beyond our control."

To our surprise, we immediately began getting input from our readers, and quickly learned what they liked—as well as what we had been omitting that they wanted to know. We also learned that the newsletter *was* being read and was developing a good following. Had we followed Nathaniel Emmons's advice and remained modestly in the background, we never would have known.

Follow the Leaders (How Others Make It Happen)

14.

       I've always enjoyed meeting other writers, trading notes: "How do you . . . ," "When do you . . . ," and "Where do you. . . ." It really doesn't matter if they're far more published than I am, or if they've never made a sale.

Writers, especially those of us who also are housewives and mothers, gravitate to each other, like grease spots on a new knit blouse.

"We know we're 'safe' when we're together," one housewife-writer said. "We can let our hair down and talk shop . . . and know the person listening really is interested.

A few years ago I was invited to a party where I knew no one except the host and hostess. Cocktail parties make me uncomfortable even when I know everyone. I took refuge in the library. After a passage of awkward time, my hostess brought someone over to me.

"This is _____ ," she said. "She writes too."

Those three little words were magical. The two of us began swapping "fish stories." She was more published than I, but we had found a common ground. No wonder so many writers enjoy the security of writers' clubs.

Another housewife-writer and I "talk shop" through the mail. (We write to each other when we should be working.) "We housewife-writers are like a sorority," she said. "We care for each other and share the highs and lows."

Many of these women also were willing to share their thoughts and experiences, describing what has been their most difficult moments in trying to blend housewife, writer, mother, wife and how they've coped.

They all took time off from their writing to help me with mine—to reflect and to comment. I appreciate it and thank them herewith for their courtesy and camaraderie.

PEG BRACKEN: (*The I Hate to Cook Book; The I Hate to Housekeep Book; I Try to Behave Myself; Peg Bracken's Appendex to the I Hate to Cook Book; I Didn't Come Here to Argue; But I Wouldn't Have Missed It for the World; I Hate to Cook Almanac—A Book of Days*)

"You ask what is the most difficult part of being a housewife/writer/mother. I note that you don't include just plain wife, and I'm wondering if that was on purpose. Certainly you can be the first three without being the fourth. It often happens, too, that if you spend too much time being the first three when you have a husband, you'll end up without one. It is a calculated risk. On the other hand, writing can be more interesting and more fun than a husband is, depending on the husband, and more rewarding too, also depending on the husband. . . .

"But that isn't answering your question. In my experience, the hardest part of being all four at once is—of course—knowing how to split your time among the four; deciding what your priorities are. It is truly hard, sometimes, when they are all screaming at once: the baby for attention; the husband likewise; ditto the book or story (because for some damnable reason it is at times like this that the writing part of you moves into high gear and you're producing a dozen ideas at once without even time to jot them down). . . . As for the poor old house, it doesn't scream, it sits there and sulks, looking like the devil, and you feel bad about that too. . . . And by the way, in spite of all the talk about liberated males and females, I don't see that things have changed much. In the young marriages or living arrangements I know, it's *still* the woman who eventually notices that the curtain ruffle is heavy with dust and something's got to be done.

"So the hardest thing, in my experience, is feeling guilty on all four fronts most of the time. From the vantage point of years now, with my children grown and my husband philosophic (and easy going) I can see that it was pretty foolish to feel as guilty as I used to feel. My writing didn't hurt anyone that I can see; the children turned out all right; they knew I loved them—and that's what mainly matters.

"As to how I resolved it or resolve it now, I didn't and don't. I muddle along. The main thing I do is get up very early, at 3:30 or 4:00, and go to my office six miles from the house and get to work. I got up early when the children were little too, because those were the only guaranteed-uninterrupted hours I had, though I didn't have an office away from the house then. I certainly recommend that, for anyone who can possibly hack it. But one must find and keep inviolate—somehow—those three or four hours, because they're certainly not going to find you."

MARJORIE HOLMES: (*Who Am I, God?*; *Hold Me Up a Little Longer, Lord*; *Two From Galilee*; *Nobody Else Will Listen*; *I've Got to Talk to Somebody, God*; and *How Can I Find You, God?*)

"For me, the most difficult part of combining writing with mothering and keeping house was the terrible tug-of-war between my desire to be at the typewriter and the love-bond that tied me to the children.

"I was an impassioned mother, savoring every minute with them, taking copious notes on everything they did (and that we did together), keeping scrapbooks of their developments and sayings, taking pictures. (All of which proved invaluable later when there was this fierce and terrible compulsion to write. An emotional and physical NEED to be productive.)

"I tried to resolve this by keeping on schedule—bathing and feeding at certain times (I nursed all my four babies), then flying to work when they were asleep, at school or supervised play. I also was able to make enough money to have household help (just barely enough at first), for I did NOT have a passionate desire to cook or keep house. But life, alas, has little respect for schedules; children get sick, or just need cuddling; maids don't show up. There were thousands of times when I thought I would go mad, mad, mad with the interruptions, the frustrations. Yet no matter what happened I managed to creep to my typewriter and turn out a little something almost every day. Even a paragraph, a scrap of an idea or observation.

"I learned not to fret and fume and scream that 'Life won't let me write.' Simply to realize that life didn't *care* whether or not I wrote—but *I* cared, and somehow, some way, I would do it. This steely 'just try and stop me' attitude is very important. It develops the patience a writer must have for the long, long haul. For the defeats and frustrations that come, not from a family, but from the whole serious business of being a professional. And just as important—perhaps more so—it establishes the writing *habit*. If you go to your desk every day and write (preferably at the same time, but if not, *some* time) you become safe from procrastination. Sheer behaviorism takes over. There never will come a time when you dread writing, or think you 'can't write.'

"Back to that original conflict . . . I can honestly say I don't think I ever neglected my children. (In fact, I overcompensated, doing a lot of things for them 'normal' mothers might think unnecessary.) But I didn't neglect my writing either. If you have genuine talent that's important. A gift God expects you to use. And I firmly believe that if you want to do anything in life badly enough—and it's worth doing—you can."

BETTE GREENE: (*Summer of My German Soldier; Morning Is a Long Time Coming; Philip Hall Likes Me. I Reckon Maybe.*)

"Handing out rules on how to survive as a housewife/writer/mother must be similar to handing out rules for surviving in an active combat zone. After two children, one husband and twenty years of writing, however, I will admit to knowing where the land mines are buried and the enemy's heavy artillery is entrenched.

"The first 'enemy' that the housewife/writer/mother may have to face is to freely and without guilt convince herself that she deserves a daily block of time that belongs only to her. Borrow, beg or steal that time, but, by all means, secure your daily quota of the stuff.

"I guess the second rule should be the first rule. Believe in yourself. I'll say it twice. Believe in yourself. Lots of time I've rendered myself impotent by repeatedly asking myself: What can I, a high school dropout from Arkansas, possibly find to place on paper that would even mildly interest anybody else?

"But sooner or later another internal voice would come along with the answer: If I can somehow find the courage to write with all the passion I feel, then people will not only read; they will respond.

"Finally, I would remind the housewife/writer/mother that nobody ever told them that writing was an easy game to play, and so they should let nothing, absolutely nothing, put them down. My novel *Summer of My German Soldier* was refused by eighteen publishers. . . ."

PHYLLIS REYNOLDS NAYLOR: (*Crazy Love*; *Witch Water*; *Witch's Sister*; *Walking Through the Dark*; *How I Came to Be a Writer*; and *In Small Doses*)

"The most difficult part of being a housewife/writer/mother for me was to find time to work without being interrupted. Noise does not bother me particularly, as long as I don't have to be involved in that noise. I can write in restaurants or train stations if I know that nobody is likely to talk to me. At home, however, when the children were young, I could never 'get into' my work and sustain the mood, because sooner or later someone would need my attention.

"I discovered, however, after the first child was born, that I was actually writing more than before, simply because I was using my time more efficiently. I wrote feverishly during nap times, early in the morning, or in the evenings. When my children reached the toddler stage and nap times were shorter, I hired a lovely woman to come in once a week and sit with them all day while I went to the library and wrote for eight hours. When I felt desperate for more time, my husband would sometimes sit with the children in the evening while I went again to the library.

"Now with the boys in school, there is no real problem. My writing day begins the moment they are out the door, and with an hour off for lunch, does not end till they get home in the afternoon. As soon as they leave in the morning, I let all housework go, and pick it up again when they are home. I can listen to them while I am making beds or washing windows, but I cannot write when they are around, so writing takes first place when I'm alone. They are old enough now, too, so that if I need additional time on the weekends, I can simply go in the den and close the door, and they respect that. But it means listening, really listening to them when I do give them time, and making sure we have many other opportunities to do things together."

LOIS DUNCAN: (*Down a Dark Hall*; *I Know What You Did Last Summer*; *Killing Mr. Griffin*; *Point of Violence*; *Summer of Fear*; *When the Bough Breaks*; and numerous articles in *Good Housekeeping*, *Ladies' Home Journal*, *Redbook*, etc.)

"I often feel that I have the best of all worlds: a husband and children, and a stimulating career; work I love, and a chance to schedule it to fit with the other parts of my life. I look at women who work an eight-hour day outside the home, and I can't imagine how they do it. (I tried it myself once for six awful months and almost had a nervous breakdown.) With writing, it's different. It can be done for an hour here and an hour there—or occasionally for long stretches of time—depending upon what other demands there are.

"When babies were small, I wrote during their naptimes. When they started school, my writing time expanded to fill the time they were away. I could still make it to all the school plays, doctor appointments, band recitals, or whatever. If children wanted to come home for lunch, I was here. If somebody threw up on the playground, I could come get him.

"Like all 'working mothers' (part time or otherwise), I have only a limited amount of free time, and it can't go everywhere. I do very little housekeeping. We have a cleaning woman who comes in on Thursday and shovels a path through the living room, changes the beds, and scrubs the kitchen floor. Aside from that, I pretty much let things pile up. I run laundry all week and fold it Saturday morning at the breakfast table while my husband has a second cup of coffee. I'm a good cook, and we eat by candlelight (that's supposed to make up for the fact that the breakfast dishes are still in the sink). But my work and my family are my life. I don't play tennis or jog or collect for charities or belong to clubs or go to luncheons; I'm not homeroom mother or Brownie leader or cookie chairman or PTA president.

"You can't do it all. You have to choose. Luckily, my husband is happy with things as they are. I was a professional writer when he met me, so he knew what he was getting into. He is an electrical engineer, successful enough in his own field so that he doesn't feel threatened by having me successful in mine."

EVELYN WILDE MAYERSON: (*Sanjo*; three medical textbooks; and stories in *Highlights for Children*)

"I've learned to be jealous of my time. Nobody else will watch your time if *you* don't. I'm not reluctant to take the phone off the hook or, if it rings before I can do that, will say 'I just can't talk now.' I work best in the early morning. I try to write at least two hours a day and, when I'm traveling, will write in longhand. You'll never get lost time back again, so it's a constant choice, a trade. 'Will I go to the beach or go sailing—or write?'

"When the kids were small, I wrote in the evening. It was hard because my energy level was low after 8 p.m. But it was important to me. Writing was and is my work. [She also is a professor of psychiatry, a communications therapist, and commutes between her home in Miami to the University of South Florida in Tampa, where she teaches at the medical school.]

"I'm not all that fussy about housework. The kids bring the clothes to the washing machine. It doesn't make sense to bother putting it in a hamper first. We have simple meals. I've learned tricks to housekeeping, like cleaning as you go. It saves time.

"I'm efficient too. When I leave a room, I take papers out with me. I only shop once a week. The secret here is to have a list and to go after you've eaten. Then you won't buy as much. I have a lot of lists: drugstore lists, clothing lists, etc.

"My sons, who are grown now, have learned to be independent. They both are excellent cooks, know how to use the washing machine and dryer, take care of themselves in general. I think we do children a disservice when we try to do all things for them. I don't have a daughter, but I think women writers who do are excellent role models for them.

"Probably the hardest part of being a writer is having to solve your own problems. A doctor or lawyer can consult with a colleague, but we writers have to be able to critique and edit our own work. But I wouldn't have it any other way. The act of composing is a joyous experience. The rewards are in the process itself; publishing, and all else that goes with it, is gravy. When you're writing, you're being your own person. . . ."

SHIRLEY L. RADL: (*Mother's Day Is Over* and *How to Be a Mother and a Person Too*)

"I would say that the most difficult part of being a housewife/writer/ mother has been being able to stay with my work despite all the interruptions. If you're a woman and you're at home, you are a housewife even if you work sixty hours a week rushing to meet a deadline. Oddly, when I stand back and look at the situation objectively, I can't really say that my children, who are very demanding, represent the major problem. It is that when you have children, they have friends, and the friends have mothers, so the doorbell and the phone are constantly ringing. . . .

"And then, because I am home, it is assumed that I don't work—I'm available. I get phone calls from the school, the PTA, and various committees asking me to bake cakes, chaperone on field trips, run over to the school and bring forgotten books, and hundreds of other things. And friends and acquaintances who want something or are just plain bored feel perfectly free to call me up or just drop by.

"It isn't just that the interruptions take time from my

work; . . . some of my most inspired passages were shattered mid-thought by a jangling phone, someone at the door, one of my children rushing in to tell me something, or even some child I've never seen before needing first-aid.

"The most important thing I've done to cope with this is to psych myself up for it, and not let it keep me from writing—even if what I turn out during the course of a day is completely unintelligible. I keep my eye on my goals, and I'm very determined. And disciplined. Unless there are unusual circumstances, I force myself to sit down and write for at least three hours a day, and try hard not to look to the right or the left. I take advantage of every minute that the children are away from home. . . .

"Another thing I have done . . . is cut back on ALL outside activities that aren't essential to the well-being of my family or to my work. I even dropped out of my writing club because going to the meeting usually meant that the day was shot. . . . I don't belong to the PTA, I don't play tennis, I don't talk on the phone unless I have to, and I don't go to a shrink (my typewriter is my shrink).

"I've told friends that they should call before they drop by and I've explained to people what one interruption can do at a critical time. And when people call up to chat, I've finally gotten up the courage to say that I can only talk for a minute or two. I've found that consistently being unavailable for chit-chat has substantially reduced the number of phone calls I get.

"I do suggest to novice writers that they have realistic expectations regarding how much they can accomplish and how difficult it is to get published. I've been quite successful in recent years, but there were a number of lean years even though I worked very hard. Right now I'm making money and yet am not working as hard as I did during the years I couldn't seem to make anything click. And I feel that I've been one of the lucky ones. Writing is like playing blackjack, only more work. A while back, for example, *New West* published a piece about a guy who sent one of Jerzy Kosinski's award-winning books to something like twenty-five agents and thirty-five pub- lishers. . . . Every one of them turned it down. . . . This man had retyped the book and put his own name on the manuscript. I am convinced that there are monumental books sitting in bottom drawers collecting dust, buried under rejection slips."

ANN TOLAND SERB: (*Mother-in-Law*; *Love, Lollipops and Laundry*; and *Stop the World . . . Our Gerbils Are Loose*, the last two books with Joan Wester Anderson)

"It's about time we housewife-writers got an entire volume to ourselves. It took me a while to sort through all those 'most difficult parts' and make a selection. Tough job, like choosing a favorite child from my tribe of eight. But I've narrowed it down to two major problems:

Problem one: finding the time. (It's probably the most common problem since it's the question everybody always asks.)

"Solution: I gave up trying to find the time six years ago, when I realized there wasn't any. When I began to write, I had an infant, a toddler, two preschoolers, and four grammar-school children home for summer vacation. It wasn't the most advantageous moment to embark on a new career. However, I was too tired for tennis, too busy for bridge, and too poor to go shopping. (I also had no babysitter and couldn't find both good shoes at once.) Writing seemed a perfect escape, while trying to hold down the family fort. I devoted the little ones' naptime to the typewriter, and squeezed in whatever other spare moments I could. (Not much TV in the evenings back then.)

"I coauthored my first book with Joan Anderson, *Love, Lollipops and Laundry* (Our Sunday Visitor, 1976) while tending two preschoolers. There wasn't time to write a book, but we did it anyway. When my youngest entered kindergarten, I celebrated by grinding out my first solo venture, *Mother-In-Law* (Carillon Books, 1978). When that was done, I finished the year by a repeat performance with Joan, *Stop the World . . . Our Gerbils Are Loose!* (Doubleday, 1979). These were totally impossible projects, but I was too busy doing them to notice it at the time.

"I grab the time I need, whenever I can fit it in. It's a priority item, ranking just behind family survival, and well ahead of Keeping Up With the House. I also turn down my fair share of volunteer projects, and do only enough Cub Scout, PTA, or community projects to keep my conscience quiet. Super-Mom, who could say 'yes' to everything, perished some time age.

"When I'm really in a crisis situation, down to the wire on a book deadline or trying to complete several magazine articles at once, I enlist my troops to help with the cooking, the laundry, etc. Sure, they grumble a lot, but I point out that if Ma can't make a living from her desk corner, she may have to get an honest outside job—in which case they'll inherit the cooking, the laundry, etc., on a permanent basis.

"I admit things are easier now by comparison, with my 'baby' finishing first grade. I've got the whole quiet house to myself much of the day, yet accomplish not much more than I did in the constant-offspring-company years. Eveything that needs doing gets done somehow. The only thing I still don't have time to do is figure out where I find the time to write. . . .

Problem two: Nobody seems to respect writing as a serious business. That includes family, friends, committees, and myself too.

"Solution: I've become happily schizophrenic. First, I convinced myself that my writing was a serious business, and approach it like a total professional. Everything that leaves my typewriter must be the best I can do. I'm also very tough when it comes to negotiating contract terms for books, etc. Because I've had to do some promotional travel with my latest book, *Stop the World* . . . , for Doubleday, I've learned to organize my household for those jaunts the same way the Allied forces approached D-Day.

"The rest of my time, however, I enjoy being 'just a homemaker.' It doesn't bother me a bit that my neighbors don't view me as a career person. I bake cookies with glee, oversee homework, and struggle to keep up with the wash. I've discovered that this 'normal' part of my life makes it far easier to keep things on an even keel, staying in touch with all the normal people just like me who are my prime audience.

"Perhaps the finest example of my schizophrenic approach to life came last March. I was gabbing with an old college chum who came in town for a couple of days, while together we cut out a wedding gown costume for my number-two daughter, who had the lead in our church teen musical. Chum also has eight children, so this seemed a perfectly normal combination of visiting and home-based production to her too. While she cut out one side of the dress and I the other, the phone rang. It was Doubleday, asking if I could fly to New York the following week to tape a show with David Susskind. Sure, I responded, then went back to the scissoring project. A few minutes later, while I was basting the bodice, the phone rang again. It was one of David Susskind's writers, asking questions about my writing career. I plied my needle while answering as all three dogs barked furiously in the background and my five youngest sons pounded in the door from school. As my old pal put it, 'This sure is an interesting place, but I don't think I'd want to live here.' Well, I live here, and I love my double life."

ALEEN MALCOLM: (*The Taming*)
"I'm disciplined in my work and write from eight to three, but don't seem to be very disciplined in any other way. I have my own study

and don't take phone calls when I'm working. I've learned to paddle through the debris.

"I don't like housekeeping so the kids and my husband took over. Naturally, since I don't do it, I can't complain about the way they do it. We have a grocery list on the refrigerator and everyone adds to it. We save laundry for the weekend. Everyone puts his own away.

"I've taught the three older children to cook. They all make their own school lunches. I'll share one cooking secret with you: When you make spaghetti sauce, make three times what you need. Have spaghetti one night, freeze one batch, and use the third one the following night for chili (with taco shells).

"I still feel guilty when guests come. I'm afraid they'll be critical about the house. I haven't learned not to take judgment from others. I don't want to be defensive, but I am.

"Sometimes I feel guilty for being 'inside myself.' I set the alarm clock half an hour before the children come home from school so I can 'come down.' It's hard for me to change roles quickly. If I don't take this time off from my writing before they get home, the kids will talk and I won't even hear them.

"My husband and I take turns with the kids when they're sick or have school activities. We have five kids in five schools so it can be fairly hectic.

"During school holidays, I forget about writing. Otherwise, when the children are around, I'll proof my work while they're doing their homework so we'll all be together. They've been self-sufficient since they were toddlers. I always felt boredom was *their* problem."

PAT LEIMBACH: (*A Thread of Blue Denim* and *All My Meadows*)
"There is a maximum potential of five free hours in a housewife/writer/mother's day—they lie between midnight and five a.m. . . . I am a writer because I learned to take advantage of them. I have not yet learned 'how to get organized, what to do about friends and family, how to simplify housekeeping.' (Though I have learned that the simplest thing to do about housekeeping is nothing.) I also have learned that if you bake enough bread, you can get away with almost anything.

" 'Where's our supper?'
" 'Shut up and eat your homemade bread.'
"Writing, of course, is 90 percent mental, and the muse is often most solicitous when one is *very* busy at other things. My five writing hours a week are flanked always by several dozen more of cogitation,

like today's stint of running back and forth in search of two 6-inch *T*s for a PVC pipe while three guys six feet down in a drainage ditch hold up the walls with their muddy palms. Eighty miles on the highway is a couple of hours of thinking time.

"A housewife who aspires to write will make her first and best expenditure for a cleaning lady. I have always had *somebody*, even before I started writing! I have always spent a great deal of time helping my husband in the farm business, and good sense told me I deserved a modicum of household help. (Often very modicum.) The best household help around here is what I married. He's very good with windows and louvered doors. He also is an excellent typist and copy editor.

"As for the resolve to *do* it (write) a commitment to a weekly column deadline has been my only compulsive motivation. The fact that every 'precious' word I wrote got published gave me the only courage I have in the face of the discipline. I do not know what motivates novice freelancers who must survive the flagellation of all those rejection slips. I lack that sort of determined masochism.

"When I was a couple of years along in the writing game (and it must be said that I didn't begin til I was thirty-eight, thereby avoiding many of the pitfalls and a lot of good years of inspiration), I spent some money and went to a first-class writers' conference. That was probably the second-best expenditure I made. I recommend that to any beginning writer.

"If journals are not your bag, then I suggest letter writing as excellent practice. Not only do you get something in return— answers—but you also have a perpetuating mechanism. If one feels that her letter prose is deathless, then carbon paper will suffice to preserve it for the archives and the posthumous 'book of letters.' (It also gives you an excellent record of how far you've come with your skills.)"

BARBARA DEANE: (*Managing Is Communication*; articles in *Highlights for Children*; *Boys' Life*; *Florida Trend*; *Ranger Rick's Nature Magazine*; and the *Floridian*)
"The most difficult part of being a housewife-writer in the beginning was convincing myself I was a writer despite meager evidence. I wasn't publishing all that much; I certainly wasn't making much money, and compared with everything else I was doing, my writing life was almost invisible. I remember once after I'd published a couple of articles telling someone that 'I wrote.'

" 'Really?' he replied brightly. 'Have I seen anything you've done? What name do you write under?'

"What a crusher. For days, I went around making up clever 'you should have saids' in my head. Next time, I fumed, I'll reply, quick as a flash, '_____.' (Fill in the name of any famous woman writer that occurs to you; it could happen to you some day.)

"Anyway, that did it. I clammed up about my writing. No more volunteering information to anybody except other writers. It became my shameful secret that I could share only with other addicts. (Writers' clubs are a lot like AA meetings, with the important difference that nobody wants to reform.)

"Like most other young women with small children who 'want to write,' I thought about it rather than did anything about it for a long time. I was caught on the endless treadmill of diaper-changing, bottles, laundry, cleaning, and meals, without household help and with a husband busy with his own career. When the children were sick, which was often, I was too sleepless and exhausted to have any energy left for writing.

"Yet I don't really feel that these were wasted years, even though I wrote nothing. The writer in me had gone underground temporarily. Though I didn't know it at the time, I was putting down a foundation for later use. Even with my hectic schedule, I could always find time to read; while waiting for laundry to finish, feeding children, sitting in doctors' offices. I read all those books you don't have time to read in college because the demands of school interfere with a writer's real education. (I remember, for example, taking William James's *The Varieties of Religious Experience* to the maternity ward.) And I thought a lot—thoughts I carried around in my head with no time to put them on paper. Mostly, by the time I got to a typewriter, the thoughts had grown tired of waiting and fled.

"When my oldest was four and the middle child two, I timidly joined a writer's group sponsored by the local chapter of the American Association of University Women. We met once a month and read each other what we had written. They liked what I read and encouraged me. I wrote more. Some of these women had been published. By golly, if they could do it, so could I. I wrote an article and in the typical scattershot fashion of the neophyte, I sent it, more or less blindly, to seventeen markets in all before it finally sold. But I did it. I got paid for something I wrote. My writers' group was ecstatic, and so was I.

"Yet, even though these women helped me a great deal, their

influence as role models was a negative one. I didn't want to be like them. Most of them were older by at least a generation; their children were away at school or had left the nest for good. A few were retired professional women. If anybody had 'time to write,' it was they. Yet what impressed me most was how little writing they produced and how lightly they treated it. Apparently, having 'enough time' was not the only thing it took to become a writer.

"It dawned on me gradually that if I wanted to write, the enemy was not the demands of husband and children, society's expectations, or household duties. It was myself. This led me to Axiom Number One:

"*The enemy is always within.*

"Axiom Number Two:

"*The time to do it is always now.*

"I was told by the inner voice every writer learns to pay attention to that there was never going to be an ideal time when I would have plenty of time for writing, off somewhere in the future 'after the children were grown' or 'when the children were in school.' If I wanted to be a writer by the time those delightful vistas of free time opened up, I'd better get cracking NOW.

"I wish I could say that this illuminating insight turned me overnight into a serious, successful writer.

"The truth is that I was still publishing only occasionally, still producing very little and very slowly, feeling my way, and allowing anything and everything to interrupt what I was doing. *But I was writing regularly.* And by writing regularly, I was improving, seeing my mistakes and beginning to correct them. Everything that I now teach others [in a creative writing class] about revising and shaping, about markets and how they work, about writing for an audience, I had to work out painfully, alone, for myself.

"By the time my two oldest were in school, lo and behold, we had a third child. All my writing time was gone again and I was back on Square One. When I tried to pick up where I'd left off, I felt as if I were stalemated.

"The answer (although I didn't realize it) was to go underground once more. This time, I went back to the university to get an M.A. in English literature and to teach freshman English. When I reemerged, the habits of thinking, researching, and working regularly at something besides housework had been reestablished. Moreover, by trying to teach others to write, I had learned more about the craft of writing than I had ever known before.

"This time, I was too old for any more fooling around. It was high time I committed myself to writing as a career. I was no longer to be contented with earning a little 'pin money.' I was ready to set myself goals and deadlines and begin thinking and acting like a professional writer.

"What in the world took me so long? The answer is very simple. I was still carrying around the old enemy within—the image in my head of myself as Superwife and Supermom, with permission to write in the spare time I had left over from satisfying the image of perfect wife and mother, suburban 1950s style, which is when I came of age and when my values were formed. No, I don't think my values were wrong. I didn't want to sacrifice my family to Fame and Fortune as a writer. But I wasted a lot of valuable time on nonessentials.

"I realized if writing time was only 'leftover' time, it was likely to be inferior quality time. Who said I had to 'finish the housework' before I could write? I did, that's who. But what if I wrote first, early in the morning when I was fresh, and did the housework in the time left over from writing, instead of vice versa?

"Money, or lack of it, was often as much of a problem as time. The fact that the housewife is not earning her own living can be a drawback as well as a plus. She is free to write without financial pressures, but because there are no financial pressures, in practice this often means she is free not to write. Then there are all the extra expenses that are hard to justify on a tight family budget: office supplies and postage, books and magazine subscriptions, courses and writers' conferences. It took years to stop feeling apologetic about spending money on my 'writing habit.'

"If there is any lesson to be learned from my experience, it's that YOU have to do it. Nobody is going to come along and give you permission to write instead of doing whatever else is taking up your time.

"Only you can make these decisions about how you will use your time and energy, and only you can carry them out. Becoming a writer is strictly a 'do-it-yourself' job."

MARION BOND WEST: (*Out of My Bondage*; *No Turning Back*; *Two of Everything But Me*; *Learning to Lean*)
"I learned to write mentally while driving the car pool, folding clothes, vacuuming, or cooking. I made myself listen to my children and tried not to write when they were at home. Now I can work out an article or chapter almost completely before ever going to the typewriter.

"I still face the problem of writing about my family. They aren't too wild about that. But I always let them read what I've written and am willing to change or omit anything they object to. They are more relaxed since they know I'll never write anything about them without permission.

"Sometimes telephone calls, letters, and visits from strangers present a problem. Sometimes people come to see me. One lady came for a week. I always get my husband's permission. As long as I ask, he almost always says yes. For a while I think he worried because I wasn't like everyone else's wife—baking cakes, making curtains, canning, and freezing. I was sitting at the typewriter or getting involved with all sorts of unusual people that I could write about. Also I was hanging around with other writers and my family thought they were strange—till they got to know them.

"I try to do things that my family likes, since they've been so understanding about my doing what I like. I've recently started to learn to understand football after hating it for twenty years, and I'm starting to bake cakes, and I even froze some beans from my husband's garden. Of course, there's a reward in this for me. All of these experiences turned into articles."

BEA BOURGEOIS: ("The Bea Hive," a regular column appearing in *Insight*, Sunday magazine of the *Milwaukee Journal*; author of numerous articles)

"First: the most difficult part of being a housewife/writer/mother is generating the patience to deal with editors who keep a manuscript anywhere from three months to a year without acknowledging or returning it. I once had a national magazine keep one of my articles for nine months (I could have produced a baby in that length of time, and with less anguish) before deciding not to use it. Another national magazine has had an article of mine for almost four months, during which time I've written twice and phoned once to inquire about its status. The most elucidation I've received is 'we have a large backlog of articles, and you'll be hearing from us.' Agony!

"Writers seem to be last on the list to be paid. Too many times I have had to put myself in the degrading position of calling or writing to inquire about a check. After all, the editors have bought a commodity—my article—and they should pay for it promptly. I can't tell the butcher I'll pay for his pork chops after we've eaten them! To belabor the obvious, without writers there would be no magzines.

"The second most difficult thing—I'll bet this is common among women writers—*is* finding "the time." I don't find the time; I make the time. For openers, I never watch TV; it's such a time-burner. Oh, there are nights when I think it would be great to flop on the couch and watch something mindless; but I'd really rather be upstairs in my small office writing a column, and so that's what I do.

"It's much easier to produce articles during the school year; the summer is horrendous because there are a zillion interruptions every day. During the school year, as soon as the last lunch bag is out the back door, I'm at my typewriter—with a few breaks for laundry and general picking up, in between.

"I love to cook, although I don't have as much time for it as I did before I began writing the column. So—I rely on simple but hearty meals (adolescent boys, as we all know, have appetites like wolverines) like oven beef stew, large quantities of homemade spaghetti sauce, chili, chicken-and-rice casseroles and sometimes, I admit, grilled cheese sandwiches or Kraft Dinner.

"If there's a woman who loathes housework more than I do, I'm not sure I'd want to meet her. At my husband's suggestion, I have allowed myself the 'luxury' of occasional cleaning help. Beverly loves housework (she must find much happiness in my house) and I feel that the twenty-two dollars a day is an investment in my sanity and my husband's happiness (he is far more tidy than I; I'm clean but messy). It is a spiritual lift to work on an article until mid-afternoon and emerge from my office into a sparkling, vacuumed, dusted home.

"A successful woman freelance writer needs an enormous amount of *stamina.* If you tire easily, or pout when your afternoon nap is disturbed, or tend to be a chronic procrastinator, you'll never make it. Writing *is* hard work, and you have to love it; you also have to be able to juggle all the unpredictable vagaries of family living, which invariably occur just as you're halfway through with the best thing you've ever written. Often, this means that you'll be sitting at your typewriter long after everyone else in the family is snoring peacefully; if I didn't love to write, I'd probably be miserable.

"I'm not sure I've resolved all of the problems in being a housewife/mother/writer; I'm lucky to have a husband who is supportive and proud of my accomplishments.

"Being an established and now a locally recognized freelance writer is wonderfully satisfying, always interesting, and sometimes zany. It's an ego trip when the grocery store checkout person recognizes my name, and it's great good fun to get fan letters from complete strangers throughout the Midwest."

TERESA BLOOMINGDALE: (*I Should Have Seen It Coming When the Rabbit Died*; weekly humor column for *Our Sunday Visitor*; and numerous articles)

"There are many difficult aspects of combining writing with the many duties of a wife and mother, but the obvious one—not enough time—is not one of them. Anybody who wants to write will find the time. My most difficult problem has been *thinking*. . . . I write my columns in my head before I put them on paper, and I need undisturbed periods of quiet time to formulate my thoughts. Since I haven't had five undisturbed minutes in the last twenty years, this does present a problem. Consequently, I do much of my thinking after I get into bed at night (a sure cure for insomnia) or while I am in church (which may present an even bigger problem on Judgment Day).

"With seven of our ten children still living at home, my days are filled with questions and crises, which give me lots to write about but not much time to write it. As many writer-mothers may feel *time to write* could be a problem, I offer the following advice: Never try to write in the evening or on weekends (or hours that are normally 'family time.') I get up at 5:30 to do my household chores and get my family off to work and school so that I may work in a neat atmosphere, with no dirty dishes, unmade beds, laundry, etc. hanging over my head while I write, from 9:00 to 3:00. I stop as soon as the first child comes home from school, and do not go back to the typewriter (except in rare cases when a deadline is pushing me) until 9:00 the next morning. I never write on the weekends, when family activity would distract me. (Thus I never have a guilty conscience about neglecting my family.)

"I realize that many would-be writers (and even established writers) still have preschool-age children at home. I wish I could remember how I solved that problem, but I must have, as I was writing two columns and two book reviews a week when I still had three babies underfoot. Admittedly, that was a difficult period for me, but I don't advise waiting to write. If a writer procastinates too long, the muse may depart for greener pastures.

"Another problem I faced (which may have been personal) was vocabulary. With an English major and journalism minor I considered myself a treasury of words and phrases—until I began to write. My vocabulary was so limited, it was frightening. I resolved this by reading anything and everything I could get my hands on, especially current fiction and nonfiction (the classics are great, but the language is outdated) and even managed to profit from my reading by selling book reviews. One cannot write unless one reads. I also recommend frequent use of a thesaurus, a dictionary, and Bartlett's quotations.

"A third problem was money. (Ain't it always?) A freelance writer must be aware of the fact that nothing has been deducted from her checks, and Uncle Sam is going to demand not only an accounting, but also most of the money. I advise setting up two bank accounts: one for saving and one for Sam. The savings account can be used for fun or bills or whatever, the Uncle Sam account should never be touched. It's painful at first, but one gets used to it, and it is nice to have the cash available come April 15. (Especially if one is married to a lawyer who has no patience or pity or understanding of how somebody could spend money on such luxuries as a cavity-filling when she knew very well that money was to go for taxes!)

"For a long time *where to write* was a problem for me. With this many children, there was no available room for writing alone, thus I did it at the dining-room table, for two reasons. Believe it or not, the dining room is the least-used room in the house, even for those who eat dinner in their dining room, as we do. Also, I felt that I would thus have to clean up my 'mess' each day; could not leave papers, manuscripts, typewriter, etc., out and about. I felt more organized, and the family didn't feel that 'Mom is always writing.' (Now I do have a small den, as one of the kids graciously moved out and joined the Marines, and it is a constant mess. Even so, I recommend finding a nook, however small, for writing.) I do not recommend (in fact I strongly advise against it) renting office space away from home; I know writers who tried it and hated it. They were under terrible pressure to 'write now, while I am here at the office' and always felt they should hurry home. When writing at home one can write when the muse strikes, and if the ideas simply won't come one can, as a last resort, do the ironing. (Nothing draws me to the typewriter faster than a basket of wrinkled clothes.)"

TERRY TUCKER FRANCIS: (Author of numerous articles)
"The most difficult part of my dual career is definitely not housework. I simply don't do it if it can be avoided, put off, or otherwise ignored. Nor is it difficult finding subject matter—the sensory bombardment of being the mother to a two-year-old and wife of a photographer/illustrator and one of eight grownup siblings and aunt to their assorted infants keeps me on the fine-honed edge of insanity essential to the working writer-mother.

"The problem is, has been, and will always be privacy—time to think uninterrupted thoughts, to chase the sparkling glimmer of an idea before it fizzles into darkness, to cling to a ghostly train of thought as it rounds hairpin turns at breakneck speed. If I ever resolve the problem I'll write a book and tell the world how I did it!

"Meanwhile I cope. Sometimes I lapse into ominous and moody silences, which can only be walked off. (I recommend a walk to the nearest nice quiet library where you can check out murder mysteries—nothing is more restful than a good Gothic!) On a more practical level: I have a button on my phone that turns off the ring while I'm working (it rings in the line, though, so callers get the impression I'm not home; it saves me from drop-in visitors who come to see if I'm all right!). I also have a rigged doorbell. With the flip of a switch (installed by my husband) my doorbell can be rendered out of order when I'm hard at work. I write regularly for two magazines and freelance for another half-dozen, so deadlines are a part of my life. We make no social commitments near deadline, and if an unexpected close deadline comes up we cancel any commitments that would interfere. Our family and friends understand, but only after months of firm policy on our part. Writing mustcome first with us, because, for the past eight months we've been living totally on our income as a writer-illustrator team. Being firm with family and friends may be one of the most difficult problems the homemaker-writer has to face—if people around the homemaker-writer don't see her work as "a real job" she must educate them by her actions to the fact that it is not only 'a real job,' it is one of the most challenging real jobs in the known world.

"Her children and husband must be taught, too. My two-year-old already knows that when Mama is at the typewriter none of her antics will tear Mama away. So she plays quietly with her toys a few feet from my desk. I don't try her patience beyond endurance, however. If she needs dry diapers or a nap or her lunch I take a break. I also make a point of spending good loving time with her between typing bouts—guilt is one trip no writing mother needs!

"When my husband and I have a photo-article assignment of some complexity or which requires a daylong trip, we hire the best babysitter in the world for Katie Rose: either my mother or one of my sisters. Note the word hire. My mother objects, but we insist that when we must leave Katie for a whole day (or a large part of the day) we will pay the person who takes care of her. It is a legitimate part of our business expenses and it saves me the guilt of feeling I'm taking advantage of someone I love. Furthermore, it is deductible. We strongly recommend hiring a competent and loving babysitter. It not only gives you physical freedom to go after an assignment you couldn't otherwise do, it gives you peace of mind.

"My final advice to homemaker-writers is this: Don't let anyone discourage you. Avoid those who mock your efforts. Consider carefully the worth of any "friend" who smirks at your career, ignores your need for time to write, or counsels you with negativity and discouragement. Either tell them that you don't care to hear their disparaging talk—or drop them. Writing is difficult enough without having to endure the slings and arrows of the jealous, the unkind, and the disrespectful. Don't give up!"

ERMA BOMBECK: (*If Life Is a Bowl of Cherries, What Am I Doing in the Pits; I Lost Everything in the Post-Natal Depression; The Grass Is Always Greener Over the Septic Tank; At Wit's End*)

"The most difficult part of being a housewife/writer/mother is the /.

"The /, which is just below the question mark on my typewriter, represents the tightropes we all walk on; the three masters we try to serve. Which one gets priority, and how much do we steal from one to compensate the other?

"In my case I took all three very seriously.

"At first, I used to think I could allot time slots in the day. From 7-8/mother . . . 8-10/housewife . . . 10-3/writer . . . 3-11/housewife/mother.

"It would have worked out fine if my son hadn't bled during my deadline with *Good Housekeeping*, grocery day clashed with a parent-teacher conference, and the oven caught fire on the same day an editor told me he wasn't laughing.

"I could fill up a book for you on the frustrations of H/W/M syndrome. But I'll limit myself to just a few.

"PROBLEM: No one takes your little part-time job seriously. Just because you write from your home, everyone assumes you have the flexibility to chuck it anytime you want. No one realizes the discipline that goes into writing. Even bad checks and grocery lists take concentration.

"SOLUTION: I have an x-rated response for people who call me up and chirp, 'You busy?'

"PROBLEM: It's lonely at the bottom. When you have no name, no contacts, no track record, how do you sustain enthusiasm for what you're doing?

"SOLUTION: Save your fan letter. I lived for years on the comment of a desk editor on the *Detroit Free Press* . . . an elderly man who said, 'I never read your stuff—but by God you have it here on time.'

"PROBLEM: How do you know how good or how bad you are? Whom do you go to for critique?

"SOLUTION: I found that if I begged my husband, wrapping myself around his leg and dragging behind him pleading for criticism, he had the good sense to keep his mouth shut and thus save our marriage. Most people who ask for criticism don't really want it. Learn to be honest with yourself. When it's garbage, say so.

"PROBLEM: Writing in a traffic area and being constantly interrupted by children who want you to stop and belt their sibling for humming/making faces/breathing.

"SOLUTION: After about five or six years, I got up the courage to say, 'Your MOTHER is busy. I will talk to you when I am finished. If this is going to bruise your ID, then I will try for some other part of your body the moment I complete this idea.'

"My family has been very supportive of me and what I do. It helps more than you know, but don't expect too much out of them. For the most part, you are your own cheerleader, coach, psychiatrist, critic, confessor, and house mother. When something has to give, you have to make your own decision as to where you can take the time.

"I let my body go.

"In 1971, I took my daughter with me to Pittsburgh where I was to receive a Headliner Award from the Women In Communications.

"As she sat in the audience I looked at her and said, 'For all the irritability when the writing didn't go well that day; for the three-pound roast that was still breathing at dinner; for the time I ironed a blouse for the school play and asked, "Which sleeve faces the audience?"; for the uncombed hair until noon; the instant icing on the warm birthday cakes; I thank you. You've seen the agony of a mother who writes from home. I'm glad you're here to see the ecstasy.' "

BILLIE SUE MOSIMAN: (Not published as yet. The following excerpts are from letters she sent to another writer from 1977 to the present. She graciously has given permission for me to reprint them here.)

" . . . You should see me! Fifteen pages of single type from top to bottom. Fifteen! . . . averaging out at five pages a working day or the equivalent of a short story a day. I'm amazed at my own progress. I wonder if I'm being an ogre. My two little girls have the house to themselves. They tear and strew and generally have their fun because Mama is busy typing. Of course, I am up every few minutes checking on them, washing a face or a fanny, or fixing a lunch. But I don't pay much attention to them, I know. I forget to eat. Dinner is the only meal my stomach recognizes now. I drink pots of coffee and smoke packs of cigarettes. I stop around four in the afternoon to straighten the mess and cook a meal. Then I'm up to one a.m. reading, listening to TV. I know it's a terrible schedule and the only thing I'm getting done is the book. Right now, that's all that matters. I don't know how long I can hold up under this set-up, but I'm enjoying it. The house can wait. And the girls can come to me in my study when they need attention from Mama. I've tried explaining to Suzanne that they must not be extraordinarily messy or noisy or plundersome so that Mama can type and write her stories. I know how her four-year-old mind must grapple with that. But at least they know I'm always here. I live in the inner landscape where my words and thoughts are all that matters. Writing is a selfish occupation, isn't it?

" . . . I've written on the novel most of the day. I've come to a part I particularly like. I'm not so much soaring over the blank pages now. I pick my way along, considering which is chaff and which is the good grain. I'm entering a wilderness and I don't know the path, so it takes more thought, less hot-headed plunging. It's getting to the climax and it has to be handled deftly. It's important that I get it right. I lose even myself and have to go back over the manuscript to see exactly what I've done so far. Is it time for this bit of information? It is necessary that this go into a new chapter? But the challenge is wonderful. . . .

This is turning out to be my off-the-record diary. Maybe you're right about keeping this, if only for my children, to show them later how their mother worked and slaved over nothing more than ideas and words.

" . . . Now I've started a brand new love affair. I'm doing the rewrite, sentence by sentence, page by page. I'm finding ways of better expressing the dialogue, making the scenes more realistic. It's a whole new ballgame. Same book, but it has a new taste because I'm still creating, still in there cranking away. I thought I knew it all, had it pat, and here we go on the rollercoaster again. A brand new insight. A dozen new imaginative words. Things chopped out and things added. But this time I know the territory. . . .

My husband seems to think the work over. The house will magically turn into a palace right out of a Spic and Span commercial.

But I'm as involved as I was before. Maybe even more so, because the first draft is a cryptic message that even I have trouble decyphering. . . . Monday night I finished the novel. Tuesday I made a monster blackberry cobbler and cleaned up the two back rooms that hadn't seen a broom in a month. Wednesday I fixed a meal right out of a gourmet restaurant's menu. He and the kids ate it like it was the Last Supper. Today I got up and realized that I had gotten no further than a draft of the synopsis on *Jesse*. This can't go on, I thought. You can't slough off the rewrite forever, or only you will ever read the book. So today I did some more work for a change. And the bed needs making and the kitchen floor needs mopping. Back to the quickie meals and the messy house. Just for awhile, I'll tell him. Give me another month. He comes home most of the time to find me sitting at the typewriter still in a daze. I always turn it off and embrace him. 'If you write on that book on the weekends, I'm going off by myself.' So macho power won again and *Jesse* had to wait. I try not to neglect him or the children. But it's possible to juggle only so many things at one time. I hope it will be worth it. I hope I can make him proud. . . .

" . . . Yesterday was a miserable failure for it to have been Mother's Day. We had dinner at my father-in-law's house and around four when we were going to leave, he seemed upset with us for leaving early. My husband said we had to take the children over to my cousin's house as they interrupted me and I needed to get the revision done as soon as possible on my novel. Dad almost choked he became so indignant. 'You can't even handle two kids. What would you do with four or five?' My husband pointed out that we didn't plan to have four or five. 'Your mother took care of *five* kids and never complained.' he said. My husband again said something to the effect that his mother had not tried to write a book either and that it was a job like any other requiring quietness at times. (I could have hugged him.) 'Humph! Writing! She can do that in her spare time. She ought to take care of her family.' All this as if I weren't even there. I felt destroyed. I had never done a thing to this man. . . .

(Two years later)

" . . . I've reread those old letters and could see all over again how hard I worked on *Jesse*, how much faith I had in it and in myself. It was during that period that I taught myself how to concentrate with three-fourths of my brain on writing and with one-fourth sitting back listening to child sounds. Was that tin clicking against the floor or a glass in the sink? Was that a giggle that sounded a little too devious? Are things too quiet? Too noisy? Will anyone love me after this? Now

I have more confidence in my family's ability to understand what I do and why I do it. I can't tell you why. I've made no money from all this messing around with words, made no big splash, couldn't sell the book my father-in-law barked at me about. But he finally understands. He asks me now with every phone call, every meeting, 'How is your writing going?' He has commented on reading an article about a writer who took a long time to reach print and how one should not give up. This from a man who two years ago said, 'Keep her in the kitchen.' Maybe he sees how I never quit, how I am determinedly serious-minded about writing. It's a sad thing to have to prove yourself to others, a sad thing for it to take years to convince a person of your calling's worthiness, but I've done it. So if those letters might help some other women-writer—then yeah, let everyone read them."

The Beginning
(Not the End)

15.

That's it! That's all there is. Perhaps you were expecting some fantastic trade secrets, a magic potion, some way to make it all easier.

I'm truly sorry if you feel you've been misled. But the only way to write is by doing it, the way a child learns to walk—step by step, stumbling and starting over, getting a little bruised along the way. The only trick is in keeping at it, learning to control your life so that the twenty-four hours in your day include some time for writing.

Writing is hardly the job I'd recommend to someone who requires instant gratification. The hours are long, the pay is usually poor and encouragement along the way is as hard to find as a kid who likes to brush his teeth.

I began writing at the age of ten, with a book entitled "Good Short Stories" hand-written especially for my mother on Mother's Day.

My older sister looked at my offering and sniffed.

"How do you know they're any good?"

Unshaken, I replied, "At least they're short."

The passing of years changed nothing. No man is a hero to his valet, nor a mother/writer to her children.

"Gee, I'm glad you're a writer, Mom," my daughter said recently.

"Really?" I said, feeling very pleased. Obviously she felt I was a good role model, she was proud of my success, etc. I should have remembered that pride indeed goeth before a fall. "Why?"

"Because," she answered in that matter-of-fact way only kids can carry off, "If you didn't write, you'd drive us all crazy."

It's no better with the younger ones. When I got the contract for this book, I was ecstatic. The only person home to share the good news with was my seven-year-old.

"Mommy's going to write a book," I said. "I'll be in the card catalogue."

He looked at me very seriously. At last he spoke. "I don't think you'll fit," he said.

Relatives are just as bad. Someone asked of my sister-in-law if we were related.

"Yes," she answered.

"Oh, I love her humorous articles," gushed my fan. "They're adorable. Is she fun to be around? Is she always making you laugh?"

Said my sister-in-law: "I don't think she's ever made me laugh."

So much for praise and garlands at your feet. The only things strewn in my path are dirty gym socks. So why? Why do it?

My oldest son wondered about that too. He was up early to study for exams, and we sat leaning on the breakfast table together.

"Why don't you sleep late?" he asked.

"I have to work."

"Do you like working?"

No one had ever asked me that before. I thought about it. Do I like working? Yes, I really do. It's getting up I don't like. I'd much rather curl back under my big, fluffy quilt and snuggle down into the warmth. Instead I force myself to get up, make coffee, and open both eyes. I mumble about having low blood pressure, poor circulation, and low blood sugar, but I get up, because that's my writing time and I like writing.

That may sound a little masochistic, and perhaps it is. It's like being hooked on the texture of typing paper, the look of red pen corrections against black type, and the smell of rubber cement. I get a high from words and how they fit together; on the irregular clacking of my typewriter; and, yes, on the chomping of my bubble gum as I write, and on the rhythm I feel in my thoughts as they tumble like long rows of dominoes, one after another. I hear my writing as I work and that's music to me, like a baby's giggle, a special voice on the phone, or a kitten's purr.

When we first got Smudge, our "inside" cat, he was a tiny kitten. I held him on my lap and stroked him. He made no sound at all.

"This cat doesn't purr," I told my younger daughter. "Maybe he's sick."

She laughed. She knows of kittens and their ways. "There's nothing wrong with him," she said. "You've just got to believe—and be patient."

She was right. He sleeps nestled against the small of my back as I type, and he purrs perfectly.

Writing's a lot like that. You have to believe (in yourself) and you have to have patience. Of course, you also have to keep stroking—that is, writing—while you're busy believing and being patient.

What am I? Writer? Mother? Housewife? Wife? I am all that and more. We all have many facets, like a stained-glass window, with the sections reflecting differently depending on the day and the angle of the sun. I am a symbiotic blend, each part dependent on the other for nourishment. Housewife and writer (and mother too) are so intertwined I find it hard to separate the identities, even though I consider myself a professional writer. The writer side of me continually appears outside my study; in the kitchen where it pops up like toast in the toaster; on the coffee table where my market lists (one for food and one for articles) nestle compatibly like the odd couple. I find notes for leads and article ideas on the backs of school permission slips and camp application forms.

My family make themselves at home in my writing, like a grown child raiding his mother's refrigerator. "Write about what you know best," the experts advise. What does any woman know better than her husband and her children? The love shared; the arguments fought, won, and lost; the heartaches and triumphs; all are part of your life and, therefore, your writing.

Writing makes me happy. It's as simple as that. It makes my "mothering" more meaningful because my children are learning responsibility—doing for others and themselves, carrying out obligations. Because my time is precious, I have to let them try for themselves and, if they fail, try again. I have no time to fuss at them for little things. We focus on important issues.

"Give your children roots . . . and wings," they say. My writing helps me give them both.

My family knows it's good for them. "It will keep you busy and happy in your old age" they tell me. (I hate to press for dates.) It helps them sit and share their thoughts "in case you want to write it up," they say. It makes communication a little easier to begin.

They all encourage me and help. We all have lives that touch and intermesh, but still we have our separate work. My life is not totally dependent on them for joy and meaning, nor theirs on me. It makes us each feel better and look forward to coming together to compare "our day."

I guess writing gives me a "sense of identity," makes me a good "role model" and all those other good things we read so much about today, but that's not why I do it. Writing gives me pleasure. What could be nicer than being in love with your work and at the same time knowing that what you do helps others by making them laugh, helping them cry, or just letting them know more about something.

If you think writing makes *you* happy, if you want to write, *really* want to write, decide that today is the day you'll begin. I guess if this book has any "message," that's it. You *can* make the time for writing if you want to, if you feel you have to. There are no obstacles too great, no schedules too frantic, no excuses too overpowering for those who *will* become writers.

Motivation! Confidence! Persistence! You *can* become a successful housewife-writer. Why not get started?

Books of Interest From Writer's Digest

The Beginning Writer's Answer Book, edited by Kirk Polking, Jean Chimsky, and Rose Adkins. "What is a query letter?" "If I use a pen name, how can I cash the check?" These are among 567 questions most frequently asked by beginning writers—and expertly answered in this down-to-earth handbook. Cross-indexed. 270 pp. $8.95.

How to be a Successful Housewife/Writer, by Elaine Fantle Shimberg. The art of being a successful housewife/writer. 256 pp. $10.95.

The Cartoonist's and Gag Writer's Handbook, by Jack Markow. Longtime cartoonist with thousands of sales, reveals the secrets of successful cartooning—step by step. Richly illustrated. 157 pp. $8.95.

A Complete Guide to Marketing Magazine Articles, by Duane Newcomb. "Anyone who can write a clear sentence can learn to write and sell articles on a consistent basis." says Newcomb (who has published well over 3,000 articles). Here's how. 248 pp. $7.95.

The Confession Writer's Handbook, by Florence K. Palmer. A stylish and informative guide to getting started and getting ahead in the confessions. How to start a confession and carry it through. How to take an insignificant event and make it significant. 171 pp. $7.95.

The Craft of Interviewing, by John Brady. Everything you always wanted to know about asking questions, but were afraid to ask—from an experienced interviewer and editor of *Writer's Digest*. The most comprehensive guide to interviewing on the market. 244 pp. $9.95.

Craftworker's Market, edited by Lynne Lapin. Over 3,500 places for you to sell and exhibit your work. Listings include names and addresses, payment rates, special requirements and other information you need to sell your crafts. 696 pp. $11.95.

The Creative Writer, edited by Aron Mathieu. This book opens the door to the real world of publishing. Inspiration, techniques, and ideas, plus inside tips from Maugham, Caldwell, Purdy, others. 416 pp. $8.95.

The Greeting Card Writer's Handbook, by H. Joseph Chadwick. A former greeting card editor tells you what editors look for in inspirational verse...how to write humor...what to write about for conventional, studio and juvenile cards. Extra: a renewable list of greeting card markets. Will be greeted by any freelancer. 268 pp. $8.95.

A Guide to Writing History, by Doris Ricker Marston. How to track down Big Foot—or your family Civil War letters, or your hometown's last century—for publication and profit. A timely handbook for history buffs and writers. 258 pp. $8.50.

Handbook of Short Story Writing, edited by Frank A. Dickson and Sandra Smythe. You provide the pencil, paper, and sweat—and this book will provide the expert guidance. Features include James Hilton on creating a lovable character: R.V. Cassill on plotting a short story. 238 pp. $9.95.

Law and the Writer, edited by Kirk Polking and Leonard S. Meranus. Don't let legal hassles slow down your progress as a writer. Now you can find good counsel on libel, invasion of privacy, fair use, taxes, contracts, social security, and more—all in one volume. 249 pp. $9.95.

Magazine Writing: The Inside Angle, by Art Spikol. Successful editor and writer reveals inside secrets of getting your mss. published. 288 pp. $10.95.

Magazine Writing Today, by Jerome E. Kelley. If you sometimes feel like a mouse in a maze of magazines, with a fat manuscript check at the end of the line, don't fret. Kelley tells you how to get a piece of the action. Covers ideas, research, interviewing, organization, the writing process, and ways to get photos. Plus advice on getting started. 220 pp. $9.95.

Mystery Writer's Handbook, by the Mystery Writers of America. A howtheydunit to the whodunit, newly written and revised by members of the Mystery Writers of America. Includes the four elements essential to the classic mystery. A comprehensive handbook that takes the mystery out of mystery writing. 273 pp. $8.95.

1001 Article Ideas, by Frank A. Dickson. A compendium of ideas plus formulas to generate more of your own! 256 pp. $10.95.

Writing for Regional Publications, by Brian Vachon. How to write for this growing market. 256 pp. $11.95.

One Way to Write Your Novel, by Dick Perry.* For Perry, a novel is 200 pages. Or, two pages a day for 100 days. You can start and finish your novel, with the help of this step-by-step guide taking you from blank sheet to polished page. 138 pp. $8.95.

Photographer's Market, edited by Melissa Milar. Contains what you need to know to be a successful freelance photographer. Names, addresses, photo requirements, and payment rates for 3,000 markets. 624 pp. $12.95.

The Poet and the Poem, by Judson Jerome. A rare journey into the night of the poem—the mechanics, the mystery, the craft and sullen art. Written by the most widely read authority on poetry in America, and a major contemporary poet in his own right. 400 pp. $11.95.

Sell Copy, by Webster Kuswa. Tells the secrets of successful business writing. How to write it. How to sell it. How to buy it. 224 pp. $11.95.

Songwriter's Market, edited by William Brohaugh. Lists 2,000 places where you can sell your songs. Included are the people and companies who work daily with songwriters and musicians. Features names and addresses, pay rates and other valuable information you need to sell your work. 432 pp. $10.95.

Stalking the Feature Story, by William Ruehlmann. Besides a nose for news, the newspaper feature writer needs an ear for dialog and an eye for detail. He must also be adept at handling off-the-record remarks, organization, grammar, and the investigative story. Here's the "scoop" on newspaper feature writing. 314 pp. $9.95.

Successful Outdoor Writing, by Jack Samson. Longtime editor of *Field & Stream* covers this market in depth. Illustrated. 288 pp. $11.95.

A Treasury of Tips for Writers, edited by Marvin Weisbord. Everything from Vance Packard's system of organizing notes to tips on how to get research done free, by 86 magazine writers. 174 pp. $7.95.

Writer's Digest. The world's leading magazine for writers. Monthly issues include timely interviews, columns, tips to keep writers informed on where and how to sell their work. One year subscription, $15.

The Writer's Digest Diary. Plan your year in it, note appointments, log manuscript sales, be prepared for the IRS. It will become a permanent annual record of writing activity. Durable cloth cover. 144 pp. $8.95.

Writer's Market, edited by William Brohaugh. The freelancer's bible, containing 4,500 places to sell what you write. Includes the name, address and phone number of the buyer, a description of material wanted and rates of payment. 912 pp. $14.95.

The Writer's Resource Guide, edited by William Brohaugh. Over 2,000 research sources for information on anything you write about. 488 pp. $11.95.

Writer's Yearbook, edited by John Brady. This large annual magazine contains how-to-articles, interviews and special features, along with analyses of 500 major markets for writers. 128 pp. $2.50.

Writing and Selling Non-Fiction, by Hayes B. Jacobs. Explores with style and know-how the book market, organization and research, finding new markets, interviewing, humor, agents, writer's fatigue and more. 317 pp. $10.95.

Writing and Selling Science Fiction, compiled by the Science Fiction Writers of America. A comprehensive handbook to an exciting but oft-misunderstood genre. Eleven articles by top-flight sf writers on markets, characters, dialog, "crazy" ideas, world-building, alien-building, money and more. 197 pp. $8.95.

Writing for Children and Teen-agers, by Lee Wyndham. Author of over 50 children's books shares her secrets for selling to this large, lucrative market. Features: the 12-point recipe for plotting, and the Ten Commandments for Writers. 253 pp. $9.95.

Writing Popular Fiction, by Dean R. Koontz. How to write mysteries, suspense, thrillers, science fiction, Gothic romances, adult fantasy, Westerns and erotica. Here's an inside guide to lively fiction, by a lively novelist. 232 pp. $8.95.

Writing the Novel: From Plot to Print, by Lawrence Block. Practical advice on how to write any kind of novel. 256 pp. $10.95.

(1-2 books, add $1.00 postage and handling; 3 or more, additional 25¢ each. Allow 30 days for delivery. Prices subject to change without notice.)
Writer's Digest Books, Dept. B, 9933 Alliance Road, Cincinnati, Ohio 45242